A
FLORIDA
STATE
OF MIND

THE AUTHOR (LEFT) AND FRIENDS AT THE ENTRANCE TO GATORLAND
IN KISSIMMEE, THE QUINTESSENTIAL "OLD FLORIDA" TOURIST ATTRACTION.
(PHOTO BY CHRISTINE STEWART)

A
FLORIDA
STATE OF MIND

AN UNNATURAL
HISTORY OF AMERICA'S
WEIRDEST STATE

JAMES D. WRIGHT

THOMAS DUNNE BOOKS ST. MARTIN'S PRESS NEW YORK

THOMAS DUNNE BOOKS.
An imprint of St. Martin's Press.

A FLORIDA STATE OF MIND. Copyright © 2019 by James D. Wright. All rights reserved.
Printed in the United States of America. For information, address St. Martin's Press,
175 Fifth Avenue, New York, N.Y. 10010.

www.thomasdunnebooks.com
www.stmartins.com

Designed by Steven Seighman

The Library of Congress Cataloging-in-Publication Data is available upon request.

ISBN 978-1-250-18565-5 (hardcover)
ISBN 978-1-250-18566-2 (ebook)

Our books may be purchased in bulk for promotional, educational, or business use. Please
contact your local bookseller or the Macmillan Corporate and Premium Sales Department at
1-800-221-7945, extension 5442, or by email at MacmillanSpecialMarkets@macmillan.com.

First Edition: April 2019

10 9 8 7 6 5 4 3 2 1

CONTENTS

ACKNOWLEDGMENTS

MY FIRST AND greatest debt is to my agent, Laura Dail, who first suggested the idea for this book to me and whose firm but gracious editing resulted in a much better book. Thanks also to the editorial staff at Thomas Dunne Books, whose advice was spot-on and whose enthusiasm for the project was refreshing. I am also grateful to my good friend David Fisher for reading and commenting on early drafts. And finally, sincere thanks to my wife, Chris, among whose many virtues is that she understands my need to write.

I dedicate this book to my first and so far only grandson, Desmond Matthew Akers Wright. Little Desmond reminds me, as Carl Sandburg said, that "a baby is God's opinion that life should go on."

PREFACE

MY WIFE, CHRIS, and I met in Massachusetts in 1980, eventually tired of New England winters, moved to New Orleans in 1988, grew weary of the poverty and crime in the Big Easy, and moved to Orlando in 2001. Having now lived in Florida for eighteen years, we qualify as veteran Floridians by state standards. Not that you need a long tenure to qualify. Only 36 percent of the state's residents were born here—the second lowest number of any state (Nevada is first at 25 percent).

When we lived in New Orleans, I would frequently remind people that the first syllable in Louisiana was "lose." But you don't live in the Sunshine State very long before you realize that the last syllable in Florida is "duh." Florida is not as poor or as crime-riddled as Louisiana, but its people are very creative at making fools of themselves.

We were in the process of deciding to move to the Sunshine State during the 2000 presidential election. The outcome of that election, recall, was not decided until December 12, when the Supreme Court ruled in *Bush v. Gore* that Florida's 25 electoral college votes would go to George W. Bush by a margin of 537 votes (out of nearly six million votes cast). The most memorable image of that election, at least for me, was the bespectacled poll worker, tweezers in one hand and magnifying glass in the other, trying to determine if the hanging chad in front of him was a legitimate vote or not.

From such absurdity was the fate of the free world decided. How is it that every state but Florida had figured out how to hold an election?

We made the move to Orlando in May 2001. Just a few months later, we woke up on a lovely September morning to the *Today* show video clip showing two Boeing 767 passenger jets crashing into the Twin Towers. Fall classes had just begun, and I was on my way to campus when it was announced that the collisions were not accidental but were a horrific terrorist attack. And in that moment of awful recognition, the world changed and has never been the same since.

Soon enough, it came to light that many of the terrorists responsible for the attack had connections to my new adopted homeland. Thirteen of the nineteen hijackers had Florida driver's licenses or identification cards, fifteen were living in South Florida at the time of the attack, and two of the four pilot-leaders—Mohamed Atta and Marwan al-Shehhi—had been spotted in Hollywood, Florida, just days before the attack. They had learned to fly in flight schools in Venice and Vero Beach. The alleged disinterest of these students in learning how to *land* a plane apparently raised no red flags.

An election outcome determined by how firmly a ballot dimple remained attached to its cardboard backing, then a terrorist attack that changed the world forever—these are the energy poles between which Florida vibrates and crackles: absurdity at one pole, tragedy at the other, with an arc in between that runs through the weird, the preposterous, the inane, the wonderful, and at times the just plain spooky. That is the state I have come to know and love and have written about in this book.

The leading Florida headline of 2002 was the execution of Aileen Wuornos, aka the "Highway Hooker" and "Damsel of Death." Wuornos, a prostitute who prowled the highways of north-central Florida and who was famously played by Charlize Theron in the 2003 crime drama *Monster,* had been convicted of killing six or seven middle-aged men (she confessed to seven but only six bodies were ever found), often posing as a stranded motorist to lure men into her death trap and then shooting them at point-blank range with a .22 caliber pistol. A Michigan native, Wuornos was a regular at the Daytona-area bars in the 1980s. The bar where she was arrested—appropriately called the Last Resort, in Port Orange—has since become a tourist attraction. Unrepentant, Wuornos demanded a year before her execution that she be put to death. "There is no point in sparing me," she said. "It's a waste of taxpayers' money."

Not all of the state's recent history is murderous or tragic. Sometimes, it's just plain zany. In February 2003, America's then–oldest living man, John McMorran of Lakeland, died of heart failure at the age of 113. Mr. McMorran credited his long life to having given up his cigar habit— at the age of 97.

In 2004, an item in *National Geographic* warned of the possible extinction of our resident mermaid population. Yes, the *mermaid* population. There's an Old Florida tourist attraction in Weeki Wachee Springs on the Gulf Coast that features women in mermaid costumes performing choreographed underwater dance routines. *National Geographic* warned that there were fewer than twenty people left "who do this for a living" and all of them lived in Weeki Wachee. One "senior mermaid" quoted in the story said that the mermaid fantasy was an incurable disease. But another remarked, "Wrinkles, cellulite, chubby, whatever—we're ready to go!"

In subsequent years, Floridians looked on as Michael Schiavo's request to have his wife's feeding tube removed was finally granted, allowing Terri Schiavo to exit her permanent vegetative state and die peacefully in a Pinellas Park hospice. We watched as notorious con man and lobbyist Jack Abramoff was sentenced to six years in prison for scamming Native American Florida casino operators out of $85 million. We collectively gagged as Orlando resident Casey Anthony was accused, tried, and acquitted of killing her two-year-old child, Caylee. Everyone but the jury seemed to believe that she did it. Right after her acquittal, there was a rumor that she had signed a contract to do a porn movie for a million bucks to pay off her legal fees, although the movie never materialized. Five years later, she was said to be living in West Palm Beach and had opened her own photography business.

Then in 2013, Sanford resident George Zimmerman was tried and also acquitted for the murder of Trayvon Martin. Showing all the class you would expect from a vicious "cracker," Zimmerman later tried to sell the pistol he used to kill seventeen-year-old Trayvon—a Kel-Tec PF9 9mm handgun—on the internet for a cool quarter million dollars. He planned to use the proceeds, he said, to oppose Hillary Clinton's 2016 presidential campaign.

Zimmerman's defense entered the national political lexicon. He invoked Florida's now-infamous "stand your ground" law and claimed, successfully, that he had killed Martin in self-defense. Martin was armed with a can of iced tea and a bag of Skittles from the nearby 7-Eleven. One wonders what Zimmerman was defending himself *against*. Despite the tragedy, "stand your ground" has been reaffirmed by the state legislature—twice—and its legality has been sustained by the Florida Supreme Court.

Then there was the news out of Key Biscayne that a man had fallen out of a private airplane and plummeted some two thousand feet to his death. This wasn't a suicide, mind you, but an accidental death. Apparently, he had unlatched the door, leaned out to get a better view, forgot he wasn't wearing his seat belt, and just tumbled out of the plane.

For every story that makes you laugh or scratch your head, there is another that makes you weep. In Orlando on a Friday night, June 10, 2016, *The Voice* runner-up and pop singer Christina Grimmie was shot to death in a small Orlando music venue called The Plaza Live as she was signing autographs. Her killer, Kevin James Loibl, then shot himself to death. No motive for the killing was ever discovered.

Then early in the morning of June 12, Omar Mateen walked into Orlando's Pulse nightclub and killed forty-nine people, at that time the deadliest mass shooting in the nation's history. Two days later, the headline concerned a youngster attacked and killed by a gator at Disney World. The victim, two-year-old Lane Graves, was playing innocently at the edge of an artificial lake in Disney World when he was snatched and killed by an eight-footer. Orlando residents (I was one at the time) longed for a day when the city's tragedies were not the lead story on the nightly national news.

Weird, tragic, ridiculous, and outright crazy stuff happens in Florida so frequently that the state's newspapers provide a steady stream of material to a very popular Twitter feed, @_FloridaMan. The feed consists exclusively of news stories with headlines along the lines of "Florida Man" does this or "Florida Woman" does that. The feed for February 11, 2017, for example, included "Florida man beats off alligator with putter";

"Floridians lead nation in head injuries"; "Florida man has to be rescued from garbage truck after falling asleep in dumpster"; "Florida man says he committed $7 billion bank fraud because Jesus wanted to make him rich"; and "Florida man shoots cat for pooping in his yard." The latter involved a sixty-nine-year-old man from Ormond Beach who said he shot the cat because it "looked at me like he owned the place."

Florida is a state where Outback Steakhouse frequently ranks as the number-one restaurant in the local Zagat survey, where college football and stock-car racing are nearly as important as God, where fifteen acres of habitat for storks, ibises, and sandhill cranes were sacrificed to build Dolly Parton's Dixie Stampede, an Orlando tourist attraction that opened in 2003, closed in 2008, and was demolished in 2012 to make way for expansion of a nearby outlet discount mall. It is a state where traffic congestion is consistently rated as the leading threat to the quality of life; whose cities are consistently rated the least safe in America for bicyclers and pedestrians; a state that leads the nation in annual shark attacks and where about a dozen people are bitten by alligators every year. Yet, despite it all, it is also a state that draws more than a hundred million annual visitors and has become one of the world's leading tourist destinations.

Whether it is the bizarre custody battle over Dannielynn Birkhead, the child of deceased model and TV star Anna Nicole Smith (potential fathers in the custody suit were Smith's lawyer, Howard K. Stern; her boyfriend, Larry Birkhead; her bodyguard, Alex Denk; a former boyfriend, Mark Hatten; and paramour Frédéric Prinz von Anhalt, Zsa Zsa Gabor's husband) or the antics of one-term congressman Allen West (an African American member of the House of Representatives who once said, "When I see anyone with an Obama 2012 bumper sticker, I recognize them as a threat to the gene pool"), the news here is never boring. Tragic and disturbing? Often. Zany and funny? Regularly. Just plain weird? Most of the time. But boring? Never.

In Florida, nothing is ever quite as it seems. Every story has a backstory, every point a counterpoint, every ugliness a contrary scene of sublime beauty. Whenever Florida purports to be one thing, it turns out to be another. Yes, Disney World can be "The Happiest Place on Earth," just as Disney wants the world to believe. But it is also a place where two-year-olds can be killed by alligators. Our coastal regions have been among the fastest-growing in the country for decades. As Andrew Ross said in his 1999 book, *The Celebration Chronicles*, "Keep the World Coming to Florida" has forever been the state's calling card. And yet those very regions have been allowed to evolve into vast, sprawling, congested, environmental disasters that get slammed by hurricanes year after year. At certain times of the year, Daytona Beach is a happening place where hundreds of thousands revel in the Daytona 500, Daytona Beach Bike Week, and spring break. Yet at other times, in the words of Dr. Sara Strickhouser, a former Daytona resident, "The place is kind of a hellhole." The rapper Vanilla Ice has mortgage and real estate interests in Florida and says that "Florida is a kinda gold mine." The actor Sidney Poitier, who was sent to Florida to live with his brother's family when he was fifteen, found it "an antihuman place."

A second theme that recurs throughout is the incessant tension between Old and New Florida. Old Florida basically is the Florida that existed prior to the opening of Walt Disney World in 1971. New Florida is everything since. The tension is whether to preserve what is traditional about the state, its culture and its lifestyle, or sacrifice everything to keep the tourists, immigrants, and retirees flowing in. I have yet to find a community in Florida that has successfully navigated between these treacherous shoals.

This book is a collection of factoids, oddments, stories, and backstories all related to my central theme, that Florida is never quite as it seems. The book is organized into four parts and eighteen chapters. Part I recounts some of the history of the state. The first chapter reviews the state's "discovery" by Ponce de León in 1513 and subsequent settlement by the Spanish. Ponce, of course, did not "discover" Florida. Tens of thousands of people were already living here when he arrived, and for the better part of two centuries, the state's Native Americans resisted the European conquest with a great deal of bloodshed on both sides.

When statehood was declared in 1845, little Tallahassee was chosen as the capital because it was near the middle of what was considered the habitable part of the state, about midway between Pensacola and Saint Augustine, two of the state's largest cities in the middle of the nineteenth century. (A third major city at the time was Key West.) The rest of the state, everything south of the Panhandle, was mosquito-infested swamplands crawling with alligators, panthers, and bears. How the state evolved from deserted swampland to an international tourist attraction is the topic of chapter 2.

Development of the state south of the Panhandle was made possible largely by Henry Morrison Flagler, a Standard Oil tycoon whose wealth and vision brought the railroad into Florida, initially from Jacksonville to Saint Augustine but eventually all the way down the coast to Miami and then along the Florida Keys to Key West. Flagler, who has been called the inventor of modern Florida, is the subject of chapter 3.

Cars were invented at about the same time Flagler was building his railroad along with a string of luxurious hotels in the state. Very early in the twentieth century, wealthy sportsmen and thrill seekers from the northern cities were coming to race their expensive toys on the flat sands of Daytona. Chapter 4 tells the story of the invention of American-style stock-car racing at Daytona Beach, much of it wrapped up in the biography of William H. G. France, the founder of NASCAR and the man who built the Daytona International Speedway.

Part II explores Florida's trillion-dollar economy. We begin with the history of tourism. Some of the Old Florida tourist attractions were opened in the nineteenth century before it was even possible to get there by train, plane, or car. As the transportation industry evolved over the early decades of the twentieth century, so did tourism. The 1971 opening of Disney World heralded the arrival of the New Florida and the state has not been the same since.

Oranges were introduced by Ponce de León sometime in the first half of the sixteenth century near present-day Saint Augustine. The fruit has since blossomed into an orange juice industry that adds about $10 billion to the state's economy each year. Today, some 8,000 commercial citrus growers cultivate about 550,000 acres of orange groves. The northern part of the county where Orlando is located, originally known as Mosquito County, was renamed Orange County in 1845.

Florida's over-sixty-five population is the largest in the nation, with the state's four million seniors making up just about 20 percent of the entire state population. (The national average is about 15 percent.) One Florida county, Sumter (west of Orlando), is the only county in America where more than half the population (56.3 percent) is age sixty-five or older. Former governor Jeb Bush once remarked that Florida thinks of "retirement as an important industry. . . . We recognize the economic and social value of current elders and the aging baby boomer population." With a welcoming climate, numerous retirement communities, more golf courses than any other state, and no state income tax, the state has become a retirement (and snowbird) mecca, a favorite place for seniors to bring their pension funds, savings, and Social Security checks and "dissipate capital accumulated elsewhere" (see T. D. Allman, "Beyond Disney" in *National Geographic*, March 2007).

Florida also sports about 1,350 miles of coastline (roughly twice the total coastline of California). Indeed, there is no spot of dirt anywhere in the state that is more than 70 miles from the Atlantic Ocean or Gulf of Mexico. And yet we also lead the nation in per capita private swimming pools. In many suburban subdivisions, it is the rare house without one. From Daytona Beach (which bills itself as the "most famous beach in the world") down the Atlantic Coast to Miami Beach (Lenny Bruce said that Miami Beach was "where neon goes to die"), around the Straits of Florida to Key West (former home of Ernest Hemingway), then up the coast to Naples, Venice, Sarasota, Saint Petersburg, and finally the fabulous beaches of the Florida Panhandle, no part of Florida is exempt from beach culture and ethos. As the author Jarod Kintz once said, "I live in Florida, and when people ask how close to the beach I am, I say, 'Twelve minutes or twelve hours. Depends on which beach you want to go to.'"

We are also the preferred launch site for America's space program, situated near the small town of Port Canaveral. Space exploration out of Cape Canaveral (known as Cape Kennedy from 1963 to 1973) began in July 1950—much earlier than most people realize—when a two-stage Bumper 2 rocket blasted four hundred kilometers into space. The point of the launch was primarily to test the rocket's various systems, but in just less than two decades, NASA scientists and engineers flew three men from the east coast of Florida to the moon and back.

The third part of the book is about the people and politics of the Sunshine State—two of the state's weirder attractions. Politically and culturally, Florida is not one state but three. North Florida forms the boundary of the true South and is the home of "crackers" and their culture. Heavily Republican, the southern boundary of North Florida is The Barn, a country-western bar and nightclub in Sanford. From The Barn north to the Mason-Dixon Line, you can always get grits with your breakfast.

South of The Barn lies Central Florida, aka the I-4 corridor, the area from Tampa in the west, up through Orlando and on to Daytona in the East. The corridor is heavily urbanized and suburbanized and can go either Democratic or Republican. How it goes usually determines the statewide political outcome.

Then finally there is South Florida, home to a large retired Jewish population and an even larger Hispanic population made up mostly of Cuban exiles and their children (and now grandchildren and great-grandchildren). Cuban exiles from Miami made up most of the crew that broke into the Watergate Hotel in 1972 and subsequently brought down the Nixon administration. Today, English-only speakers make up less than a third of the Miami–Dade County population, and Miami has not elected a mayor of non-Cuban origin since 1973. Throughout Miami, Spanish is the predominant language, and despite the deeply anti-Castro and anti-Communist sentiments of the Cuban exile community, South Florida is reliably Democratic in national political contests.

Chapter 11 recounts the weirdness that was the 2000 presidential election, the election finally decided by 537 votes. As a percentage of the total vote, the two candidates differed only in the second decimal place (48.85 percent for Bush, 48.84 percent for Gore). The recount brought to light a number of disturbing election "irregularities," among them the "butterfly ballot" in Palm Beach, possibly illegal preelection purges of tens of thousands of potential voters from the voter registration lists, a large number of so-called overvotes (ballots with what appeared to be multiple markings), the infamous "hanging chads," and a great deal more chicanery, voter manipulation, and borderline corruption.

Florida's greatest living writer, Carl Hiaasen, has written, "The Florida in my novels is not as seedy as the real Florida. It's hard to stay ahead of the curve." We are, it seems, the last stop on the tour for deviants and derelicts of all descriptions. But the state has also produced its share of big thinkers and creative entrepreneurs. From Juan Trippe (the founder of commercial air travel) to the crooner Pat Boone, from Bruce Rossmeyer, owner of one of the world's largest Harley-Davidson dealerships, to Lewis Powell, coconspirator of John Wilkes Booth, the state has always been home to oddballs and unforgettables of every description. Stories of some of Florida's first, best, wildest, and weirdest conclude part III.

In part IV, we turn to the natural environment. For millions of years, hurricanes have swept across the peninsula with little but Everglade jungle and swampland in their path. Today, more than twenty million people are in the way. One of the most destructive hurricanes of all time, Hurricane Andrew, inundated South Florida in August 1992, leaving sixty-five people dead and $26 billion in damages in its wake. Andrew was a major force in the rewriting of the state's building codes and therefore an important factor in the late-twentieth-century development of the state.

Andrew tore through the Miami MetroZoo (now Zoo Miami) and various other public, private, and research enclosures that housed a variety of non-native species, species that have since gone feral and have taken up various niches in the state's ecosystem. The storm resulted in the introduction of the now-infamous Burmese python into the Everglades, where the predator has flourished. The python and other invasive species are the subject of chapter 15. Another chapter in part IV introduces the state's many lethal species—sharks, bears, gators, and snakes. These species really seem to bring out the stupid in people: the man who lost a hand trying to pet a wild bear; the many people bitten by alligators because they looked like they were asleep; the eighteen-year-old Tampa guy who captured a four-foot water moccasin, kept it in a pillowcase under his bed, and periodically expressed his affection for the snake by kissing it—until the day the snake "kissed" back. A chapter on roadkill, one on famous foods, and a concluding speculation complete part IV.

A book that discusses everything from politics to alligators to murderous prostitutes and corrupt politicians defies easy summary, so rather than recapping the book's common themes and takeaways, I conclude with an essay on what makes Florida so off-kilter in the first place. Various theories have been advanced: some merit serious attention; others are mainly laugh lines. In the end, I settle on a three-factor explanation: the very large numbers of outsiders in the state, the widespread perception that "the rules are different here" (at one time, this was a state marketing slogan), and a climate that often leads to weird, impulsive, and desperate behavior.

Some have dismissed my adopted state as just "America's hot, moist land-wang" (the quote is from author Chuck Wendig), but this conclusion is facile. Florida is equal parts amusement, frustration, horror, and wonderment, all of which wend their way through my narrative.

PART ONE

SOME BITS AND PIECES OF HISTORY

THE EARLY HISTORY

THE LIES BEGIN at the border. When you cross over into Florida from Georgia or Alabama, there are large signs that read WELCOME TO THE SUNSHINE STATE. (They also announce that Florida is OPEN FOR BUSINESS, an addition at the behest of the very conservative Governor Rick Scott.) But contrary to the implication of the state's famous motto, Florida is not the nation's sunniest state. Not even close. The state's percent-sun number (the average percentage of time between sunrise and sunset that the sun reaches the ground) is a respectable 66 percent, but that is exceeded by Arizona (85 percent), Nevada (79 percent), New Mexico (76 percent), Colorado (71 percent), Hawaii (71 percent), California, Wyoming, and Oklahoma (68 percent each). Florida averages only ninety-seven clear days annually (days with no clouds, a number that depends in part on where in Florida you live), which is fewer than the number of clear days in twenty-two other states. Where we do shine, so to speak, is in the number of hot and humid days, but somehow, "Welcome to the Muggy State" or "Florida: The Partly Cloudy State" just don't work as marketing slogans.

Also contrary to popular perception, Florida was not named for its abundant flowering species. *Florido* is the Spanish word for "flowery" (also "florid," incidentally), so many people assume that Florida means "the land of flowers." Not so. The name Pascua Florida was bestowed upon the state by the Spanish explorer Ponce de León on Easter Day, 1513, as Ponce and his crew sailed into what is now Matanzas Bay. In Spain, the Easter Celebration is known as the Feast of the Flowers, and a literal translation of Pascua Florida is therefore "Flowery Easter." The name Ponce chose for the state was not intended to refer to the orchids, violets, wild petunias, and other flowering plants that are native to Florida, but rather to the Catholic celebration of the death and resurrection of Christ.

THE SPANISH INCURSION

Juan Ponce de León led the first Spanish expedition into what is now Florida, and so he is often said to have been the state's "discoverer." Of course, Florida was occupied for twelve thousand years or so before Ponce and his hardy band of *conquistadores* showed up. Ponce did not "discover" the state, he only initiated (or rather, tried to initiate) the European conquest of Native American lands in the region.

Ponce's 1513 expedition came ashore somewhere near present-day Saint Augustine. This was when the name Pascua Florida was bestowed. He then sailed south and eventually came upon what we now know as the Florida Keys, the outermost of which are the Dry Tortugas. *Tortuga* is Spanish for "turtle," and Ponce evidently chose the name because of the turtles he observed there. (It was "dry" because there seemed to be no fresh water anywhere on the island.) He then turned north, landed near what is now Port Charlotte, ran into some very unfriendly natives, and hightailed it back to Puerto Rico.

Ponce returned to the Port Charlotte area in 1521 with the intention of establishing a colony but again ran afoul of the local tribesmen, the Calusa. Ponce was fatally wounded in this confrontation, and the Spanish colonization effort was abandoned until 1565. After the face-off with the Calusa, the *conquistadores* withdrew to their base in Cuba, where Ponce de León died from his wounds. His remains were interred and subsequently moved to Puerto Rico, where his burial crypt can be viewed today in the Cathedral of San Juan Bautista in Old San Juan.

It is often said that Ponce came to Florida to find the mythical Fountain of Youth. More lies, of course—not that you would know it if you went to Saint Augustine to visit a tourist attraction called Ponce de León's Fountain of Youth Archaeological Park. The park houses practically nothing of genuine archaeological significance, and one assumes that the reference to archaeology in the park's name is intended to impart a faux impression of scientific merit or importance. In fact, there is no legitimate historical evidence to suggest that Ponce was looking for anything like a Fountain of Youth. As was true of all the Spanish explorers of the New World, he was looking for gold and silver to seal his favor with the Spanish Crown. The whole Fountain of Youth business is a myth likely perpetrated by one Gonzalo Fernández de Oviedo y Valdés, who is said to have despised Ponce and cooked up the Fountain of Youth story to depict Ponce as a gullible, dim-witted fool. Even in sixteenth-century Spain, the idea that water could reverse aging was considered pretty unlikely.

As for the park, it showcases a primitive fountain (a stone well from which hundreds of tourists imbibe daily), a number of reconstructions ("historically correct examples") of native Timucuan villages (the Timucua were another tribe that inhabited Florida at the time of the European "discovery"), a reconstruction of a 1587 church, a Founders Riverwalk, miles of natural beauty, and a new three-thousand-square-foot pavilion "perfect for weddings and other events."

Between 1513 and 1559, there were numerous efforts to colonize the region for Spain, but they all ended in abject failure. Hernando de Soto and his *conquistadores,* for example, wandered around the region near present-day Tallahassee for four years searching for silver and gold, found nothing, gave up, and headed west toward the Mississippi, where the explorer died in 1542. In 1559, another Spanish adventurer, Tristán de Luna y Arellano, tried to establish a colony near present-day Pensacola, but this effort came a cropper when a hurricane blew through and destroyed a supply ship. After the 1559 failure, King Philip II of Spain ordered a halt to all further colonization efforts, but the moratorium lasted only six years.

Colonization began anew in 1565 when Pedro Menéndez de Avilés came ashore at what is now known as Matanzas Bay and founded the Presidio of San Agustin, America's first and oldest continuously inhabited European-origin city. Saint Augustine was established decades before the founding of the first English settlement in Jamestown, Virginia, in 1607, or the landing of the *Mayflower* at Plymouth Rock in 1620.

Matanzas is Spanish for "slaughters," and that alone tells us something about the city's violent origins. French Huguenots (Protestants) had established a colony near the mouth of the Saint Johns River in territory claimed by Spain, and Menéndez had been dispatched by the Spanish Crown to dislodge the French settlers and kill any Protestants he came across. He landed near Saint Augustine, then marched his army of a thousand soldiers overland for a surprise attack on the French Fort Caroline near present-day Jacksonville. The surprise was successful, and virtually all the French men were slaughtered (the women and children were spared). Menéndez also got word of a band of French castaways who had shipwrecked farther south along the coast and dispatched a force to hunt them down. Once found, the castaways surrendered immediately since they had neither arms nor strength nor will to resist. They too were killed. These slaughters occurred near the banks of the river that opens into the bay, so both the river and the bay were named *Matanzas*.

Menéndez chose the name San Agustin for his Presidio because his force sailed into the bay on August 28, 1565, which happened to be the feast day of Saint Augustine. Augustine is remembered mostly as the theoretician of the "just war," a doctrine invoked repeatedly by the *conquistadores* to justify the forcible conversion of heathens to Christianity and the wanton slaughter of those who resisted. Saint Aug was a big fan of Romans 13:4: ". . . rulers do not bear the sword for no reason. They are God's servants, agents of wrath to bring punishment on the wrongdoer."

Saint Augustine (the city) rapidly became the center of Spanish Florida and was a frequent target of attack. The city (really, little more than a fort in the early years) was burned to the ground in 1586 by the British explorer Sir Francis Drake, then burned numerous times by pirates (and occasionally by the British) in succeeding years. In most cases, the town's residents were killed or driven away. The city remained vulnerable until the Spanish completed the Castillo de San Marcos in 1695 and Fort Matanzas in 1742.

The Castillo and most of Fort Matanzas remain today and were declared national historical monuments in 1924. Often overrun by tourists, Fort Matanzas is rated by Trip Advisor as #29 of 191 things to do in Saint Augustine. The Castillo is rated #11.

HEY, WE WERE HERE FIRST!

Spain's troubles in colonizing Florida were of two sorts: unfriendly conditions and even less friendly natives. Wresting ownership of the peninsula from its indigenous inhabitants, both human and otherwise, was harder here than almost anywhere else in North America. All the Spanish colonies in Florida were built on the coasts and near or at the mouths of rivers, for reasons that would be obvious to today's beachgoers. In addition to the obvious transportation advantages, there are sea breezes on the coasts that keep the temperature and humidity tolerable and the mosquitoes at bay. In the sixteenth through eighteenth centuries, venturing even a few miles inland would bring you into impassible swampland, suffocating heat and humidity, vast swarms of mosquitoes, and alligators, crocodiles, bears, and snakes galore.

Contrary to popular mythology, Native Americans were not docile bands of primitives, certainly not in Florida and not in the rest of the country, either, and in no way was Florida "easy pickings" for its conquerors. Native North American technologies included quarrying, stoneworking, ceramics, grinding, lumbering, manufacture of wood products, hunting and butchering, canoe manufacture, food preservation, leatherworking, some metalworking, food processing, and weaving, among other things—hardly a "primitive" collection of skills. The native culture also included song and dance, jewelry and art, religion, calendars, medical practices, rituals and celebrations, and elaborate horticultural understandings—not really a "primitive" collection of cultural traits, either. Nor were the natives unorganized politically. Many tribes and coalitions of tribes evidenced advanced forms of social organization, and many could deploy highly capable warriors to defend their interests. The European incursion into native lands involved two centuries of wars, skirmishes, battles, clashes, and massacres between the natives and their colonizers. And it wasn't always the colonizers who came out on top. Ponce de León's troubles with the Calusa were only the beginning. Indeed, of all the Native American groups and tribes that were eventually subdued and displaced by the

Europeans, the Florida natives resisted most successfully. Even today, no peace treaty with the Seminoles has ever been signed.

Although today the Seminole is a federally recognized tribe, they were originally a coalition of Native American tribes that formed specifically to fight off the Europeans. Among the tribes in the coalition were the Apalachee, Calusa, Choctaw, Creek, Miccosukee, Tequesta, Jeaga, Ais, and Timucua. (Historians think there were about sixty tribes, bands, and culturally independent groupings of Native Americans in the state when the Spaniards arrived.) Many similar coalitions were formed all over the United States, and for the same reason, to resist European (and later American) expansion into native lands. Notable in this connection are the Miami Confederacy in Indiana, the Iroquois Confederacy in New York (later known as the Six Nations), the Three Fires Confederacy in the Great Lakes region, and the Wabanaki Confederacy in Maine. The formation of the Seminole coalition was not a singular event, either, but rather a process of "ethnogenesis" that occurred in the early 1700s as more and more native groups recognized their common interests. The word "Seminole" itself is a corruption of the Spanish *cimarrón,* "wild."

Three full-scale wars were fought between the Seminoles and the new United States government. The first was waged in 1817–1818, and the US effort was led by Andrew Jackson two years before dominion over Florida was ceded by the Spanish to the Americans. Florida was slave territory (and later a slave state), and the willingness of the Seminoles to provide sanctuary to escaped slaves was a key issue in the First Seminole War. The second war began in 1835, as the American government moved in to stabilize the territory and relocate unfriendly natives. More and more colonists were demanding that the natives be forcibly removed and relocated on reservations west of the Mississippi, an idea of which Andrew Jackson wholeheartedly approved when he became president in 1829. The Indian Removal Act of 1830 was signed by President Jackson two days after it was enacted by Congress and was pursued vigorously from the Great Lakes to the swamplands of South Florida.

Chief Osceola led the Seminole resistance to Jackson's forcible relocation policies in what came to be called the Second Seminole War (1835–1842). The Seminoles were vastly outnumbered by the US Army and its associated local militias and thus resorted to guerrilla warfare, which they deployed to devastating effect. When Osceola finally approached the American forces, white flag in hand, to negotiate a truce, he was arrested, jailed, and died a year later. In an action worthy of an @_FloridaMan entry, he was then decapitated and his body and head were buried separately. This was not a burial custom of the Spanish, the Americans, or the natives, just sheer barbarism.

Between 1831 and 1850, most of the American Southeast was cleared of its Native American population via voluntary or forced relocation along what came to be called the Trail of Tears. Tribes vacated along the infamous trail included the Cherokee, Muscogee, Chickasaw, Choctaw, and, of course, the Florida Seminole. Nearly all of these tribes provided some resistance to relocation.

The most common estimate for the number of lives lost on the Trail of Tears is four thousand, though this figure is unverified and disputed by some. By the end of the Second Seminole War, death, disease, and relocation had drastically reduced the Seminole population and the remaining Seminoles retreated into the Everglades and continued their resistance to the Americans. The Third Seminole War broke out in 1855 when US Army scouting parties deliberately provoked a confrontation in the hopes of driving the few Seminoles that remained out of the state. This war, mainly a series of raids, skirmishes, and reprisals rather than full-scale battles, persisted until 1858, when the war-weary Seminoles agreed to be relocated to reservations in Oklahoma. Even then, a hundred Seminoles (or maybe several hundred—historians disagree) refused to leave and retreated deeper into the Everglades, at which point the US government simply gave up and allowed the few Seminoles remaining in Florida to stay.

Today, the Seminole Tribe of Florida, the Seminole Nation of Oklahoma (descendants of those relocated along the Trail of Tears), and the Miccosukee Tribe of Indians of Florida are all that remain of the aboriginal Florida population. The Seminole was recognized as a legitimate Native American tribe in 1957, the Miccosukee in 1962, and today members of the two tribes reside on six Florida reservations. Upon the grant of legal status, the tribes opened tax-free tobacco operations and high-stakes bingo games on their reservations that evolved into the large Seminole and Miccosukee casinos that the tribes operate today. They are the only land-based casinos in Florida, and according to a 2016 report, they reel in more than $2 billion annually.

The Miccosukee have proven particularly adept at marketing and tourism. Their Miccosukee Resort & Gaming hotel in Miami–Dade County has 302 rooms and rakes in hundreds of millions of dollars annually. The tribe sponsored several NASCAR race cars from 2002 to 2010. There is also a Miccosukee Indian Village Museum, founded in 1983, which offers tourists native paintings and handicrafts, photos and artifacts from the tribe's past, an "authentic" Indian camp reconstruction, alligator shows, and airboat rides. Trip Advisor rates the Miccosukee Indian Village as #1 of one things to do in Tamiami. It is, in short, the only game in town.

Today, there are some 72,000 Floridians who claim "American Indian" as their sole ethnic or racial heritage and more than twice that number who claim American Indian heritage in combination with some other ethnicity. Either way, this is a whopping increase from the numbers that remained at the close of the Third Seminole War (several hundred at best). Perhaps as compensation for the predations of the nineteenth century, the twentieth and now twenty-first centuries have been reasonably good to these "First Floridians," at least demographically.

Up until 1763 and the Treaty of Paris that ended what Americans know as the French and Indian War, most of the eastern seaboard was ruled by the British, a vast swath of the interior from Quebec to New Orleans was ruled by the French, and Florida and the territories of the Southwest (present-day Texas, New Mexico, Arizona, and Mexico) were ruled by the Spanish. Unlike the British, the Spanish were pretty relaxed about racial matters, and while there were slaveholders throughout Spanish America, including in Florida, the Spanish were also keen to "steal" population from the British by offering sanctuary in Florida to runaway slaves from the north. In 1693, Spain's King Charles II offered freedom to runaway slaves from British territories, the only condition being that they convert to Catholicism. In 1738, the Spanish governor of Florida approved construction of a settlement for ex-slaves to be built north of present-day Saint Augustine. The settlement was named Fort Mose (Moh-say, although today in American usage, the pronunciation rhymes with dose), and it was the first legally approved town for free blacks in North America. Fort Mose precedes the Emancipation Proclamation by more than a century.

Today, Fort Mose is a state park featuring an archaeological excavation begun in 1986 and three replicas of historically significant items: a cooking hut, a small "historic" garden, and a Spanish *barca chata* (flatboat). The park also features picnic areas, a boardwalk for birding, a kayak launch, a visitor center, and an annual reenactment of the 1740 Battle of Bloody Mose. Admission to the park is free, but it costs adults two bucks to get into the visitor center.

Spain traded Florida to the British in 1763 in exchange for control of Havana, which had been captured by the Brits in the Seven Years' War (aka the French and Indian War). So at the outbreak of the American Revolution in 1776, Florida was in British (not Spanish) hands, and Floridians remained loyal to Britain. This loyalty explains why there were thirteen original colonies, not fourteen. Florida had been invited to the Continental Congress but refused and served as an important refuge for British loyalists throughout the Revolution. Saint Augustine housed thousands of British loyalists during the war, and effigies of John Hancock and Samuel Adams were burned in downtown Saint Augustine to protest the Declaration of Independence. One loyalist even organized a militia force, the East Florida Rangers, which fought numerous battles against the American forces, among them the battles of Thomas Creek and Alligator Bridge.

The treaty officially ending the American Revolution was another Treaty of Paris, signed in 1783 (almost two years after the British surrendered at Yorktown). Since Florida was not one of the thirteen newly independent colonies, control of the state was returned to Spain, although with no specific boundaries. Spain in turn ceded Florida to the Americans in 1821, just in time for Andrew Jackson to begin the long bloody process of moving the natives out. The region was granted the status of a formal US territory in 1822, and Florida became the twenty-seventh state in 1845. Tallahassee was chosen as the territorial capital, and subsequently the state capital, because it was midway in what was considered the habitable part of the state, midway between Pensacola to the west and Saint Augustine to the east. With a few exceptions, everything south of what we now call the Panhandle remained mostly the territory of the mosquitoes and alligators well into the twentieth century.

2

THE TWELFTH HAPPIEST STATE IN THE NINETEENTH HAPPIEST COUNTRY

THE *CONCEPT* OF Florida is a mixture of myth, metaphor, and reality. Mythical Florida is Disney's "Happiest Place on Earth," the Florida of unparalleled growth and boundless opportunity, the Florida of warm sunshine, alluring suburbs, and a government that gets by without a state income tax. Florida has also become a metaphor for unplanned growth, sprawl, congestion, and automobile dependence—a vast blob of indistinguishable suburban developments loosely coupled to cities that are congested warrens of concrete, glass, and steel and devoid of vernacular appeal. The reality of Florida is that while many people have gotten rich off tourism, construction, retirement, and unchecked growth, the wealth has been very unequally distributed and has resulted in a labor economy dominated by low-wage jobs in the service industries and a construction sector comprised in substantial measure of illegal immigrant workers. This chapter separates the state's marketing falsehoods, misdirection, and half-truths from the economic and demographic realities of what is now America's third most populous state.*

At the time of statehood (1845), the Florida population amounted to

---

*Readers interested in learning more about the contemporary economic realities of Florida will be well served by James D. Wright and Amy M. Donley, *Poor and Homeless in the Sunshine State: Down and Out in Theme Park Nation* (New Brunswick, NJ: Transaction Publishers, 2011).

about 66,500 people (this in an area of 58,560 square miles, or a bit more than one person per square mile). There were a few reasonably populous towns along the coasts—Jacksonville, Saint Augustine, Miami, Key West, Tampa, and Pensacola. Key West was the largest city in Florida, with about 3,000 residents, and Saint Augustine was second, with just a couple thousand. The only inland town of any significance was the territorial capital Tallahassee (established 1824). Florida's interior cities and towns were all established after statehood: Ocala in 1846, Gainesville in 1869, Orlando in 1875. The state's economy in 1845 was predominantly agricultural, and cotton harvested by slaves was the main cash product.

Even as late as 1900, the state's population was just over a half million. A population of one million was first recorded in the 1930 census and even at mid-century, the entire population of the state was fewer than three million people. Today, more than twenty-one million people call Florida home. Three important factors in the explosive twentieth-century growth of the state were the building of the Florida East Coast Railway between 1885 and 1912 (discussed in chapter 3), the opening of Walt Disney World in 1971 (chapter 5), and the completion of the Dixie Highway from Chicago to Miami (chapter 12). Exaggerating only slightly, the first and third gave people a way to get to Florida, and the second gave them something to do once they got here. Over the course of the twentieth century, Florida was transformed from a rural agricultural backwater to an international tourist destination. These days, a hundred million tourists visit Florida each year (five times the resident population), and tourism is the backbone of the state's economy.

The transformation from rural boondocks to major tourist and retirement destination did not happen overnight. For the first several decades of the twentieth century, Florida was infamous for brazen land swindles that attracted thousands under false and fraudulent promises. Florida real estate was a classic con game for much of the twentieth century. Advertising photos ran in northern papers showing lovely lakes and golf courses and inviting families to buy Florida property for as little as one thousand dollars down and ten dollars a month—more affordable than buying a car. Thousands were sucked into these schemes, only to learn once they came to Florida that their "land" was under water or in the middle of a gator-infested swamp. Some of the more notorious real estate scams included the Golden Gates Estates near present-day Naples, and Cape Coral near present-day Fort Myers, although land scams went on throughout the state. Ironically, both Cape Coral and Golden Gates Estates (and many other one-time scams) have evolved into thriving suburbs of the sort that have come to define Florida's "suburban sprawl."

The real estate scams of the forties, fifties, and sixties gave way to explosive population growth beginning about 1970. Since 1970, the state has added an average of about two million additional residents each decade: from 1960 to 1970, the state population jumped from about 5 to 7 million, and then in succeeding decades from 7 million to 10 million (1980) to 13 million (1990) to 16 million (2000) to more than 21 million today. In most of these decades, Florida was the fastest growing state in the nation. Tourism, retirement, and construction were the wellsprings of this growth.

The *myth* of modern Florida has also grown rapidly since 1970, stimulated in large measure by Disney and the tourist economy. Mythical Florida, as the Disney marketing slogan has it, is "The Happiest Place on Earth," a place where the sun always shines, jobs are plentiful, taxes are low, and people are friendly—a state of magnificent sprawling homes near rolling golf courses in spectacular gated communities with screened-in swimming pools in every backyard. One local referred to mythical Florida as "pixie dust." When asked to explain, she noted that millions of people come to Florida each year for their vacations, somehow convince themselves (this is the pixie dust working) that their vacation experiences are the reality of life in the state, then uproot themselves and move to Florida, only to discover that it was all a fantasy—a wonderful, upbeat, glorious fantasy, yes, but a fantasy nonetheless.

The growth that tourism has stimulated has been the basis of the Florida economy for the last forty or fifty years. Population growth on the scale Florida has experienced demands housing and infrastructure—lots of it, in a hurry. The state's developers rapidly created a booming secondary economy based on construction—of homes to house new arrivals, strip malls to cater to their needs, schools to educate their children, churches to pray for forgiveness, and, always, highways, streets, and roads to get everyone from place to place.

Rapid development and suburbanization also turned Florida into a leading metaphor of the twenty-first-century postindustrial city: a congested,
unplanned, and overbuilt growth machine that has created hundreds of
thousands of square miles of metro-area suburbs, often enough with little
or no urban core. With only a few exceptions, the state has become a gigantic collection of suburbs that are connected to businesses, employment
centers, shopping opportunities, and cultural amenities by endless miles
of toll roads and interstates. As T. D. Allman put it in a *National Geographic*
article, Florida's suburbs have become "blobby coalescences of look-alike,
overnight, amoeba-like concentrations of population far from city centers.
These huge, sprawling communities are where more and more Americans
choose to be, the place where job growth is fastest, home building is brisk-
est, and malls and mega-churches are multiplying as newcomers keep on
coming. Who are all these people?"

Andrew Ross says, "The damage wrought by thirty [now fifty] years of
this kind of market-driven development, propelled by short-term profit and
asleep-at-the-wheel planning, is painfully evident on all sides." And so it
is. Florida cities all rank relatively high in urban sprawl. One consequence
of sprawl is long commuting times and traffic congestion, especially since
public transportation in Florida has been largely an afterthought. A 2017
study of traffic congestion in US cities ranked Miami fifth, Orlando twenty-
eighth, and Tampa thirty-first. In earlier studies, Fort Lauderdale, West
Palm Beach, Jacksonville, and Pensacola were also singled out for their traffic congestion. There is also a 2017 list of US cities that are the most dangerous for pedestrians (and bicyclists). Of the ten most dangerous cities for
pedestrians, eight are in Florida. Really. In order, they are Fort Myers, Palm
Bay, Orlando, Jacksonville, Daytona Beach, Lakeland, Tampa, Jackson
(Mississippi), Memphis (Tennessee), and then Sarasota.

The transformation of Florida from swamp to sprawling suburbanized
megalopolis was the result of hardheaded, profit-driven business decisions
abetted by a local political atmosphere of indifferent planning and an almost religious devotion among state and local policy-makers to growth at
any cost. One result is a kind of social and human (not to mention environmental) devastation. Much of Florida has evolved through land-
development schemes that often exacerbated relations between the wealthy

and the state's sizable and growing poverty population. Employment opportunities in construction, tourism, and the like have enticed millions of people, many of them economically marginal, into the region to take jobs that do not alleviate and often heighten their marginality.

The Florida economy was hit hard by the 2007–2008 recession. The rate of state population growth began to slow in 2007, just as state planners were forecasting continued exponential growth through to mid-century. Growth essentially halted entirely in 2008, and in 2009 some counties lost population for the first time in sixty-three years. (The state has since recovered and has begun adding population again, but for the last decade, population was basically flat.) So starting in 2007, everything in the state that lived on continued, and rapid population growth—and that was just about everything—suffered. Several major developers (e.g., Levitt and Sons, Engle Homes, and numerous others) pulled out of Florida entirely. Many development projects were halted mid-construction. New home start-ups fell to all-time lows.

The impact of the economic recession, reduced construction, and flagging tourism on the state's budget was brutal. The projected deficit for the 2009–2010 fiscal year was about $2.4 billion, which the state legislature "covered" with severe cuts to education, health services, law enforcement, and transportation. (The Florida Constitution does not permit the state to run deficits.) Fiscal year 2010–2011 was even worse, with statewide budget deficits initially projected to be in the $4 to $6 billion range; thus more budget cuts. Then in late 2010, Florida elected ultraconservative Rick Scott as its governor, and cutting services and budgets became an ideological mandate as much as an economic necessity.

Scott was formerly the CEO of Columbia/Hospital Corporation of America, the largest private for-profit health-care company in the nation. He resigned in 1997 in the middle of a controversy surrounding the company's Medicare billing practices, a controversy that was finally resolved when Columbia/HCA agreed to pay back about $630 million to the federal government—the largest health-care fraud settlement up until that time. Scott avoided personal prosecution in the case by pleading the Fifth Amendment in his deposition *seventy-five times*.

Upon taking office in 2011, Scott set about stripping welfare, education, and health-care spending out of the Florida budget to make room for huge tax breaks for his superwealthy friends. He later turned down some $2 billion in federal funding to build high-speed rail service in the state, cut $1.75 billion from the state's education budget, tried to get the state to mandate drug testing for welfare recipients, declined federal funds to expand Medicaid in Florida, and brushed up against some rather serious corruption allegations involving state contracts being awarded to his cronies. As punishment for his heartless misdeeds, Scott was reelected in 2014.

The good news about the Florida reality is that there are always lots of jobs. (When my research shop interviews homeless people who came to Florida from out of state and asks them why they came, a common reply is, "We heard Disney was hiring.") The bad news is that most of these jobs don't pay very well. The result is that Florida ranks thirty-fourth among the fifty states in overall poverty rate and thirty-sixth in its child poverty rate. Yes, taxes are low. Florida is one of seven states that have no state income tax. But as a result of low taxes, Florida ranks tenth from the bottom in per-student expenditures on public education, at the very bottom in state spending on mental health services, and somewhere in the middle (at best) in overall spending on health. As with everything else in life, you only get what you pay for. And Florida does not pay for very much.

Gallup-Sharecare has developed a "Well-Being Index" that they use to determine which states are the happiest. The index captures multiple dimensions of well-being. The most recent of their surveys did not show Florida to be "The Happiest Place on Earth," not even the happiest place in the United States. In this poll, Florida was the twelfth happiest state, and in other surveys and rankings has come in as low as fortieth.

There was also a 2016 study ranking the various nations in the world according to aggregate national happiness. In this particular study, the United States ranked nineteenth, well behind Denmark, Switzerland, the Netherlands, Canada, and several others. (In other similar studies, we've ranked as low as twenty-fourth.) So come to Florida, the Twelfth Happiest State in the Nineteenth Happiest Country!" Somehow, that too falls flat as a marketing slogan.

3

HENRY FLAGLER'S RAILROAD

AT THE TURN of the twentieth century, the entire paved road system of the United States amounted to well less than a thousand miles of highway, little of it to be found in Florida. There were, of course, millions of miles of roadways at the time, all unpaved. In the cities, roadways were sometimes surfaced with wooden or granite blocks, gravel, or cobblestones "harvested" from sailing ship ballast, none of which provided a particularly smooth or long-lasting surface. Driving on these surfaces was a difficult, bone-jarring experience. In the countryside, the "roads" were little more than dirt cattle paths, deeply rutted, impassable in wet weather and barely navigable when dry. As the nineteenth century morphed into the twentieth, transportation was by horse, boat, oxcart, or on foot—none of these well suited to the rapid movement of large numbers of people, least of all into the nation's interior. The expansion and growth of much of the American interior, and certainly much of Florida, awaited the development of the railroads. And no one was more instrumental in bringing the railroads to Florida and opening the state to tourism than Henry Flagler.

It is no exaggeration to say that Flagler invented the Florida we know today. His ventures were instrumental in establishing Florida as a tourist destination: the farms he developed to feed his small army of workers were to become the basis of Florida's agricultural economy; the housing projects he constructed to provide shelter for his workers evolved into many of

Florida's present-day cities and towns. *Sun Sentinel* reporter Wayne Roustan says, "If it weren't for the railroad, there might not be a South Florida." And Cully Waggoner of the Gold Coast Railroad Museum says, "Without Henry Flagler and his railroad, we wouldn't have the Miami that we have today." More than any other single person, Flagler opened up Florida to the rest of America, and that made it possible for the weirdness to come flowing in.

The practicability of a steam locomotive capable of pulling large loads along metal rails had been demonstrated in 1829, and as locomotives replaced horses, mules, and oxen for overland transit, rails came into general use and a national system of railway transport emerged. For most of the nineteenth century, urban development followed the railroads, whereas previously it had followed the rivers. At the same time, the rail lines tended to run parallel to nearby rivers because that is where the people were when the railroads were first developed.

Construction of a rail network in the United States began in 1828, when work was started on the first section of the Baltimore & Ohio Railroad. This 14-mile line was opened to traffic in 1830. By the end of that year, the country had a total of 23 miles of railroad in operation. Five years later, the national total was 1,098 miles. By 1848 there were nearly 6,000 miles of track, virtually all of it in states along the Atlantic seaboard.

A trans-Florida railroad was first proposed in 1842. At the time, to get by ship from the Atlantic Ocean into the Gulf of Mexico required navigation through the treacherous Straits of Florida, where many a laden cargo ship ran aground and sank. Indeed, a principal industry in Key West in this era was salvage from shipwrecks. In 1842, the US Congress commissioned a study of the practicality of a railroad to run from the mouth of the Saint Marys River (note: Marys, not the frequently encountered misspelling Mary's) at the Florida-Georgia border overland to Cedar Key (near present-day Tampa). Not only would this allow cargo to avoid the dangerous Florida straits, it would also lop about eight hundred miles off the trip.

Construction of the railway started from the eastern side in 1855, near present-day Fernandina on Amelia Island at Florida's northernmost point. By 1858, the line was opened between Fernandina and Starke (site of the state's largest maximum-security prison, where Florida's numerous executions are carried out), but further progress was halted by the Panic of 1857, which left the railroad in near bankruptcy. A major rearrangement of the railroad's financial affairs let construction resume in 1858. The line was extended to Gainesville by 1859 and reached Cedar Key on Florida's west coast by 1861. In all, the line extended 156 miles from one side of the state to the other.

Getting goods, food, war supplies, and troops efficiently across the Florida peninsula was a definite strategic advantage for the South in the early days of the Civil War, and so the little railroad quickly became a target for Union forces. The Union's USS *Hatteras* raided Cedar Key in 1862 and destroyed all the engines, cars, and buildings it could. In March 1862, the railroad was besieged on its eastern side by a Union raid at Fernandina that shelled the last train leaving the town and killed or injured numerous passengers. Miles of track were torn up on the western side by Union soldiers, and miles more were torn up on the eastern side by Confederate soldiers to build a new and more strategically important line from Florida to Georgia.

Operation of what was called the Florida Railroad was resumed after the war, but the extensive war-related damages to the rolling stock, buildings, and track made the railway unprofitable, so it was sold off, reorganized, amalgamated, and otherwise restructured numerous times until it emerged as part of the Florida Central and Peninsular Railway about 1893. Rails operated by this company connected Jacksonville with Tallahassee and Pensacola across the Panhandle; Jacksonville with Gainesville, Cedar Key, and the Gulf Coast to the southwest; and Gainesville with Tampa along a southern route. Florida's east coast was conspicuously absent from the list—mainly because there was little or nothing along the east coast that was worth connecting to.

Between 1863 and 1869, three private companies with rights of way provided by the US government completed the Transcontinental Railroad that connected Omaha with San Francisco. Many eastern railroads serviced Omaha and its immense cattle-processing industry. So beginning in 1869, one could get from most urban areas in the East all the way to the West Coast by rail. This stimulated what could be called the Golden Age of railway construction in America. Between 1880 and 1910, railroad mileage was added to the American landscape at the rate of about seven thousand miles per year. The railroads connected the major US cities long before paved roads did. At its peak in 1916, US railroad route mileage amounted to more than a quarter million miles. Auto-friendly (that is to say, paved or gravel) road mileage in the same year amounted to barely thirty-six thousand miles. So if you needed to get quickly and painlessly from point A to point B almost anywhere in the United States, the railroads were just about the only way to go.

The opening up of Florida's east coast for development and as a vacationer's paradise is largely due to Henry Morrison Flagler (1830–1913). Born in New York as the child of a Presbyterian minister, Flagler moved to Ohio after completing eighth grade to work with his cousins in a grain store. During the Civil War, he and a brother-in-law opened a salt-mining business in Michigan, but the business collapsed when the demand for salt fell. (Salt was in high demand during the war as a food preservative. When the Union Army dissolved, so did the demand for salt.) Nearly bankrupt, he returned to Ohio and reentered the grain-merchant business, where he soon befriended another Cleveland-area grain merchant, one John D. Rockefeller.

During and just after the Civil War, Cleveland was emerging as a center of oil refining in America, and Rockefeller abandoned the grain business to open an oil refinery of his own. At the time, the principal market for oil-based products was kerosene to fuel lamps, not gasoline to power cars, which had not yet been invented. (The car was invented in Germany in the 1880s.) Initially, gasoline was an unwanted and unused by-product of the oil-refining process, useful mainly as a solvent, but dangerously flammable. The advent of the automobile changed all that.

Not yet the "richest man in America," Rockefeller needed investors to get his first refinery open, and his new friend Henry Flagler was just the man. For an investment of a hundred thousand dollars (all of it borrowed), Flagler was made the 25 percent owner-partner in a new company, Rockefeller, Andrews, and Flagler. Rockefeller was the entrepreneur and Flagler was the financier. Samuel Andrews was a chemist who is credited with inventing the process of fractional distillation, on which the modern oil industry is based. He was the technical genius behind the new joint venture. In

1870, this partnership was reorganized as a joint-stock corporation named Standard Oil. When Rockefeller moved his headquarters to New York City in 1875, Flagler, now wealthy almost beyond description, moved with him.

In 1878, Flagler was advised by his doctors to take his beloved but tubercular wife, Mary, to Florida for the winter. His wife's health was rapidly deteriorating, and her doctors feared that another winter in New York might do her in. Railroad travel between New York City and Jacksonville, Florida, was possible at the time, so the couple visited both Jacksonville and Saint Augustine during their stay. Flagler recognized at once the potential of Florida's east coast as a wintering-over spot and tourist destination for his wealthy pals in the north. While his friends were hacking their way through the winter cold and snow, Henry and Mary were sunning themselves on the white sands of the Jacksonville and Saint Augustine beaches. Alas, the region, although charming and temperate in the winter, was lacking hotel facilities and a local transportation system.

Flagler's wife died in 1881, and a few years later Flagler (now remarried) surrendered his day-to-day involvement in the affairs of Standard Oil and moved to Florida to pursue his development interests. He began by buying up, modernizing, consolidating, and extending a bunch of small local railroads so that visitors to Jacksonville would have efficient rail service to points south. A key accomplishment was his railroad bridge over the Saint Johns River, a bridge that opened all of Florida's east coast.

Flagler soon began work on an exclusive luxury hotel in Saint Augustine, the Hotel Ponce de León, completed in 1887 and opened in grand style the following year. In Flagler's words: "How to build a hotel to meet the requirements of nineteenth-century America and have it in keeping with the character of the place? that was my hardest problem." The Ponce de León was the first such building to be built entirely from poured concrete and was wired for electrical service from the outset. Instructions to the builders, engineers, and decorators were to spare no expense. Notables who stayed in the hotel include Mark Twain, Theodore Roosevelt, Somerset Maugham, and Babe Ruth. Today, the Ponce de León is the central building of Saint Augustine's Flagler College, a small liberal arts college founded in 1968. Among Flagler College alumni, probably the best known is the American model Laura Croft, whose claim to fame is that she was *Playboy*'s Playmate of the Month in July 2008.

The Ponce de León proved an attractive location for America's burgeoning film industry. Parts of *Stolen Moments,* starring Rudolph Valentino, were filmed there, and the hotel was a favorite location for romantic garden shots and anything else that required elegance in design and decor. For a brief period, Saint Augustine was as important to the American film industry as Hollywood.

The Ponce de León was the first but by no means the last of Flagler's luxury hotels. An Ormond Beach hotel, the Hotel Ormond (where stock-car racing was invented), was purchased and refurbished. A second Saint Augustine hotel, the Alcazar, was built to accommodate the overflow from the Ponce de León. (The Alcazar today houses the Lightner Museum and its collection of antiquities.) Still another luxury hotel project was the 1,150-room Royal Poinciana Hotel in West Palm Beach. To get guests to the Royal Poinciana, Flagler extended his rail service southward by about 250 miles. At the time, the Royal Poinciana was the largest wooden structure in the world and the largest resort hotel. Still another luxury hotel was opened two years later in Palm Beach proper. Because of these hotels and the development they spawned, Flagler is considered the father of Palm Beach and West Palm Beach.

Flagler's developmental strategy was very simple. He would spot a small village in a promising location—Ormond Beach, Daytona, Palm Springs, Palm Beach, Miami—acquire as much land as was available, build a luxurious hotel, and extend rail service to the location. And thus did he transform eastern Florida from gator-infested mangrove swampland into a wintering-over paradise, a chain of luxurious beachside hotels connected by train to the wealthy northern cities. In short, he invented the Florida we know today.

Flagler was a man of his times, and in the Deep South at the end of the nineteenth century, that meant a certain indifference to the conditions and dignity of the state's large population of ex-slaves, a racism that persists, undeniably, in much of Florida today. Guests at the Royal Poinciana were ferried about the property by African Americans pedaling bikes outfitted with large wicker chairs. They were called "Afrimobiles" and were a popular hotel amenity.

Of all his Florida sites, Flagler was most enamored of the South Florida town of Palm Springs, and that is where he chose to build his luxurious personal estate, Whitehall (built originally as a wedding present to his third wife). Whitehall sported seventy-five rooms and one hundred thousand square feet of living space and was described in *The New York Herald* as "more wonderful than any palace in Europe, grander and more magnificent than any other private dwelling in the world." Whitehall became the Flagler winter retreat from its opening in 1902 until Henry died in 1913. The annual arrival of the Flaglers opened the Palm Beach social season for the wealthy vacationers of America's Gilded Age. After Flagler's death, the property was acquired by an investment company, which converted the entire structure to a hotel. Today, the building houses the Flagler Museum, showcasing a collection of Flagler memorabilia including his completely restored private Railcar No. 91, the property's original 1,249-pipe Odell organ, and many other items of historical significance.

Flagler's original intention was that Palm Beach would be the terminus of his railroad, hotel, and tourism empire, but an unusual winter in 1894–1895 brought freezing temperatures to the Palm Beach area. About seventy miles to the south, however, was the little town of Miami (1900 population: 1,681) and it was untouched by the freeze. So by 1896, Flagler's railroad had been pushed south all the way to Biscayne Bay and became a major factor in the development of Miami into the world-class city it is today. When the city of Miami was finally incorporated as a city in 1896, locals wanted to name it Flagler to honor the man whose railroad had brought people and riches into the region. Flagler declined and persuaded the city fathers to name the place Miami, from Mayaimi, an old Indian name. Flagler is still considered the founding father of the modern city of Miami.

By 1905 or so, Flagler had decided that he might as well push his railroad all the way out to Key West, a project that involved connecting by rail a large number of islands, some of them miles apart. The Panama Canal was under construction at the time, and Key West, the southernmost location in the continental United States, was the closest American city to the Gulf side of that canal. Why not connect the mainland to Key West by rail, thus establishing Key West as a major international port?

The Key West project required causeways, bridges, roads, and trestles all built across open waters—at one point, almost seven miles of open water. Nothing of the sort had ever been done before, and the project soon came to be known as Flagler's Folly. Still, Flagler persisted, and the Florida Overseas Railroad was completed in 1912. The railroad connecting Miami to Key West was and remains the most ambitious feat of engineering ever undertaken by a private citizen (at least until Elon Musk came along). Flagler died at the age of eighty-three, about a year after the Key West Line was opened.

In the process of developing his railroad and hotel system, Flagler also created what he called the Model Land Company to develop real estate and agriculture along his railway routes. He hired agronomists, horticulturalists, and other specialists to create farms and citrus groves, the purpose of which was to provide food for his workers. These farms and citrus groves became the basis for Florida's modern-day agricultural economy. In the process, he also built a lot of housing for his workers, and these settlements eventually became the towns of Delray Beach, Deerfield Beach, Dania Beach, Ojus, Perrine, Homestead, Kenansville, Okeechobee, and Stuart. He was instrumental in the settlement of Fort Lauderdale, Miami, and West Palm Beach. Flagler also made generous donations to establish hospitals, churches, schools, and libraries in these emerging communities.

The transportation infrastructure Flagler built, the tourism that his chain of hotels made possible, and even the agricultural enterprises he established in the process of doing everything else remain the foundation of Florida's economy to the present day. Among other things, it was his vision (and his railroad) that allowed the rich playboys and wealthy sportsmen of the North to bring themselves and their race cars to Daytona by train and to spend their days there in the luxury of some of the finest hotels ever built in the post–Civil War south. So in an important sense, Flagler also made auto racing on the beaches of Daytona possible.

4

GREEN, YELLOW, CHECKERED

AUTO RACING GETS ITS START

NOT LONG AFTER Henry Flagler's railroad reached Daytona Beach, automobile racing began on the beach's twenty-three miles of flat, hard-packed sand. Most sandy beaches have loose, fluffy sand that would be impossible to drive on, but in a very few places in the United States, the sand has peculiar physical properties such that the receding tide leaves the beach dry and hard-packed, and Daytona Beach is one of those places. (New Smyrna Beach, a bit to the south of Daytona, is another.) So for a century now, Daytona Beach, speed, and automobile racing have been interwoven in the public mind.

NASCAR champion Richard Petty once confessed that he really didn't know when the car was invented, but "there is no doubt about precisely when folks began racing each other in automobiles. It was the day they built the second automobile." The first automobile race in the United States took place in Chicago in 1895 (on Thanksgiving Day) and featured five competitors—two electric cars and three gasoline-powered Benz machines imported from Germany. The race was won by Frank Duryea, one of the Duryea brothers (Frank and Charles) who are often credited as America's first home-grown car builders. Frank covered the fifty-four-mile course in a little more than ten hours and averaged about 7 mph (taking into account stops for gasoline and in at least one case a passing train).

Many of the early automobile races on both sides of the Atlantic were less about speed than reliability. The manufacturers of these newfangled machines were anxious to show that their "horseless carriages" were reliable forms of transportation that could be counted on to convey passengers safely and relatively quickly over long distances. But soon enough, they turned into speed contests in which racers competed for bragging rights as "the fastest on four wheels." And so they have been ever since.

The American automobile industry sprang to life in the 1890s. The Duryea brothers were manufacturing cars in Springfield, Massachusetts, as early as 1893. Elsewhere in the country there were literally hundreds of manufacturers in the business, almost all of whom fell by the wayside before the end of the 1920s.

For their first couple of decades, cars were almost exclusively playthings of the affluent. The earliest automobiles had price tags of $2,000 and up, more than $40,000 in current dollars. A truly affordable car did not come along until Henry Ford's Model T in 1916. The list price of the Model T was $875 (about $19,000 in today's dollars); by 1925, the list price was down to $260 ($5,600 in today's dollars). It is therefore often said, with justification, that while Europeans invented the automobile, Americans democratized it. By the mid-1920s, a car was within the reach, or nearly so, of most American families. Then came the Depression.

AUTO RACING COMES TO FLORIDA

The first automobile race ever on Daytona Beach took place in 1902. One of the guests at Flagler's Hotel Ormond had arrived with a car in tow. His name was Ransom Eli Olds, founder of the Olds Motor Vehicle Company and the progenitor of both Oldsmobile and REO automobiles. His car was an Olds Pirate that he had shipped all the way from Michigan to see how fast he could drive it on the smooth sandy beach.

The exact date of Olds's first timed run is in dispute, but he and his Olds Pirate clocked in at the breathtaking speed of just over 50 mph. Olds returned to the library at the Hotel Ormond and babbled with great animation to his friend Alexander Winton, "You have no idea, Alex, what a thrill it is out there. Do you know what it feels like to go 50 mph?!?" (The quotation is taken from William Neely's "official history" of Daytona and is almost certainly an imagined reconstruction.)

Winton was a Scotsman and, like Olds, a bicycle and automobile manufacturer and an early automotive pioneer who held more than a hundred patents for innovations in cars and engines. Also like Olds, Winton saw auto racing as a means to promote his product and to advertise his cars' reliability and speed. He had also shown up at the Hotel Ormond with a race car, a Winton Bullet. A natural question arose between the two old friends: Whose car would be the fastest up and down the beach? And thus was side-by-side auto racing on the sands of Daytona invented.

Legend has it that the pair first shared a breakfast in the elegant columned dining room of the hotel, then repaired to the beach, where a crowd of some fifty onlookers had gathered to watch the contest. The course was generally southward toward Daytona Beach, with a subsequent turn back north to Ormond; the race was to be one lap. The cars were neck and neck at the start, neck and neck at the turn, and neck and neck at the finish. Daytona's first automobile race ended in a dead tie. The average speed over the entire course was 57 mph.

A lovely story, yes, but probably more legend than fact. Far from having arisen as a spontaneous challenge between two friends, the potential of the Ormond Beach site for auto racing had been heavily promoted to northern automobilists by the managers of the Hotel Ormond, John Anderson and Joseph D. Price, and by two winter residents of the hotel, C. W. Birchwood and J. F. Hathaway, evidently as a way to stimulate hotel business. At the time, auto racing, although fairly widespread (remember Petty's comment), was confined to rutted dirt roads built for carriages or to dirt-track ovals originally built for horse racing. Daytona Beach offered twenty-three straight miles of smooth white sand. Olds and Winton were merely two of many wealthy northern sportsmen who succumbed to the allure of a racing venue where speeds were limited only by horsepower and engineering, not by track conditions. In at least some versions of the 1902 event, Olds did not even drive his car in the race; one of his mechanics did.

The 1902 event came to the attention of a New York sportswriter, William J. Morgan, who immediately sensed the potential and traveled to

Ormond Beach to meet with Anderson and Price. Morgan worked for *The Automobile* magazine, and its owners were eager to stage an annual Florida racing event. What became the Winter Speed Carnival would be staged in early winter. A second beach race was held in 1903, and a small phalanx of cars and wealthy sportsmen showed up. Winton returned with a much improved race car and easily bested the field with an average speed of 68.9 mph, but the race, according to Ed Hinton (author of *Daytona: From the Birth of Speed to the Death of the Man in Black* and a highly reliable Daytona historian), "essentially was a flop."

Undeterred, Morgan and his associates tirelessly promoted the 1904 event. These efforts bore fruit: entries for the 1904 Winter Speed Carnival poured in from all over the world, and the Hotel Ormond became the "it" place to be for wealthy sportsmen and East Coast society types, just the sort of patron Flagler hoped to attract. Not unlike the Kentucky Derby today, the well-to-do from all over traveled to the Hotel Ormond to "see and be seen" and to watch the racing.

One highlight of the 1904 Ormond Beach racing season was the Mercedes-Daimler machine driven by William K. Vanderbilt, grandson of Cornelius Vanderbilt, the patriarch of the Vanderbilt fortune. Vanderbilt's imported Mercedes was a 90-horsepower monster racing in the over-two-thousand-pound class and with "Willie K." at the wheel it set a new world speed record through the measured mile of 92 mph.

Winton too had returned to Ormond Beach for the 1904 event, but with a new driver for his race car, a backwoods Ohio bumpkin named Barney Oldfield, a daredevil who had been driving for Ford's nascent racing team. According to Ed Hinton, Oldfield had bested Winton not once but twice in Ohio exhibition races and so, unable to beat the commoner, Winton hired him and took him to the Winter Speed Carnival of 1904 as his driver.

The contrast between Willie K. and Oldfield could scarcely be sharper. Vanderbilt was the archetype of the wealthy amateur whose racing prowess was based mainly on his ability to buy the fastest, most powerful cars available anywhere in the world. Oldfield had dropped out of school in the eighth grade and worked as a water boy, volunteer fireman, kitchen helper, and orderly at a mental asylum before signing on as a driver for Henry Ford. He was the Dale Earnhardt of his time. Hinton says Oldfield "had . . . a set of balls on him that wouldn't fit in a fifty-five-gallon drum." Also like Earn-hardt, he did not own the equipment he drove and therefore "had no qualms about driving it to, and then past, its limits." Inevitably, the final race of the 1904 Winter Speed Carnival season pitted Vanderbilt against Oldfield. Oldfield won by a hundred yards and thus, virtually in a single race, did auto racing begin its transformation from an amusement of the very wealthy to a sport associated with the working classes and the common man.

By 1905, the Ormond Garage had opened not far from the Hotel Ormond, and the stretch of dirt road between it and a nearby dormitory for mechanics was christened Gasoline Alley (years before the opening of the better-known Gasoline Alley at the Indianapolis Motor Speedway). The 1905 racing was memorable for two main reasons. A new land-speed record was set at 110 mph, the first time the record exceeded the 100 mph barrier. The more significant "first" was the death of wealthy New Yorker Frank Croker, who veered on the beach to miss a bicyclist and drove his car into the surf at 90 miles an hour.

Whether because of Croker's death, the bumpkin Oldfield's successes, or the ever-increasing speeds (and therefore danger), wealthy playboys soon realized that auto racing was not a game but a blood sport that demanded high levels of courage and skill. By 1906, most of them had begun to follow the lead that Winton had established in 1904: they hired professional drivers to pilot their race cars. So 1906 witnessed the emergence of the professional Daytona racer. It also marked the beginning of the end for the great Winter Speed Carnival at Daytona.

The nature of motorsports was evolving toward longer races on closed courses, the prototype for which was the Indianapolis 500, first run in 1911 and won by the American Ray Harroun at an average speed of 75 mph. The Indianapolis Motor Speedway had been built in 1909 by Carl Graham Fisher (more on Fisher in a later chapter) and a group of Indianapolis businessmen. The revolutionary "Brickyard" was a 2.5-mile nearly rectangular track that initially hosted 100-mile events. These 100-milers were very popular, and Fisher began to wonder if an even longer event might not be possible. The constraint was that people would need to get into the track, watch the race, and get out while the sun was shining. Making reasonable assumptions all around, he figured that this would mean about seven hours of racing, and with average speeds those days around 70 mph, a 500-mile race seemed like it would be about the limit. In 1911, the Indianapolis 500 replaced Daytona as the center of American motorsports, a position it would retain for decades.

LAND-SPEED RECORDS

From the very beginning, auto racing was not one sport but two: side-by-side racing around a closed course to see who could finish first, as at Indianapolis; and one-car-at-a-time straight-line racing through a measured distance, to see which car was the fastest. For its first thirty years, beach racing at Daytona was more about the latter than the former. There was side-by-side racing at the Winter Speed Carnivals, of course, but the real interest was in setting ever-higher speed records over a measured distance. For this purpose, Daytona was ideal: racers could use the first ten or eleven miles of smooth hard sand to get a race car completely up to speed, blast through a measured mile, then use the last ten or eleven miles to bring the car safely to a stop. Most of the national publicity surrounding the Winter Speed Carnival was focused on who did best through the measured mile. Who won the side-by-side races was less interesting (and conferred less prestige and prize money).

The evolution of the land-speed record traces that of the cars themselves. The very earliest records were attained in France by electric vehicles. In 1902 and again in 1906, the record was broken by steam-powered vehicles. The first to break the record with a gas-powered internal combustion engine was Willie K. in a French Mors in 1902; the second was Henry Ford in his famous Ford 999 racer in 1904. From the advent of the land-speed record in 1898 to the appearance of jet- and rocket-powered cars in 1964, the record was broken eight times on the Daytona sands.

The 1906 record-breaking run by Fred Marriott in a Stanley Steamer Rocket was notable. Contrary to the modern image of steamers as slow, cumbersome teapots on wheels, the Stanley race cars were eerily quiet and astonishingly fast. Marriott's speed was 128 mph over the measured mile. The anti-steam, pro-gas forces used the car's dominance as evidence that races between steam-powered and gas-powered autos were unfair, and that led ultimately to the banning of steam-powered vehicles in Daytona racing.

The last land-speed record set at Daytona was by Major Sir Malcolm Campbell in 1935 with a top speed of 301 mph, and that was the end of land-speed-record racing at Daytona. Thereafter, all US efforts at the land-speed record took place at Utah's Bonneville Salt Flats, the dry and extremely smooth, flat bed of an ancient saltwater lake that offered even better racing conditions than Daytona.

The 1935 speed trials were not to be the end of all racing on east Florida's flat white sands, though, not by any means. Among the spectators at Campbell's last Daytona run was a tall young man—William H. G. France—and "Big Bill," as he was known, had big plans for Daytona racing.

WILLIAM FRANCE AND DAYTONA BEACH

By 1935, Daytona was known internationally as the Speed Capital of the World, and the city's business class was eager to retain some sort of annual racing event to maintain that reputation and pump up the local economy. The city had invested as much as thirty thousand dollars (a lot of money in those days) for some of the big-name speed trials and always seemed to feel that they had gotten back their money's worth. But with Campbell exiting Daytona for Bonneville, record-setting speed trials at Daytona were a thing of the past. Now what?

Big Bill France was born in Washington, DC, on September 26, 1909. He and a buddy built France's first race car when Bill was just seventeen. By 1927 he was employed as a mechanic at a DC service station and then shortly thereafter as a front-end specialist at a local Ford dealership. He was passionately interested in everything about cars: how they worked, how they failed, how they could be repaired, and above all else, how they could be made to go faster.

As a part-time amateur dirt-track racer, France found two aspects of auto racing disturbing. One, race promoters were almost universally sleazeballs and crooks who would routinely make off with the gate money before paying off the racers. Two, as we have seen, racing in the early years was a rich man's sport, featuring expensive imported racing machines that a common man could neither identify with nor afford. Two decades later, these would be the animating sentiments that created NASCAR.

The Depression fell hard on Washington, DC, as it did in the rest of the country. With the District an increasingly unpleasant place to be, France decided to move south, where he could continue working as a mechanic without freezing in the winter. He and his wife, Annie, used most of their cash reserves to buy a small mobile home, and in 1934, they made their way down the coast to Daytona Beach.

Legend has it that they ended up in Daytona Beach because that's where the car broke down, but France himself repudiated that. "Hell, I was a mechanic," he told Ed Hinton. "If my car had broken down, I would have fixed it." The young France family settled in Daytona because Bill just liked the place, and because being there would connect him to Daytona racing history, of which he was well aware. When Malcolm Campbell made his last run at Daytona in 1935, France was there to witness the event. The following year, he was racing on Daytona Beach himself.

As the Depression deepened, Daytona's movers and shakers were struggling to come up with some sort of winter speed event that would bring tourists and money to the city's hotels and restaurants. They approached a well-known local racer and garage owner, Sigurd "Sig" Haugdahl, and asked him to come up with a concept that would retain the luster of Daytona racing. Sig contacted France and together they developed the idea for a road race that would have one leg running along Highway A1A, the (by now) paved road that ran adjacent to the beach, and a second leg on the beach itself. France's contribution was to suggest that the race feature cars that common people could relate to, cars right off the showroom floors—that is, *stock cars*. The first stock-car race on Daytona Beach occurred in March 1936, a year after Campbell's last Daytona appearance.

Everything about that first stock-car race was ridiculed: the proposed course was preposterous (half highway, half beach—c'mon!), and the idea that people would pay good money to watch men race family jalopies didn't seem very promising either. But the race went on as planned because, as William Neely says, "nobody else suggested anything better."

With a heavily promoted purse of five thousand dollars (seventeen hundred to the winning driver—princely sums during the depths of the Depression), the race drew plenty of well-known entrants, among them Indy 500 winner Bill Cummings, several dirt-track and midget-car champs, an international racing star or two, a handful of Southeast dirt-track racers, and Bill France. The track layout was 3.2 miles, 1.5 miles down A1A, then a turn onto the beach, another 1.5 miles up the beach, with a final turn back onto the highway. Because Indianapolis had demonstrated a large market for longer races, the event was promoted as a 250-miler—seventy-eight laps around the 3.2-mile course.

In all respects, the inaugural stock-car race on Daytona Beach was a disaster. On the management side, the race had become a political football, and there was a possibility that city officials would cancel the event even after the cars were on the beach. City ticket takers showed up to charge for admission, only to find that thousands of fans were already in place. Another faction in city government had sequestered the prize money. When all was said and done, however, the race went ahead as scheduled, the promised prize money was distributed—and the city of Daytona Beach came out twenty-two thousand dollars in the red. So far as city officials were concerned, that was the end of their enthusiasm for auto racing, but Sig and his partner were undeterred. Stock-car racing on the beach had its problems, yes, but the potential was enormous. So the pair, full of assurances that the problems of the 1936 race could be fixed, convinced a local Elks Club to sponsor a similar event in 1937. Beach racing at Daytona would continue, with or without the support of local government.

The year 1937 was not quite the financial disaster that 1936 had been, but it was a big enough loser that the Elks Club declined to continue their sponsorship. Now what? When other possibilities failed to pan out, France teamed up with a local restaurateur, Charlie Reese, to promote Daytona stock-car racing themselves. Two races were slated for 1938: the first in the early spring, the second on Labor Day. This marked the beginning of France's transition from racer to racing promoter.

The spring race was largely uneventful until the winner, a local bar owner named Smokey Purser, crossed the finish line and then just kept on going. At the time, France was still adamant about his "strictly stock" concept, and he suspected that Purser had made illegal modifications to the car. A subsequent search proved him right, so Purser was stripped of the win and the second-place finisher would be declared—but wait! The second-place finisher had been France himself. How would it look if the race promoter named himself the winner and claimed the winner's purse? France resolved the dilemma by awarding himself the victory but ceding the victor's purse to the third-place finisher.

There were nine more races on the sands of Daytona between 1938 and the suspension of racing after the Japanese attack on Pearl Harbor in December 1941. Each race saw higher speeds and higher-quality racing. But racing conditions changed dramatically from race to race and year to year, a constant source of frustration to France and one among several motivations to build large, modern speedways.

The Japanese attacked Pearl Harbor on December 7, 1941, and all of a sudden, young American men were presented with other means to test their manhood. Wasting steel, rubber, and gasoline racing cars around in a circle seem frivolous and unpatriotic. The 1942 Indianapolis 500 was canceled and so too was all racing at Daytona for the duration of the war.

Once the war ended, automobile racing resumed, not just in Florida but across the nation. Young men who had stared down Nazis in Europe and Japanese kamikaze pilots in Asia came back to the States riddled with testosterone and needing a place to make use of it, and racing cars was just the thing. But as a sport with a national following, stock-car racing was in utter disarray. There were scores of sanctioning bodies, dozens of race sponsors, the rules differed from track to track, and there was no method of determining a national champion.

With the idea of unifying the sport in mind, France organized a meeting at the Ebony Bar atop the Streamline Hotel in Daytona Beach on December 14, 1947. It was at this meeting that the National Association for Stock Car Automobile Racing (NASCAR) was formed. The idea of bringing discipline, order, and stability to the sport, or at least making a profit from it, was clearly on the minds of many all over the country (not just in Florida), because several rival sanctioning organizations were forming at about the same time: the National Stock Car Racing Association, National Championship Stock Car Circuit, Stock Car Auto Racing Society (acronym: SCARS—bad choice of name), National Auto Racing League, National Auto Racing Club, American Stock Car Racing Association, United Stock Car Racing Association, United States Auto Club, and, according to *The Official NASCAR Handbook,* "literally dozens of others." For a variety of reasons, not least Big Bill's unflinching dictatorial hand, NASCAR eventually emerged as the most successful of these competing organizations and is, of course, the dominant force in American stock-car racing today.

NASCAR raced on the beach course at Daytona from the end of the war until 1958. By then, beachfront development in Daytona had brought more hotels, restaurants, and private residences near the racecourse and it was becoming obvious that some sort of permanent racing facility would soon be needed to hold the increasingly large crowds. And so, with NASCAR on a firm initial footing, France set out to build the sport's premier showcase, the Daytona International Speedway. Construction began in 1957.

France took huge risks and incurred enormous personal debt to get the speedway built. But with his characteristic perseverance and financial assistance from oil magnate Clint Murchison and Pepsi chairman Don Kendall, build it he did. It was nearly twice as long as the stock-car track at Darlington, South Carolina (the sport's first super speedway), and featured banking in the turns three times steeper than the venerable Brickyard at Indianapolis. Then as now, people marveled at the sheer immensity of the thing. And yet despite the size, nearly every grandstand seat afforded a clear view of the entire track. France's super speedway at Daytona permanently transformed the sport.

The Daytona 500 remains the sport's premier event and is held every February to open the new NASCAR racing season. A second race is held at the track every year over the July 4 weekend. A second NASCAR track in Florida was opened in 1995 in Homestead (near Miami) and now serves as the traditional venue for the final race of the NASCAR season. (The Homestead track was part of the redevelopment of southern Florida in the aftermath of Hurricane Andrew.) So in every sense, NASCAR begins and ends in Florida.

WHAT REMAINS OF THE EARLY ERA
IN DAYTONA TODAY?

Although auto racing made Daytona Beach what it is today, very little of the early era remains. The original Ormond Garage, the anchor of Daytona's Gasoline Alley, burned to the ground in 1976. A facsimile now stands near the original site, at the corner of Atlantic Avenue and Granada Boulevard in Ormond Beach, and serves as the focal attraction of the Birthplace of Speed Park. It promotes itself as "a wonderful setting for wedding ceremonies and gatherings."

The Hotel Ormond was placed on the National Register of Historic Places in 1980 but was torn down in 1992 to make way for luxury condo development. All that remains is the building's cupola, which now stands in a park just west of the original site.

Soon after his move to Daytona, Bill France opened a car repair shop at 316 Main Street in Daytona Beach. The building still stands and today serves as a bar and entertainment venue. Their website emphasizes music, motorcycles, and hot women more than the shop's role in the early history of Daytona stock-car racing.

By far the most extensive collection of early Daytona Beach memorabilia is to be found at the ISC Archives and Research Center, just up the road from Daytona International Speedway. ISC is Bill France's International Speedway Corporation, founded in 1953 as the arm of the France empire concerned with building, owning, and operating race tracks. ISC owns thirteen of the NASCAR venues, the Motor Racing Network (radio broadcasts of NASCAR events), and the Daytona USA theme park (now called the Daytona 500 Experience). The archive has a collection of racing memorabilia so vast that no complete inventory of the holdings is even possible. Alas, the ISC Archives and Research Center is not open to the general public but a visit inside is included in the Daytona International Speedway VIP Tour, available only by reservation and priced at fifty-two dollars per person (as of 2015).

The number-one destination for fans of Daytona's earliest years, by far, has to be the restaurant and bar known as Racing's North Turn, located at

4511 South Atlantic Avenue in Ponce Inlet. The site is the precise location of the north turn of the original Daytona Beach road course. To say that Racing's North Turn is a NASCAR-themed restaurant is a complete understatement. The racing memorabilia on the restaurant's walls is a racing education unto itself. The equally historic south turn is in the middle of a bunch of high-rise condos and single-family dwelling units, but there is at least a plaque (and a large checkered flag) to mark its location and significance.

And you can still drive your car on the Daytona beaches. Day passes to the beach are twenty dollars per car. In the early days, you could drive up and down the entire twenty-three miles; today, driving is only allowed in designated sections. Restrictions on beach driving reflect multiple considerations. The dunes at the back of the beach are fragile and contain threatened species of sea grasses, so various driving and parking restrictions prevent them from being disturbed. Also, many species of sea turtle nest along these beaches; restrictions protect the nesting sites. (In the 1990s, nine miles of beach were permanently closed to autos to protect sea turtle nesting sites.) Finally, a great deal of the beach is now lined with luxury condos and hotels whose patrons expect unfettered beach access. It would not be good for Daytona's image to have fun-loving sunbathers mowed down by passing vehicular traffic. For the same reason, nighttime driving on the beach was banned in the 1980s. Driving on the beach is described on the "Things to Do" web page of daytonabeach.com as "one of the most popular and iconic activities beach goers have come to enjoy as part of their Daytona Beach vacation tradition."

PART TWO

FLORIDA ECONOMICS: THE TRILLION-DOLLAR STATE

5

THEME-PARK NATION

FLORIDA'S TOURIST ECONOMY

THE EARLY YEARS

Tourism in Florida dates to April 2, 1513, when Ponce de León came ashore at Saint Augustine. Ponce landed with a couple hundred men, and as his experience with the Calusa shows, he was not a welcome visitor. This year, a hundred million tourists will visit the state and will be welcomed with open arms. What's the attraction? What makes them come?

The weather, of course, has always been Florida's biggest draw. When icy winds off Lake Michigan are sweeping across Chicago on a wintry January day (locals call that wind "The Hawk"), Orlando will very likely have clear skies, low humidity, and temperatures in the seventies. When northern freeways are clogged with snow, snow plows, overturned semis, and salt-and-sand trucks, Florida freeways are clogged with tourists and snowbirds looking for relief. When the "lake effect" is dumping four feet of snow on Buffalo, the sun is dumping sixty-six thousand square miles of warm sunshine onto the peninsula. It is almost impossible to view the nightly weather map during winter anywhere north of the Mason-Dixon Line without looking at the Florida peninsula and wishing you were here.

But why Florida rather than, say, Alabama or Georgia, as the top tourist destination for Yankees seeking relief from the northern winters? Probably because Florida stretches farther to the south than any other southern state, and the weather is predictably more temperate the further south you go. Orlando, for example, is a hundred miles farther south than New Orleans. Tampa is two hundred miles further south than Mobile. All of Florida lies within the tropical or subtropical climate zone, the only continental state of which this can be said. So a winter escape to Miami or Tampa is a much safer bet than a trip to Birmingham or Atlanta.

A second factor in Florida's prominence as a winter getaway is that everywhere in the state is within an hour's drive of the nearest coast. Alabama has 53 miles of coastline, Mississippi 44, Georgia about 100, and Florida 1,350. So if your winter fantasy includes some time on the beach, Florida is by far your best bet. The winter weather along the coasts is even more temperate than inland, and, besides, what could possibly be a sweeter revenge against the snow and ice than sitting beachside in the warm winter sun sipping a margarita?

Mild winter months were definitely part of Henry Flagler's tourism promotion along Florida's east and southern coasts, but Flagler's target market was well-to-do Yankees from the affluent northern metropolises. Wealthy sportsmen were also attracted to the state to race on Daytona Beach—again, during the winter. But there are not enough rich people or daredevil sportsmen to sustain an entire economy. What transformed warm but swamp-riddled Florida into an attractive vacation destination for middle- and working-class tourists?

The main answer is cars and highways to drive them on. Once cars began to replace horses as the prime method of personal transportation, the demand for smooth, navigable roads shot up, and road building became something of a national frenzy. After about 1912, there were far more miles of roads being built each year than there were miles of railroad track being added, in Florida and everywhere else. And once it was possible to motor into the Sunshine State in the family sedan, a Florida vacation became a real possibility for the Average Joe and his family. No expensive train tickets were required, just a couple of tanks of gasoline and you were off. Florida, here we come!

There were "roads" in, out, and around the state since precolonial times, of course, many of them simple dirt paths spontaneously formed by humans walking the same trails over and over to get to water and food. The first *paved* roads did not come to Florida until the twentieth century. The first serious paved highway built in the state was the Dixie Highway, conceived in 1914 and built between 1915 and 1927, mainly by Carl Graham Fisher, the same man who built the Indianapolis Motor Speedway. The objective of the Dixie Highway was to connect Miami near the southern end of the state with metropolitan centers as far north as Chicago. The highway was a network of interconnected roads, not one single highway of the sort we know today.

The Dixie Highway was bold in its conception. The road was to leave Chicago and connect to Indianapolis via Danville in Illinois. In Indy, the road was to split into eastern and western portions. One branch went from Indy to Louisville, to Nashville, and on to Chattanooga, Atlanta, Macon, and Jacksonville. The other branch went straight to Tallahassee, then to Jacksonville, then down the coast to Miami. A later revision brought the western route from Tallahassee to Orlando, Kissimmee, and Arcadia, then across the state to Jupiter and Miami.

A second major route into Florida was US Highway 1, the great American highway that eventually ran from the Canadian coast all the way to Key West. (Highway 1's marker MILE 0 is a popular Key West tourist site.) Various sections of US 1 were opened at different times, but the entire route was complete (except for a stretch between Jacksonville and Augusta, Georgia) by 1926. Still a third major north–south route through Florida was the Tamiami Trail from Tampa to Miami, completed in 1928, which opened up the west coast of Florida for tourism and development.

These three major Florida highways were massive undertakings. US Highway 1 runs for nearly 2,400 miles, the longest north-to-south road in the country. The Florida portion alone is 545 miles. The Chicago-to-Miami Dixie Highway (the "Western Route") was longer still. In comparison, the Tamiami Trail was a mere 275 miles, but the highway ran through some of the most forbidding real estate anywhere in America, the Florida Everglades. Today, when it is a simple matter to hop onto the Interstate Highway System and motor around the country at 80 mph, it is difficult to appreciate the rigors of automobile travel in the early twentieth century or the incredible engineering achievements these early highways represented.

Highways into the other southern states were being built around the

same time, of course, but none of the other states ever had the tourist allure of Florida. A week in Fort Lauderdale or Miami had a cachet that a
week in Mobile or Charlotte or Chattanooga lacked. Sure, there was (and
is) winter tourism throughout the South, and places like New Orleans,
Charleston, and Savannah have long had thriving tourist businesses. But
no place developed the reputation as a tourist haven as well or as aggressively as Florida.

In the 1920s and 1930s many other smaller highways were being built
between the populated areas of Florida, but many of them were one- and
two-lane affairs that frequently ran through marshy swampland and
served as nice warm places for the alligators to sun themselves. Until Disney World opened in Orlando in 1971, most of the state's interior roads
were poorly maintained two-lane blacktops that mostly served to connect
one orange grove to the next. Still, by the time of the Great Depression, it
would have been possible to drive into Florida from pretty much anyplace
east of the Mississippi and get around much of the state by car.

Florida's first road-building law was passed in 1922 and required only
that road builders leave no stump higher than twelve inches in the right-
of-way. In 1931, Florida slapped a gasoline tax of six cents per gallon on
the state's motorists, with three cents going to new construction and maintenance and the other three to retiring highway debts incurred by the
counties. In the 1940s, federal highway construction funds became available, and in the 1950s, the first steps were taken toward the Interstate Highway System so familiar to motorists today. Along the earliest paved (or
often gravel) roads, 30 mph was a breakneck speed. State-to-state travel was
slow and treacherous. But this too improved dramatically as the twentieth
century wore on.

About the same time that cars were starting to appear in America in
significant numbers, two Dayton, Ohio, bicycle builders, Wilbur and Orville
Wright, built and flew the first successful airplane near Kitty Hawk,
North Carolina, on December 17, 1903. By 1919, there was an airplane
hangar at the yacht basin in Saint Petersburg, and within the following decade, commercial air service was available to most of the state: to and from
Jacksonville in 1927; to and from Key West, Miami, Tampa, and Orlando
in 1928. Initially, these airports served mainly one another (the Key West

airport featured flights to Havana), but soon enough air traffic from out of state (and from various Caribbean and Latin American destinations) was pouring into Florida, bringing lots of goods and people with them. So by the time of the Great Depression, people with enough money could fly into Florida as well as drive or take the train.

OLD FLORIDA TOURIST ATTRACTIONS

As it became progressively easier for tourists to get to Florida, entrepreneurs were busy developing tourist attractions to amuse, entertain, and educate them while they were there. Many attractions were opened during the Depression, evidently in an effort to bring money into the state. Indeed, the state's very first tourist attraction opened in 1878, well before tourists could get there by train, much less by automobile or air (neither planes nor cars had yet been invented).

Most of the early tourist attractions took advantage of Florida's unique flora, fauna, and other natural features. The very first tourist attraction was the now-famous glass-bottom boats that ply the waters of Silver Springs (near Ocala). Silver Springs is the largest of more than a thousand natural artesian springs in Florida, many of which were developed as tourist attractions or parks. At Silver Springs, which was a private attraction until 2013, at which point it became a state park, the attraction is that the water is astonishingly clear (as it is in most of these natural springs) so with a glass-bottom boat, you can view all sorts of fish, turtles, other water creatures, and exotic aquatic plants. Alligators too are native to Florida, and tourists seem fascinated by them, so alligator farms and gator-related attractions have been prominent tourist attractions at least since 1893. Other similar attractions featured snakes, turtles, bears, panthers, and other native animal species. Florida's tropical climate also sustains numerous plant species from which spectacular tropical gardens are fashioned, and these gardens were also important in the early tourism history. A final natural feature that tourists have always found fascinating are the state's marine mammals, mainly the dolphins and manatees. Tourist attractions featuring dolphins date from at least 1938.

The alligator farms, artesian springs, serpentaria, marine-mammal shows, and tropical gardens define what are now called "Old Florida" tourist attractions. These attractions dominated the state's tourism industry until the opening of Walt Disney World in 1971. Disney completely transformed the Florida tourism industry, so everything added since 1971 is considered "New Florida." A key difference is that unlike the Old Florida attractions, most of which were built around some feature of the state's natural bounty, the New Florida attractions are mostly, to use the Disney term, "imagineered." So while an Old Florida attraction such as the Lowry Park Zoo in Tampa (opened in 1957 and now known as ZooTampa) will display live Florida black bears, Disney's Country Bear Jamboree features an assemblage of animatronic "bears" with names such as Liver Lips McGrowl, Beary Barrington, and Reed Thimple playing ersatz musical instruments and singing kitschy country tunes. Old Florida could be tacky but at least it was *real*. New Florida has proven a far bigger draw, but everything is fake: fake bears at the Country Bear Jamboree, fake fish at the 20,000 Leagues under the Sea Submarine Voyage (a Disney attraction that was closed in 1994), fake cowboys at Dolly Parton's Dixie Stampede (closed in 2008), fake knights at Medieval Times, even a fake Crucifixion at the Holy Land Experience. In the New Florida, appearance is everything. Reality is to be shunned.

As I already mentioned, the first of the Old Florida tourist attractions was Silver Springs and its famous glass-bottom boats. These boats afforded a magnificent view through thirty feet of water bubbling up from the Floridan Aquifer. The aquifer underlies an area of almost one hundred thousand square miles stretching from southern Mississippi to South Carolina and including all of Florida. The aquifer is, in essence, a gigantic limestone sponge, and every so often, it bubbles up out of the ground to form beautiful natural springs that provide wetlands habitat for many species of fish, mammal, bird, and reptile. Silver Springs is one of these natural springs (indeed, it is the largest artesian spring in the world, disgorging hundreds of millions of gallons of pure spring water daily to form the Silver River) and is one of about a thousand such springs that dot the state, many of which are now state parks. Silver Springs is where *Creature from the Black Lagoon* was filmed in 1954, where several Tarzan movies were shot in the

1930s and 1940s, and also where much of the footage of television's *Sea Hunt* was shot.

The glass-bottom boats were the invention either of Hullam Jones or Phillip Morell. There is no consensus among Silver Springs's historians on the point. A credible origin story is that Jones used his version to search the bottom for sunken cypress logs, which were then in great demand as building material. Whoever thought up the idea, it fell to the entrepreneurs William Carl Ray and Shorty Davidson to realize the tourist potential. For more on Silver Springs history, I recommend Tim Hollis's delightful book, *Glass Bottom Boats & Mermaid Tails: Florida's Tourist Springs.*

Today, Silver Springs, like many other natural bodies of water, is being threatened by nitrogen runoff from overfertilized fields and by pollutants from aging septic tanks. Residential and commercial development, all of which has historically tapped the Floridan Aquifer for water, appears to have reduced the flow out of Silver Springs by as much as half. Various cleanup and conservation efforts are under way, but in the meantime, the park remains open to tourists and features various animal exhibits (gators, of course, and also giraffes, Florida panthers, and Florida black bears) in addition to the glass-bottom-boat rides, some live shows, a Lost River Voyage, and more. The park attracts more than a third of a million tourists a year. Entrance to the park is a mere two bucks, but there are additional charges for almost everything.

Many of the Old Florida tourist attractions feature the state's best-known reptile, alligators. Gator-based tourist attractions date from at least 1893 with the opening of the Saint Augustine Alligator Farm Zoological Park. (The biggest gator attraction today is Gatorland, near Kissimmee, as fine an example of Old Florida as you will ever find.) The original Saint Aug gator park was promoted as a "thing to do" by the railroad into the city. By 1916, the park housed thousands of reptiles, mostly harvested locally and donated. In later years, the park was destroyed by fire and hurricanes but was always rebuilt bigger and better than before.

With an estimated 1.3 million alligators living wild in the state, one might wonder why the creepy reptiles are "farmed" rather than simply hunted. God knows, they're not hard to find. But back in 1973, the gator population had been decimated by hunting because gator hunting had always been (and remains) a favored cracker sport and an important test of cracker manhood. "Cracker" is a term originally used to refer to Florida cowmen and pioneers but is now used to describe people whose families settled in Florida before the invention of window screens, air-conditioning, insect repellant, and the Interstate Highway System. Because of over-hunting, the Florida alligator was listed as endangered in the Endangered Species Act. Since then, they have made a spectacular comeback. Today, gators are a federally "protected" species and can be legally hunted only with the proper license and permits.

Since the demand for alligator products exceeds the legal hunting limits, alligator farming has emerged as a volatile but profitable business enterprise. The reptiles are harvested for their tail meat (see chapter 17, "Famous Foods of Florida"), their hides (alligator skin is a fine and ex-pensive leather used for shoes, boots, belts, purses, and luggage), and their skulls (desiccated white gator heads can be purchased in virtually every Florida souvenir shop). In 2015, the state's gator farmers produced 116,000 gator hides worth nearly $7 million and 190,000 pounds of gator tail meat worth about $1.7 million. On average, every harvested gator netted its taker $394.85 in 2015, according to the web page on alligator farming maintained by the Florida Fish and Wildlife Conservation Commission. (Today, the figure is higher at $552.82.) And yes, gator tail meat "tastes like chicken." Really. Almost all alligator farms and attractions feature fried gator tail at their eateries, and it is considered déclassé if you visit a gator attraction and don't eat some.

The glass-bottom boats of Silver Springs and the Saint Augustine Alli-gator Farm Zoological Park seem to be the state's only surviving tourist attractions that date to the nineteenth century. But by the time the twen-tieth century got rolling, planes, trains, and automobiles were bringing enough visitors into the state to spawn a vast array of often cheesy, some-times educational, but always interesting attractions. Some highlights:

Bok Tower Gardens opened in 1929 and is named for the Dutch im-migrant Edward Bok, a successful publisher, author, and humanitarian. Bok was the editor of *Ladies' Home Journal* for thirty years and a steadfast champion of social causes ranging from housing for the working and middle classes to the preservation of Niagara Falls. Bok was enamored of the area around Lake Wales and created a lush garden and bird sanctuary featuring a sixty-bell carillon. Originally named the Mountain Lake Sanctuary and Singing Tower, the carillon was renamed Bok Tower after Bok's death in 1930. He is buried at the base of the tower that now bears his name. The gardens surrounding the tower were designed by the famous landscape architect Frederick Law Olmstead.

The Sunken Gardens at Saint Petersburg opened in 1935 and is described on the Saint Petersburg "things to do" web page as "a botanical paradise in the midst of a bustling city." The gardens were created by a local plumber, George Turner, who purchased six acres of swamp in 1903, figured out how to drain it, and then began gardening in the rich muck left behind. Neighbors were fond of strolling through the lush grounds, so fond, Turner soon learned, that they would pay a nickel apiece for the pleasure. The gardens were purchased from the Turner family by the City of Saint Petersburg in 1999. The Sunken Gardens hold pride of place as the first remaining tourist attraction opened on Florida's west coast.

The Everglades Wonder Gardens in Bonita Springs was opened in 1936 as The Reptile Gardens, a roadside attraction along the newly opened Tamiami Trail, which showcased the region's reptilian and amphibian wonders. As the exhibits grew to include more and more animal and plant species, the attraction was renamed the Everglades Wonder Gardens. It was the first tourist attraction in or around the Florida Everglades. The site of the gardens is a former Calusa Indian village, but all traces of Native American habitation are long gone. The Calusa burial mounds formerly on the site were recycled into roadway surfaces. Everglades tourism was also stimulated by the opening of the Everglades National Park in 1947. President Harry Truman officiated at the opening ceremony.

Once world famous, Cypress Gardens and its fabulous water-ski show opened in 1936, Florida's first tourist theme park. Cypress Gardens became known as the Water Ski Capital of the World because of the ski shows and numerous water-skiing "firsts" and world records that happened there: first barefoot skiing exhibition (1947), water-ski-jump records (49 feet in 1947, up to more than 300 feet today), largest pyramid of skiers, and so on. Many movies were also shot in the park, most notably the numerous Esther Williams films in the 1950s and 1960s. Cyprus Gardens was easily Florida's most alluring tourist attraction until Disney World opened in 1971, a mere thirty miles to the north. Competition from Disney caused the garden's attendance and profits to fall, and despite a series of ownership changes, the park closed in 2003, reopened in 2004 as Cypress Gardens Adventure Park, was sold off in a bankruptcy auction in 2007, reopened as a water park in 2009, closed again the same year, and was purchased by the LEGO Group in 2010. The former Cypress Gardens is now part of LEGOLAND Florida Resort.

Marineland Dolphin Adventure in Saint Augustine opened as Marine Studios in 1938, evidently the first marine-mammal park in the state. It featured a single bottleneck dolphin but attracted tourists by the thousands and paved the way for many subsequent parks with the same theme. Among the original entrepreneurs that opened Marineland was Ilya Andreyevich Tolstoy, the grandson of Leo Tolstoy, and that fact made Marineland and the surrounding bars and restaurants favorite hangouts of Florida authors such as Marjorie Kinnan Rawlings and Ernest Hemingway. The addition of trained dolphins and dolphin shows in the 1950s increased the park's popularity even further.

The Islamorada Theater of the Sea opened in 1946 and was the first of Florida's many marine-mammal parks to feature a "swim with the dolphins" opportunity that lets visitors jump into a large tank and swim with dolphins, sea lions, and stingrays. This was one of the first tourist attractions opened in the Florida Keys. The park property is a former stone quarry opened to supply rock for Henry Flagler's Overseas Railroad.

Marineland and the Theater of the Sea are the precursors to a number of marine-mammal parks in Florida: Discovery Cove (part of SeaWorld in Orlando, opened in 2000), the Dolphin Connection (in Duck Key, opened in 1990), Dolphins Plus (two locations in Key Largo), Dolphin Research Center (Grassy Key), the Gulfarium Marine Adventure Park (Fort Walton Beach, opened in 1955), Gulf World Marine Park (Panama City Beach), the Miami Seaquarium (1955), and, of course, SeaWorld, a major Orlando tourist attraction much in the news a few years ago because of the movie *Blackfish*. The movie tells the story of Tilikum, a performing orca that caused the deaths of several of his trainers. The controversies surrounding Tilikum and his treatment have caused SeaWorld to discontinue the orca shows "sometime in 2019." It is not clear whether this applies to all Sea World locations worldwide or just to their shows in the United States.

Weeki Wachee Springs State Park is another of Florida's many natural crystal-clear springs. Its world-famous mermaid show opened in 1947. Basically, large viewing windows were embedded in the limestone rock on one side of the spring, which afford tourists a panoramic underwater view. Young women dressed in mermaid costumes and breathing through underwater air hoses perform choreographed dance routines to recorded music. Each performance lasts about a half hour. Weeki Wachee Springs is now a Florida state park with lovely gardens, a short "educational" boat trip, and a water park (Buccaneer Bay).

I mentioned earlier a 2004 item in *National Geographic* warning of the possible "extinction" of the Weeki Wachee mermaids. Not to worry! The last time Chris and I visited, the Mermaid Roster (the show's cast) contained the names of at least twenty women. And enough young girls still fantasize about growing up to be mermaids to sustain the park's Junior Mermaid Camp, where children ages seven to fourteen can learn the basics of mermaidology "while getting a fascinating behind-the-scenes look at what it takes to put on a show." The price for this two-day adventure is three hundred dollars and includes a mermaid makeover and self-portrait.

As a southern state, Florida was racially segregated well into the 1970s, and that included schools, housing, churches, beaches, seats on the streetcars, and, of course, tourist attractions, many of which were for whites only. The first tourist attraction built specifically for the enjoyment of African American people was Paradise Park, about a mile south of the resort at Silver Springs and opened in 1949. The park's owners saw untapped profit potential in providing recreational opportunities for the approximate fifth of the state population that was of African descent. Paradise Park was advertised as "for colored people only" and featured numerous tropical gardens, a sandy beach for swimming, a pavilion with a very popular dance floor, picnic tables, and a softball field. It was one of only three beaches in the state that catered to African American clients. About a hundred thousand visitors came each year from as far away as New York and even California. Paradise Park closed in 1969.

Other pre-Disney tourist highlights include the state's first wax museum, Potter's Wax Museum, which opened in Saint Augustine in 1949; the Circus Hall of Fame in Sarasota (opened in 1956); and Busch Gardens in Tampa (opened in 1959). Busch Gardens was originally conceived as a marketing venue for Anheuser-Busch products, of which Budweiser beer is the best known. The park had an African savannah theme and was known as "Busch Gardens: The Dark Continent" from 1976 until the 1990s. In the 1990s, the park was renamed Busch Gardens Tampa Bay and in 2006, the subtitle was changed to "Africa." (In 2008, it went back to Tampa Bay.) At 335 acres, the park is one of the nation's largest zoological installations and among the first to put visitors in cages and let the animals roam free. Today the park features twenty rides including six roller-coasters and more than twelve thousand animals. In 2002, a zookeeper had her arm bitten off by a lion as she was conducting a "behind the scenes" tour.

Mention must also be made here of the Florida Highwaymen—not a gang of bandits but rather twenty-six self-taught African American artists who painted vivid Florida scenes and sold their products to tourists and passersby out of the trunks of their cars. Their paintings, shunned at the time by local galleries and derided as "primitive" by critics, are now quite valuable and have received national attention and acclaim. One imagines that many of these paintings now lurk in the attics and basements of Florida tourists from decades past, long forgotten, purchased for twenty or thirty bucks and now worth thousands. The Highwaymen were incredibly prolific, often knocking out a painting in less than a half hour and selling it before the paint was dry. The surviving oeuvre is a small fraction of the estimated two hundred·thousand paintings they created.

Today, we might wonder just what there was about these Old Florida tourist attractions that was worth several days of driving over primitive two-lane highways. But the whole point of owning a car was that you could go places, and for much of the American population through much of the twentieth century, about the most exotic place you could go was Florida. You are never going to see a spectacular flowering bougainvillea in Iowa or a twelve-foot alligator in Michigan or a live mermaid show in Indiana. Nope, you have to go to Florida to see any of these things. So go to Florida they did, by the millions.

Many of the early tourists could not afford to spend their nights in the new hotels and motels or eat in the fancy new restaurants, so they slept in their cars and fed themselves from tin cans, and thus became known as "tin can tourists." Others would tow small trailers behind their cars, trailers just large enough to sleep a couple of adults and their children. From these humble beginnings, the RV industry and culture were born. (An excellent source on the modern RV culture in America is James B. Twitchell's *Winnebago Nation: The Peculiar Place of the RV in American Culture.*

By the time Disney World opened in 1971, the tourist industry was already Florida's biggest source of income. Most tourists did not come specifically to view turtles and fishes through glass-bottom boats or wander through tropical gardens; most came mainly to relax and soak up the sunshine. Still, the Old Florida attractions certainly added to the allure. Also alluring was the state's sense of adventure and even lawlessness, the sense that in Florida, pretty much anything goes. For a while, the state's official marketing slogan was "The Rules Are Different Here." *Tampa Bay Times* journalist and author Craig Pittman says that Florida is "the Land of a Thousand Chances," a place where you can go to reinvent yourself if you need or want to.

IN THE SHADOW OF THE MOUSE

Tourism has been a key part of the state's economy since the late nineteenth century but never more than in the years since 1971, when Walt Disney World opened in Orlando. Disney transformed the city of Orlando and Orange County into a major international tourist destination. About fifty-five million people visit the Disney theme parks in Orlando each year, making the area one of the most popular tourist destinations in America and, indeed, in the world. With a total employment of more than 60,000 workers, Walt Disney World in Orlando also claims to be the largest single-site employer in America.

Disney opened on October 1, 1971, the culmination of eight years of legal machinations, land acquisition, engineering, and construction. In those eight years, Disney purchased, mostly through dummy corporations, 27,300 acres of land (about 43 square miles) in the southwestern part of Orange County, Florida. Land acquisition began in 1964, when Disney's real estate agents, unaware that they were working for Disney, began making offers to regional landowners. Maintaining a strict secrecy about Disney's theme-park aspirations allowed Disney to acquire land at ridiculously low prices. Over the entire project, the average cost of land was a mere $185 per acre.

Although various rumors swarmed around the acquisition process, Disney was able to get the largest share of its property under contract before filing paperwork that identified the new owners. A rumor that Disney was behind the property acquisitions was pooh-poohed by the local paper, the *Orlando Sentinel*, because they had interviewed Walt Disney himself and Walt said he had no interest in building a Central Florida theme park. Many locals assumed that the land would be used for expansion of the Kennedy Space Center.

Why Orlando? The original Disneyland in Anaheim, California, was doing well, but market surveys showed that fewer than 5 percent of Disneyland's clientele came from east of the Mississippi, where three-quarters of the population lived. Clearly, an eastern alternative would make sense (and money). In order to keep the turnstiles humming year-round, a warm-weather site was also a given. New Orleans was in active consideration but eventually rejected because the city's notorious corruption would have made development of the park difficult. Orlando was near the planned intersection of I-4 and Florida's Turnpike and so would be easily accessible by car. The city was also developing an old air force base into a world-class airport, was blessed with a temperate climate, and was already a tourist destination because of nearby Cypress Gardens. So Orlando it was. Disney's intention to build "the greatest attraction in the history of Florida" was announced in November 1965.

Initially, Disney World featured the Magic Kingdom, two golf courses, two resort hotels, and a "wilderness resort" (campground). Since the original opening, the mega-park has added Epcot Center (1982); Typhoon Lagoon, the first of what are now several on-property water parks (1989); MGM

Studios (1989); Pleasure Island (1989); Downtown Disney (the latter has been rebranded many times going back to the 1970s but opened as Downtown Disney in 1997 and was recast as Disney Springs in 2013); the Disney Wide World of Sports complex, complete with baseball diamonds, a track-and-field venue, and tennis facilities (1997); the Richard Petty Driving Experience on Disney's own 1.5 mile racetrack (1997); and the fourth complete theme park, Animal Kingdom (1998), along with numerous additional resort hotels and other attractions. Between the four theme parks, multiple water parks, assorted miniature-golf courses, regular golf courses, movie theaters, restaurants, and countless other activities and attractions, the Disney visitor need never leave "the property," and in fact is encouraged not to do so. One thing you absolutely *cannot* do at Walt Disney World is rent a car. Even passengers on the Disney Cruise Line are ferried some sixty or seventy miles to and from the Port Canaveral cruise terminal by Disney buses. Asking people to drive themselves to or from the cruise ships might expose them to non-Disney attractions, and Disney doesn't want its visitors spending money elsewhere.

Disney was soon followed by other Orlando-area theme parks and tourist attractions, including SeaWorld (1973), Universal Studios (1990), the Kennedy Space Center Visitors Complex (1995), and the Holy Land Experience (a biblically themed attraction that opened in 2001). These are the survivors, the parks and attractions that are still with us. Quite a number of others have come and gone: Circus World (opened 1973, closed 1986); Splendid China (opened 1993, closed 2003); Boardwalk and Baseball (opened 1987, closed 1990); the Guinness World Record Experience (opened 2000, closed 2002); Stars Hall of Fame (opened 1975, closed 1984), and on through quite a list. To all the above, add scores of water parks, golf courses, bowling alleys, wax museums, dinner theaters, and related attractions, plus all the hotels and motels required to house the influx of tourists, plus all the restaurants to feed them once their frolics were over, plus all the rental car agencies so visitors could get from airport to hotel to theme park and back again, plus all the churches where the pious sought redemption for their theme-park excesses, plus all the roads and highways necessary to connect the dots, and you end up with a pretty big chunk of economic activity. It sometimes seems that the entire post-1971 economy of Central Florida developed mainly to give people something to do once they were done doing Disney.

Disney World is known everywhere as the "Happiest Place on Earth." The slogan was originally developed as a marketing catchphrase for Disney-land in Southern California, but is now used to describe all things Disney. It is the most famous but by no means the only Disney marketing slogan over the years. 2006 was the "Year of a Million Dreams" (the name of a promotion that began October 1, 2006, and ended December 31, 2008— so it was about twenty-seven months of a million dreams . . . but never mind). Other Disney slogans have included "Where Dreams Come True," "Where Friends Share the Magic," "Where the Party Never Ends," and "Where the Magic Began," but none of these have the immediate appeal or staying power of "The Happiest Place on Earth."

Walt Disney's original vision was not just a tourists' theme park. He also wanted Disney World to serve as a "vision" of a better life in the future. The Experimental Prototype Community of Tomorrow, or EPCOT, was intended to be part of the Disney World complex from the beginning. Disney had developed the Carousel of Progress for the 1964 New York World's Fair and intended EPCOT as an extension of that project. The city Disney envisioned was never built (Walt died before his vision could be realized), and EPCOT itself became a future-oriented theme park alongside the Magic Kingdom. Today, locals say that EPCOT stands for "Every Person Comes Out Tired."

The featured attraction at EPCOT comprises the eleven national pavilions highlighting the world's cultures. Represented are Mexico, Norway, China, Germany, Italy, the United States, Japan, Morocco, France, the United Kingdom, and Canada. Each pavilion features themed souvenir shops, restaurants, and native garb to give visitors an "authentic" taste of these various nations. One guest was heard to say, "It's just like being in Europe but here everyone speaks English." The World Showcase is very popular, and proposals for additional pavilions (Puerto Rico, Russia, Spain, Israel, Venezuela, and others) have been made, although no new pavilions have been added since 1988. EPCOT also features a nightly fireworks display over its central artificial lake, which makes Disney World the largest consumer of fireworks in the world. If you were looking for a perfect example of the New Florida preference for fake over authentic, the World Showcase would be it.

Walt Disney's fondness for the planned community of the future eventually found expression in the Disney-inspired, Disney-owned, Disney-built town of Celebration, just south of Walt Disney World. To an urban sociologist like me, Celebration looks and feels like a small town that was sent up from central casting. Built on the principles of the New Urbanism, appropriately Imagineered, Celebration originally consisted of about eleven hundred prim houses and townhomes all neatly arranged on broad boulevards that sweep gracefully to Celebration Place, a "business district" that houses the town's commercial enterprises, all of them within an easy walk of every occupied home. Unfortunately, most of these commercial enterprises are more cutesy or trendy than useful. Celebration residents complain that while they have a very convenient "family resort-wear" store right downtown (Soft as a Grape), a Once Upon a Time outlet (children's designer clothing boutique), the Wonderland Cookie Dough store, numerous galleries and frame shops, a number of high-end restaurants, and even a gourmet food store, they do not have a Target, a large supermarket, or a Home Depot.

One story that circulates about Celebration is that when homes there first went up for sale (the original home buyers were chosen by lottery, incidentally), the developers hired young boys to sit by the central (artificial) lake with fishing poles in hand and lines in the water, just to drive home the Norman Rockwellian serenity that residents could expect to encounter. There is also a deed restriction stipulating that all owners must pay a monthly fee to the official landscape maintenance company so that adjacent lawns are all mowed at the same time and to the same height. House colors are chosen from a common palette; landscape plantings must be approved by a central landscape-planning committee. It certainly wouldn't do for the roses in front of one house to clash with the gladioli in front of another.

What does Celebration "celebrate"? Bland but proper uniformity seems to be the animating vision. And yet studies of Celebration residents have shown them to be real people engaged in real-world struggles as they deal with real-world problems. According to Andrew Ross (*The Celebration Chronicles: Life, Liberty, and the Pursuit of Property Value in Disney's New Town*), the residents worry about property values, show up at school board meetings, wring their hands over their unruly children, and wonder if a big supermarket will ever come to town. It is, as Ross says, both "the best and worst of towns."

A more-recently added tourist attraction is Orlando's Holy Land Experience, a Christian theme park opened in 2001 by Marvin Rosenthal (who was born a Jew and converted to Christianity). The park was savagely satirized by Bill Maher in his 2008 documentary *Religulous*. There are some forty exhibits and attractions in the park, all "themed" around Jesus, including the Scriptorium Center for Biblical Antiquities and a daily eighty-minute reenactment of the Crucifixion. The park's opening was protested by the Jewish Defense League on the grounds that the whole purpose was to convert Jews to Christianity, a charge that the founder vehemently denied. A one-day pass to the Holy Land Experience will set adults back fifty bucks.

An even more recent addition to the Central Florida tourist armamentarium is LEGOLAND Florida, which opened in 2011 on the former Cypress Gardens site. Virtually the entire park is built from LEGO "bricks" (or artful facsimiles). Visitors have fifty rides, attractions, and shows, as well as exhibits, a restaurant, and gift shops to choose among, as well as the remains of the Cypress Gardens botanical park and a water park.

Disney and its imitators have enjoyed fabulous successes in the American market, and that has caused Disney in particular to open theme parks and attractions in Paris, Tokyo, Hong Kong, Shanghai, and Hawaii, with several more international venues currently in the planning phases. Currently, more than 150 million people each year pay handsome admission prices to be entertained by a giant plastic rat in one of Disney's global theme parks. I have met people in the Disney World parking lot in Orlando who told me they had traveled to California, France, Japan, and China just to "do Disney" at every available location. Can there be a more apt symbol of the homogenization of world culture than that?

Disney-like inauthenticity has also come to some of the tourist attractions in Europe. I once spent an afternoon in Gretna Green, Scotland. In historic times, this little village was the closest Scottish settlement to the English border and became a Reno-like attraction for underage English lovers who could marry without parental permission under Scottish but not English law. The "attraction" at Gretna Green is the eighteenth-century blacksmith's shop where many such marriages were allegedly performed. Tourists get to participate in a mock "anvil wedding" featuring bride-and-groom volunteers from the tour buses, an irate father with a musket, and a group "wedding photograph." This faux wedding ceremony takes about twenty minutes. The rest of your time in Gretna Green can be spent in "quaint traditional shops" that feature anvil-shaped ashtrays imprinted with GRETNA GREEN, SCOTLAND, Scottish woolen goods with tourist slogans woven into them ("We Renewed Our Vows at Gretna Green!"), assorted "authentic" jams, teas, and cheese trays ("Makes a great gift! We ship anywhere!"), even canned haggis. Watching all this reminded me of the souvenir trailers at the NASCAR races.

In Stratford-upon-Avon, you can buy a T-shirt that reads MY GRANDMA VISITED THE BARD'S BIRTHPLACE AND ALL I GOT WAS THIS LOUSY T-SHIRT. At the Tower of London, you can buy chintzy plastic forgeries of the Crown Jewels. In Cambridge, you can buy a plastic replica of King's College Chapel.

The sociologist George Ritzer is best known for his 1992 book, *The McDonaldization of Society*, one of the best-selling sociology books of all time. McDonaldization reflects four basic underlying principles: efficiency, calculability, predictability, and control. The Disneyfication of world leisure is probably second only to the spread of McDonald's itself as the leading example of what Ritzer has in mind.

6

ORANGE CRUSH

MY MOTHER-IN-LAW MOVED from Massachusetts to rural Kissimmee (south of Orlando) in 1971, just as Disney was opening, and witnessed with dismay the incessant suburbanization along Narcoossee Road, the Orange Blossom Trail, and US Highway 192, the three major routes into and through Kissimmee. "All these houses!" she would exclaim, and then state her unequivocal preference for the longhorn cattle ranches and orange groves that she remembered from the early 1970s. She called it the "real" Florida, "natural" Florida, the way Florida was "supposed to be."

But oranges are not native to Florida. Neither are longhorn cattle. Both cattle and oranges came to the New World with Christopher Columbus on his second voyage in 1493 and were introduced into the Florida peninsula by Ponce de León sometime early in the sixteenth century. Neither species was native to Europe, either. The cattle aboard the *Santa Maria* were descended from Middle Eastern aurochs; the orange trees were native to ancient China and Malay.

During the Age of Exploration (late fifteenth century to the end of the seventeenth century), adventurers such as Columbus and Ponce de León set out on ships laden with the plant and animal species that grew on their native lands and that they hoped to cultivate wherever they landed. Sometimes they were successful, sometimes not. Modern-day issues surrounding invasive species would have struck these explorers as ridiculous. If something from Spain or Portugal thrived in Massachusetts or Florida, well, that was where those species were supposed to be.

Oranges originated in China and elsewhere in continental east Asia but over the centuries were carried by traders to Japan and the South Pacific, and much later to the Middle East and Africa, and then to ancient Greece and Rome. Oranges were known to Plato and Socrates, and by the time of Columbus and Ponce they were grown widely in Spain, Portugal, and Italy, as well as in North Africa. The original orange trees had a bitter fruit and were mostly planted as ornamental shrubs until Portuguese explorers introduced a sweeter variety of orange into Europe. These sweet, juicy oranges became very popular and would have been a natural item for early explorers to include in their onboard inventories, along with wheat, sugar, coffee, cows, pigs, and much more. In return, these explorers took beans, corn, squash, potatoes, tomatoes, peppers, pumpkins, and peanuts back to Europe.

One question that always comes up in discussions of oranges is whether the fruit is named for the color or the color is named for the fruit. With some certainty, the color is named for the fruit, not the reverse. The first use of the word "orange" to describe the fruit dates to the thirteenth century; the first use of the same word to describe a color dates to the sixteenth century.

Orange trees from Ponce de León's original seeds were growing profusely in Saint Augustine by 1579. Tampa in the west and Saint Augustine in the east both had good growing conditions for citrus and had large, active seaports, so these two cities (barely towns at the time) were the centers of the Florida citrus industry in the early years. Orange groves were soon supplemented with tangerine, lemon, and lime groves, and in 1823, a French adventurer named Odet Philippe brought grapefruit from the West Indies into the state. Philippe is said to have been the first permanent European settler in the peninsula that is now Pinellas County, the region encompassing Saint Petersburg and Clearwater. He was also instrumental in introducing cigar production to the Tampa region. He is buried in his former plantation, now Philippe Park, in the town of Safety Harbor.

Trains, as we have already seen, were crucial in the development of Florida's east and southern coasts and were equally instrumental in the evolution of the Florida citrus industry. Citrus does not tolerate a hard freeze, so oranges, lemons, grapefruit, limes and other citrus could only be grown in the most temperate climates: Florida certainly, also in California, Arizona, and Texas. The early development of the state's railway system gave Florida a competitive edge in bringing citrus fruit to home tables elsewhere in the nation.

The citrus industry in Florida has suffered numerous setbacks over the years. One of the earliest was the Great Freeze of 1894–95, a back-to-back pair of bitter cold snaps that practically wiped out the citrus business. In December 1894, Orlando witnessed its all-time record low temperature of 18 degrees; a second bitter freeze came along the following February. Fruit froze on the trees and numerous trees were completely destroyed. The effect of the Great Freeze was to drop production from about six million boxes of fruit annually to barely a hundred thousand in 1895. It took more than fifteen years for the industry to recover. Many growers gave up on Florida, resettled in California, planted citrus trees, and boosted the growing California citrus industry.

The Florida citrus industry weathered several other biological and meteorological crises throughout the twentieth century, and so far the twenty-first century has been even less kind. In 2004, Hurricane Charley blew through Florida and destroyed not only the crop on the trees but many of the trees themselves. And just as the industry was about to recover from Charley, along came citrus canker and "greening disease," a bacterial citrus disease, borne by tiny insects, that has spread widely across the state and afflicts every citrus crop. These infestations cause citrus leaves to turn yellow and mottled, retard the development of the tree's root system, reduce fruit development, and cause the fruit that is produced to be asymmetrical and to drop prematurely. The fruit may also contain infertile seeds and have a bitter, almost salty, taste.

The latest hit on the citrus industry was Hurricane Irma in 2017. The hurricane passed through Florida in early September and knocked half the fruit off the trees. Flooding left many citrus trees standing in as much as four feet of water, weakening and in some cases destroying the roots. In the meantime, competition from Brazil has further eroded the industry's economic base.

In the twelve years since the most recent arrival of the little Asian citrus psyllid (a species of louse) that carries the disease-causing bacteria, Florida citrus production has declined precipitously. The 2016–17 harvest was fewer than seventy-eight million boxes (4.2 million tons), the smallest yield in a half century. Right now, the only real hope for the Florida citrus industry is a genetically engineered orange that is resistant to greening, but these trees will not be available commercially until at least 2022 and are certain to encounter stiff consumer resistance. So for several years now, Florida media have periodically featured alarmist stories with headlines such as HOW LONG CAN FLORIDA'S CITRUS INDUSTRY SURVIVE? and FLORIDA WITHOUT ORANGES? and most recently (in October 2017) FLORIDA'S ORANGE INDUSTRY, SYMBOL OF A STATE, IS DYING.

The alarm is justified. Citrus growers say that 90 percent of their acreage and 80 percent of their trees are infected, and research from the University of Florida's Institute of Food and Agricultural Sciences backs them up. Canker and the greening disease have resulted in billions of dollars of lost revenue, more than a hundred thousand acres taken out of production (from a base of about 500,000 acres), and tens of thousands of jobs in the industry lost since the disease was first detected. In 1977, Florida sported fifty-three orange juice–processing plants. Today there are seven.

Weapons to fight greening are few and expensive. The only way to make sure an infected tree does not become a source of further infection is to remove it and all the other citrus trees in the vicinity. The "vicinity" is the surrounding 260 acres or thereabouts. So if a homeowner has a backyard tangerine tree that is found to be infested, all the backyard citrus trees in the entire neighborhood have to be cut down and destroyed. Inevitably, Florida homeowners are fond of their backyard citrus and took great umbrage at the state's chainsaw tactics. At the outset of the current citrus canker crisis in 2000–01, crews would sometimes show up without warning to remove infected trees. The issue evolved into a classic showdown between private property rights and the rights of government to protect an industry vital to the state's economic health.

The Florida Supreme Court resolved the issue in favor of the government tree-removal program but also ordered the state to compensate citrus tree owners for the damage. Between the trees that had already been cut down and those slated for removal, and making reasonable estimates of the economic value of backyard citrus trees, state economists quickly determined that the removal program was going to cost the state somewhere between a half billion and a billion dollars. And besides, the Florida hurricanes of 2004 (and since) were very effective in spreading the disease all over the state despite various containment efforts. So the tree-removal program was eventually halted. Still, even in 2017, homeowners were in court trying to get their "just compensation" for trees removed by the state nearly twenty years ago.

When visitors go into Florida grocery stores, they are sometimes astonished to see that all the oranges for sale were grown in California (or, increasingly, Brazil or China, the major international competitors to the domestic citrus industry). So they frequently ask, "Why can't you buy Florida oranges in Florida grocery stores?" The answer is simple: Florida oranges are grown mainly to supply raw material for the state's orange juice industry, not to supply fresh oranges for home consumption.

An ideal juice orange is very juicy, very sweet, and uniform in size. The Valencia orange is considered to be the ideal juice orange. An ideal table orange is less juicy (less messy to eat) but sweet and easy to peel. Here, the navel orange is the archetype. In 2016, almost 90 percent of Florida's citrus crop was processed into juice. In the same year, only 20 percent of the California crop became juice. In short, Florida grows juice oranges and California grows table oranges.

The Florida orange juice industry is a year-round enterprise, and that too surprises many people who seem to believe that all the oranges must ripen at about the same time. Not so! By planting multiple varieties, many of which have been bred to ripen at different times, Florida orange growers can harvest fruit from early October through June, with only a brief hiatus in the summer months.

As if canker and greening disease were not bad enough, the orange juice industry is also in its worst slump in a century because orange juice, once considered a mainstay in a fresh and healthy diet, has come under the nutritionists' fire for being laden with sugar (there is about as much sugar in a glass of OJ as there is in a glass of regular Coke) and incompatible with a low-carbohydrate diet (a large orange might contain 22 grams of carbohydrates, about the same as a potato). The idea that oranges and orange juice in particular are healthy essentials in the modern diet has always been a convenient marketing fiction cooked up by the citrus industry to increase orange consumption when the industry was overproducing. Frozen orange juice concentrate used up a lot of oranges and could be marketed as "fresh-frozen" health food in a can. It was also a great convenience to pull a can of frozen OJ concentrate out of the home freezer and have tasty table-ready juice in minutes.

Alissa Hamilton, author of *Squeezed: What You Don't Know about Orange Juice*, points out that many people look on orange juice as a natural, unprocessed, healthy breakfast drink. Not so. S-o-o-o not so. An article about orange juice in *Cook's Illustrated* magazine (March–April 2014) points out the problem that has to be overcome in the OJ industry: "how to produce (and profit from) a juice that has a fresh and consistent flavor 365 days a year and a shelf life long enough to withstand transport to and storage in supermarkets. Mind you, this is all from a seasonal fruit crop with natural variation in flavor and that is susceptible to whims of disease, bugs, and volatile weather patterns."

Anyone who squeezes their own juice from fresh oranges knows that no two batches are ever the same: one batch is sweeter, the next is on the sour side; one seems to have lots of pulp, the next has practically none. So how is it that whenever you buy a gallon of your favorite orange juice, it always tastes exactly the same?

It turns out that squeezing juice from oranges is only the first in a very long series of steps to get to the bottle of OJ in your fridge. First, the juice must be pasteurized to kill off any nasties that might cause the juice to spoil. Pasteurization involves heating the juice to about 160 degrees ("gentle" pasteurization) or higher. Most manufacturers go higher just to be on the safe side. The next step in processing is storage. Since different varieties of orange ripen at different times of the year, maintaining consistency in the final product means that most table-ready orange juice is a blend of the juices of several different varieties. So oranges are squeezed when they are ready to be squeezed, but the juice must then be stored for months to assure a steady supply for mixing into the final product.

During storage, the key issue is preventing oxidation, which turns the juice rancid. Most companies accomplish this by a process of "deaeration," a process that strips off the juice's oxygen for storage in million-gallon tanks for as long as a year. The storage tanks are "topped off" with nitrogen to assure an oxygen-free storage environment. How's that glass of OJ tasting now?

But there's more. It turns out that stripping away the oxygen also removes the juice's flavor compounds, so deoxygenated OJ tastes thin and watery. "That's where the blend technicians . . . come in." Their job is not just to blend various juices from various tanks to achieve a particular balance of sweetness and acidity, although that is certainly part of OJ processing technology. But more important, the blend technicians add highly engineered "flavor packs" to achieve the desired taste. These packs are made up of additives harvested from fresh fruit and fruit peels and then chemically processed by various "fragrance companies" to compensate for the effects of pasteurization and deaeration. The result: a highly processed, chemically engineered product that meets a manufacturer's particular "flavor profile." Minus these flavor packs, commercial OJ would be undrinkable.

Cook's Illustrated reports that Coca-Cola, the parent company of Simply Orange and Minute Maid orange juices, "has developed a staggeringly precise algorithm" by which their juice is processed. The algorithm is said to contain a *quintillion* variables that can affect the taste of orange juice. (One quintillion is 10^{18}, an unimaginably large number.) Among the variables are six hundred different volatile compounds that influence the flavor of orange juice. Satellite imagery tells the company when fruit should be harvested, and the production algorithm tells them exactly how to chemically engineer the final product to be pleasing and familiar to the consumer. If conditions change—if a hurricane wipes out a bunch of fruit in Florida, a cold snap threatens production in California, or the Brazilian crop is under attack by insects—the company can reconfigure its entire production process in less than ten minutes.

An orange is about half juice. The rest is peel, pulp, membrane, and seed, and while a small fraction of the waste is used to manufacture flavor packs (or is processed into cattle feed), the larger share by far is just plain waste. The state's citrus-processing plants produce about five million tons of citrus waste each year. Florida scientists have been working for a decade to figure out how to manufacture ethanol from this waste. Unlike corn, which is the feedstock for most US ethanol production but has many alternative uses, orange waste has no other economically viable use. Maybe someday in the not too distant future, you will be able to fuel up your body in the morning with a glass of Florida orange juice and drive to work burning ethanol manufactured from the peels.

Despite the many setbacks, citrus remains an important staple in the Florida economy and will likely remain so for the foreseeable future. There are, after all, seventy-five million citrus trees in the state. Citrus in Florida is a $10 billion a year industry and employs nearly fifty thousand people either directly or indirectly.

Citrus trees of all varieties are also landscaping staples and an important element in Florida culture. They are handsome, well-contained evergreen trees with a pleasing fragrance and are found as ornamental plantings in backyards all over the state. Ornamental or not, they also produce fruit, often in quantities far beyond what a household can consume. So one downside to backyard citrus trees is that most trees are surrounded by rotting fruit much of the time. Rotting citrus is in turn a major food source for Florida's rats. So if you begin to see a lot of rats in your backyard, you might want to rethink your citrus investment. (You'll know you have rats if you find hollowed out pieces of fruit on the ground with a hole in one end about the size of a half-dollar.)

Because rotting fruit attracts rats and insects, many backyard citrus owners make an effort to stay ahead of their trees' fruit production, often by gathering up ripe fruit daily and distributing it to friends and coworkers. I have a colleague with a giant grapefruit tree in his backyard, and for about a month each year, he brings two or three plastic grocery bags jammed with fruit into the office each day, all of it free for the taking. So it's a good thing that freshly squeezed Florida Ruby Red grapefruit juice makes a delicious salty dog. To make one yourself, rim a highball glass with kosher salt and fill with ice cubes. Pour in a quarter cup of good vodka and fill the glass with freshly squeezed grapefruit juice. Each drink will use up three or four grapefruits. Swap in freshly squeezed (not processed!) OJ for the grapefruit juice and you have a killer screwdriver. These are the drinks that make backyard citrus worth the trouble.

7

RETIREMENT PHANTASMAGORIA

THE DISSIPATION OF CAPITAL
ACCUMULATED ELSEWHERE

THERE ARE MORE than four million Floridians over the age of sixty-five, about 20 percent of the state's entire population. Our percentage of elderly is the largest of any state in the nation, so in Florida, retirement is an industry just the same as tourism or citrus production or aerospace. The state actively markets itself as a retirement haven. Mild climate, low taxes, and senior-friendly housing and retirement communities have made Florida the "final destination" for millions of retirees.

What makes retirees appealing to the state is that they bring their 401(k) accounts, pensions, investments, and Social Security checks with them and spend those funds on housing, food, health care, and country club fees, but they don't need jobs to do so. So the state can grow its population and its consumption base without having to add to the productive labor economy. As T. D. Allman put it in his *National Geographic* article on Orlando, retirement is the "dissipation of capital accumulated elsewhere." Growth without the need to accumulate capital—a developer's dream!

Retirees come to Florida for the weather, the relatively low cost of living, the absence of a state income tax, and the many leisure-time pursuits that appeal to the over-sixty crowd. Florida has more golf courses than any other state (more than 1,250 of them), and the state is home to twelve of the nation's remaining eighteen active dog-racing tracks. The capital pumped into the state for senior housing, services and amenities, health care, and recreation creates a bonanza for the local economy and a great deal of economic growth without the social and environmental downside of factories, coal mines, or assembly plants. Retirement is a clean and lucrative industry. Many retirees also bring a commitment to volunteerism and a devotion to spending their remaining years in the service of others, and that certainly enriches the social and cultural capital of the state.

Florida usually comes out as the best state in the nation for retirement—when someone in Florida is doing the rankings, that is. A more objective analysis based on measurable factors such as cost of living, walkability, crime rates, quality of health care, taxes, and the weather put only one Florida city, Cape Coral, in the top ten (of 187 cities that were ranked). An item about the study in *USA Today* was titled "The Best Place to Retire Isn't Florida." In fact, three Arizona cities were in the top ten (Phoenix, Prescott, and Tucson), as were two Colorado cities (Denver and Colorado Springs), compared to Florida's one. Florida's comparatively poor showing was attributed to too much rain, insufferable humidity for much of the year, and the comparatively high cost of living in many Florida cities.

Florida faces increasingly stiff competition for retiree dollars from other warm-weather states. Many Californians, for example, head to Arizona once they retire, and east of the Mississippi, Florida has to compete with the likes of Georgia, Tennessee, and North Carolina. Georgia recently acted to exempt the first $65,000 in retirement income from state income tax for persons over 65 and twice that for married senior couples. (Florida counters: we don't have a state income tax!) Tennessee is aggressively marketing its "Retire Tennessee" campaign, encouraging seniors to relocate to twenty-two largely rural Tennessee communities chosen for their senior-friendly amenities and lifestyle, and sending state representatives to retirement trade shows. North Carolina has a large number of planned retirement communities in development.

According to United Van Lines (who would presumably know), "more retirees than ever are relocating," and despite the increasing competition from other states, Florida remains a favored destination. When asked why, "the weather" always dominates, even though Florida seems to have about one month of fall, one week of winter, one month of spring, and almost ten months of summer each year. Next to Florida comes Arizona, a western version of Florida, with warm weather, low taxes, gorgeous scenery, and a modest cost of living. Somewhat surprisingly, third place (in a Market-Watch survey on the topic) goes to South Carolina.

An article in the *Orlando Business Journal* ranked the retirement industry as the third major source of the "boomlet" in local employment, just behind construction and tourism. And, of course, the number of retirees will skyrocket as the baby boomers reach retirement years. By convention, the baby boom encompasses all the extra-large generations born between 1946 and 1964, some seventy-eight million Americans. The retirement boom in the making virtually guarantees a measure of prosperity to Florida until mid-century.

At times, the Florida retirement industry can be every bit as Disney-esque as Disney itself and as cheesy as the tackiest tourist trap. A case in point: The Villages, allegedly the largest retirement community in the United States, occupying about 10,000 acres sprawled over five counties and marketed aggressively throughout the nation as "Florida's Friendliest Retirement Hometown." For several years now, The Villages have been the fastest growing community in the country. The 2000 population of the legal entity The Villages was 8,333. In 2010, it was 51,442. In 2016, the population of The Villages Metropolitan Statistical Area exceeds 157,000. You can't grow much quicker than that.

One might think that The Villages would be a loose confederation of separate small towns, but no, it is a master-planned age-restricted community consisting of eleven separate Community Development Districts (CDDs), each about a thousand acres in size and roughly corresponding to a "village." "The Villages" was chosen as the name to suggest a traditional small-town lifestyle, but as of the 2010 census, the place was designated as a Metropolitan Statistical Area, the Census Bureau's euphemism for a city. And it is growing by leaps and bounds.

Development of The Villages began in the 1960s when the principals, Harold Schwartz and Al Tarrson, began selling tracts of land via mail order. The mail-order end of the business was halted in 1968 when the federal government outlawed mail-order land deals. Schwartz and Tarrson then tried to develop their land into a mobile-home park, but that too was unsuccessful. Struck by the successes of retirement communities such as the Del Webb Sun City developments, which offered well-maintained units with lots of amenities and commercial outlets, Schwartz bought out Tarrson, appointed his own son, Gary Morse, to the governing board, and began upgrading the holdings and marketing them to retired seniors. The development was named The Villages in 1992 and it is still controlled by descendants of Schwartz and Morse.

Eighty percent of the homes in The Villages must be occupied by at least one person fifty-five years of age or older. Persons under the age of nineteen years are allowed to visit but for a maximum of thirty days per year. There are some family dwellings that are exempt from these restrictions, but not many. The exceptions are made for the laborers who maintain The Villages' grounds and commercial enterprises. Each neighborhood is governed by a Declaration of Restrictions that covers landscaping, lawn maintenance, paint colors, placement of items such as satellite dishes, boats, and RVs, and so on—all this to assure a pleasing uniformity throughout. The Villages are the quintessential retirement community.

Each of the CDDs features central squares surrounded by retail establishments and multiple golf courses, some of them world-class. Golf is the leading activity, possibly challenged only by pickleball. In all, there are about fifty golf courses and practice facilities operated by The Villages and "Free Golf for Life" is one of The Villages' best marketing slogans.

Pickleball is a sport most people have never heard of but is a big deal in Florida's retirement communities. It is a geriatric version of tennis played with Ping-Pong paddles and a Whiffle Ball on a court similar to a badminton court. According to the USA Pickleball Association (yes, there is such a thing), "The growth of pickleball is on fire."

Jeff Laughlin, a North Carolina sportswriter, visited a pickleball match and reported that "the absurdity of the name can only be rivaled by the absurdity of the sport itself." Because the rackets are pretty lightweight and the Whiffle Ball is, well, a Whiffle Ball, no one can hit the ball hard enough to get it past an opposing player. The result is a game featuring "long, arduous volleys" that seem to end mainly once someone gets tired of swinging the racket or it's time for lunch. Laughlin characterizes the sport as "incredibly easy and boring," but to aficionados, apparently, it is a great way to work up a thirst for an afternoon martini.

The Villages are full of dining, recreational drinking, and leisure-time venues and opportunities, even lectures by professors from nearby University of Florida. Residents routinely refer to their community as "The Happiest Place on Earth" or sometimes as "Disney for Adults." Certainly, the place has a Disney-like air about it.

A characteristic Villages feature is Lake Sumter Landing, a shopping and restaurant complex complete with an ersatz lighthouse. The absurdity of the Lake Sumter "lighthouse" becomes apparent when you realize that it is more than seventy miles from the nearest open water, as close to land-locked as you can be anywhere in Florida. Marketing materials boast that "Lake Sumter Landing's colorful waterfront setting reminds many folks of quaint seaside villages they visited during their childhood." The "colorful waterfront" opens onto a man-made lake. In the lighthouse town square, retired people can dance, swill beer purchased from open-air beer carts, take a boat tour of the fake lake, even visit a fake shipwreck in the middle of the fake lake. Everything is made to look old—the Old Mill Playhouse, Cody's Original Roadhouse. Each business sports a plaque with a fake founding date and a fake history, and the streets are paved in fake cobblestones. Lake Sumter Landing, redolent with nostalgia, evocative of America's simpler small-town past, was built in 2004. In The Villages, at Disney, and throughout Florida, the motto seems to be "Why bother with the real thing when the fake works even better?"

Life in The Villages often seems to begin and end with golf, or sometimes to begin with a round of golf, then a brisk pickleball contest, then a round of cocktails. Driving through, you notice immediately that there are more golf carts (referred to there as golf cars) than cars. Golf cars have the right of way everywhere, their own lanes on Villages roadways, and sometimes their own garages—and almost every home has one. The town website, thevillages.com, assures visitors on one web page: "Our residents say it's like being a kid again: golf, recreation, shopping, dining, medical and professional services—everything you need to live life to the fullest— just a golf-car ride away, in a beautifully designed and gated community. You'll make friends, you'll make memories, and you can ultimately make yourself a happier, healthier person too! These are the good old days, so why not enjoy them right now—each and every day!" This glowing self-promotion is followed by a resident on video who says, "I don't know how much happier I can get than right now."

As one might imagine, politics in The Villages are pretty right-wing. Republicans outnumber Democrats by at least two to one. The Villages are a regular stop on the tour for Republican hopefuls. Marco Rubio, Governor Rick Scott, Sarah Palin, Mike Huckabee, Mitt Romney, George W. Bush, Newt Gingrich, John McCain, Rick Santorum, Ron Paul, and other conservative politicos have all made stops there, as have conservative TV personalities Glen Beck and Sean Hannity. The former chairman of the local Republican Club once said, "The road to Washington goes through Tallahassee—you have to win Florida—and the road to Tallahassee goes through The Villages." The few liberal Democrats who live there complain not just of their numerical disadvantage, but of harassment, ostracization, even mild repression. When Governor Rick Scott went to The Villages for the ceremonial signing of his first state budget, members of the local Democratic Club were barred from attending, and sheriff's deputies cleared out anyone sporting anti-Scott signs or "liberal looking pins and buttons" (according to a *Miami Herald* story).

The Villages were hard-core Trump country in 2016. The sharp influx of affluent white retirees into The Villages partially offset the Democratic advantage in fast-growing ethnic minority communities. A particularly notable feature were the many Trumpmobile golf cars on Villages streets. That pesky Declaration of Restrictions forbids political lawn signs and door-to-door canvassing or solicitation, but there are no restrictions on what you can put on your vehicles. So many of The Villages' Trump enthusiasts adorned their golf cars with giant pro-Trump signs front, back, and sides. Many said they were supporting Trump because of his anti-immigrant position. Said one, "We hate to see the country taking in so many people who are immigrants who have not followed the rules." The Villages' population is more than 98 percent white. The Trumpmobiles also apparently served as "gay-dar" for some residents. One said that almost everywhere he went, people would give him the thumbs-up, but "You can tell who is gay. 'Cause all the gays give you thumbs-down."

Besides golf, pickleball, drinking, and Republican politics, a favorite Villages pastime appears to be sex. Life expectancies for women are some five to seven years longer than life expectancies for men, and men marry on average at later ages than women. So in any collection of seniors, women will outnumber men, usually by a substantial margin. So any old geezer who can still "get it up" is a hot commodity. Or so says Stefani Cohen in a 2009 essay on "Florida's wild retirees' getaway." The Villages, she says, are "a widower's paradise, and the word on the street is that there's a big black market for Viagra. . . . Getting lucky is one of the residents' primary pastimes." Alex French, writing for BuzzFeed, talks about mystery dates arranged by pulling golf-car keys from a bowl, prostitution rings, senior orgies, public sex, and not-so-subtle signals of one's availability. "I'm told that sticking a loofah on your cart antenna signifies you're into swinging. So does wearing a crimson button. According to multiple people, wearing gold shoes or letting your shirt tag stick out in the back signals you're on the prowl."

In the 1990s, when The Villages started growing exponentially, the STD rate shot up along with the population. Between 1995 and 2005, syphilis, gonorrhea, chlamydia, and HPV cases approximately doubled among Florida's seniors. A local gynecologist said that she treated more cases of herpes and HPV in The Villages than she ever did during her stint in Miami.

One Villages stud, seventy-year-old Dave, brags that he gets "offers for sex all the time." Most propositions come from women in their seventies. Mr. Midnight, another senior studmuffin, boasts of a long series of one-nighters. He's particularly fond of a woman who "comes over, takes a shower, jumps in bed, and then gets dressed and leaves." And the women seem to confirm what the men boast of: "A lot of the women are extremely brazen. Some girls will go into the parking lot with a man and come back a half-hour later like nothing happened!"

More confirmation comes from local law enforcement. Not only is there rampant sexual conquest but also drunk driving in golf cars on the way home from the bars, illegal drug use, even fistfights. A former dancer said, "Whatever you know about twenty-year-olds, it's the same with seniors." At times, The Villages bars seem more like college fraternity parties than establishments catering to seniors. A hottie walks through (in The Villages, a hottie is apparently anyone with a pulse), the juices begin to flow (well, trickle), and suddenly "You see two seventy-year-olds with canes fighting over a woman and you think, 'Oh, Jeez!'"

8

FLORIDA'S BEACHES AND BEACH CULTURE

IF YOU GOOGLE "What do people like most about Florida?" dozens of sites pop up with titles such as "23 Reasons Florida (Yes, Florida) Is Quite Possibly the Best State in America" (*The Huffington Post*), "Top 10 Reasons Why People Love Florida" (bkadventure.com), "27 Things That People in Florida Love" (Movoto), "10 Things to Love about Florida" (TripSavvy), and numerous items in a similar vein. And while the items that appear on these lists vary from the Kennedy Space Center at Cape Canaveral to Joe's Stone Crab restaurant in Miami to Key West's Duval Street Pub Crawl to the submarine sandwiches at the local Publix, the two items guaranteed to appear on every list are the weather and the Florida beaches.

Florida sports more than 1,350 miles of coastline, of which about half are sun-drenched sandy beaches. This is more coast than any other state except Alaska and a third again the length of the California coast. You can get to a beach from almost anywhere in Florida in an hour or so, and fully three-quarters of the state's population live within ten miles of the coast (although on busy beach weekends, those ten miles can sometimes take an hour). Many tourists come to Florida specifically to enjoy our beaches, and beach tourism is estimated to add $15 billion a year to the economy.

I wrote in an earlier chapter about the decline of Old Florida that came about because of Disney and "Theme-Park Nation." The one place where Old Florida continues to thrive everywhere is at the beach. Sure, you can spend your weekend at the beach holed up in a Holiday Inn or a Howard Johnson's or some other national chain establishment instead of a mom-and-pop motel, but plenty of fifties-era accommodations remain if you are into that sort of thing, and the beach experience itself—the surf, sand, water, and warm breezes—has not changed appreciably since the state was first settled. If you want an enjoyable and authentic taste of the Old Florida, book a room at the Bon-Aire Resort Motel on Saint Pete Beach (it's been a Saint Pete Beach landmark since the 1950s), grab a grouper sandwich at Sandbar Bill's Bar & Grille (a come-as-you-are bar where flip-flops are the footwear of choice), and kick back for the rest of the day on a folding beach chair overlooking the Gulf of Mexico. This has been a favored Florida pastime since there was a Florida, and it's the general topic of this chapter.

Locals love to argue over which of the state's beaches is "best," a subjective assessment that admits of many different answers. Truth is, all the Florida beaches have something special to offer. The west coast beaches (those on the Gulf of Mexico) are more staid and upscale and the waves are more placid, while the east coast (Atlantic) beaches sport a younger and rowdier crowd, more drinking, and more of the Old Florida panache and mentality. If driving on the beach is your thing, you are locked into Daytona Beach, New Smyrna Beach, or Saint Augustine Beach, all on the Atlantic. No west coast beach allows cars. Metaphorically, the east coast beaches are fried shrimp and hush puppies; the southern beaches, particularly Miami Beach, are Beautiful People sipping mojitos; and the west coast beaches are ceviche and broiled grouper. But there are nude beaches on both coasts, great deepwater fishing, all sorts of beach amusements (paddleboarding, kite sailing, surfing, sailing), a profusion of beach bars and eateries everywhere, and plenty of sunshine (most of the time).

In an essay on Florida's fifteen most popular (not necessarily best) beaches, Matt Meltzer points out that "Florida does a lot of things wrong." His list of indictments includes being unable to figure out how to put on an election, assaulting one another with live iguanas, and the occasional alligator in the backyard swimming pool. But no one, he says, does beaches as well as Florida.

Meltzer's vote for most popular Florida beach goes to Siesta Key, just south of Tampa. Siesta Key is near Sarasota, so there are plenty of things to do when the sun, surf, and sand get to be too much. *Condé Nast Traveler* says that Miami's South Beach is the best Florida has to offer, and once you are done beaching, all of Miami is within your grasp. The beaches of Key West get the Travel Channel's vote, and you can end your day there with a crowd of crazies watching the sun go down at Mallory Square. *U.S. News & World Report* once liked Saint Pete Beach the most: "miles of relaxing shorelines and an urban cityscape—perfect for those looking to escape to the beach without feeling disconnected." (I agree with this assessment, but then, Saint Pete Beach is where I now live. The latest ranking from *U.S. News & World Report*, however, lists the Panhandle beach at Destin as number one.) A little googling easily turns up "best beach" votes for several of the Panhandle beaches, for the beach at Naples, for Clearwater Beach, Daytona Beach, Cocoa Beach (best surfing in the state), or the beaches on Amelia and Sanibel Islands. The fact is, from Pensacola Beach around the perimeter to Miami and then up the Atlantic Coast, every beach has something special to offer.

Old Florida beach culture is not the same as the New England or California beach cultures. All the Florida beaches have a laid-back Caribbean feel to them, and many beach bars add to the ambience by featuring reggae music, especially on the weekends. "Trop rock" entertainment in the style of Jimmy Buffett is also very popular. Florida beaches exude a party atmosphere, whereas the vibe on California beaches is healthy lifestyles. Overweight men and women of any age will feel right at home on any Florida beach (Miami's South Beach a possible exception). On California beaches, if your body-fat percentage is greater than about 15 percent, you may be subject to fat shaming. Drinking is allowed on many Florida beaches and generally tolerated even where it is not allowed (just so long as things don't get out of hand). The drink of choice is beer. In California, only a few beaches allow alcohol and the drinks of choice are pale ale, champagne, or superchilly white wine.

Florida leads all the warm-weather states in per capita annual alcohol consumption, at least according to the National Institute on Alcohol Abuse and Alcoholism. Among all states, Florida ranks sixteenth in per capita consumption of booze. But the states that drink more booze are cold-weather states: New Hampshire, North Dakota, Wisconsin, Montana, Vermont, Alaska, Idaho, and so on. Clearly, these people drink to stay warm. In Florida, people drink to enhance the vibe, the good time.

Everywhere in Florida, proper beach garb is a pair of flip-flops, a swimming suit, and perhaps a T-shirt. No restaurant on any Florida beach has a dress code that goes beyond "shirts and shoes required," and in many Florida dives, the prevailing attitude is "No shirt? No shoes? No problem!"

During your time on Florida's beaches, you may well encounter a wedding party since Florida beach weddings are common. On the Pass-a-Grille beach where I live, there are a couple of beach weddings each week. Proper etiquette is to accede to whatever the bride requests, including moving your gear someplace else if you've set up camp on the bride's preferred spot. The wedding party will be fully dressed—the only people on the beach not clothed in swimming suits and T-shirts. By tradition, onlookers are part of the fun and form a circle around the wedding party at a distance of perhaps five or ten yards—close enough to hear the vows over the roar of the surf, but not so close as to be intrusive. When the ceremony ends, the onlookers cheer and clap. Many newly married couples conclude their ceremony by wading into the surf—tuxedo, wedding dress, bridesmaids, and all. Most of the hotels that overlook the coast will gladly arrange the details of a beach wedding for you, and if you want to marry on a public beach, companies such as Tide the Knot or Florida Beach Weddings will get you all set up—everything from on-the-beach altars to seating, flowers, catering, music, and the like.

If you find yourself on the Daytona, New Smyrna, or Saint Augustine beaches, remember that beach driving is allowed. Driving on the beach is a classic Old Florida amusement that combines two favorite Old Florida activities: driving and hanging out on the beach. Pedestrians have the right-of-way in all cases, but that is little comfort if you get run over. On beaches where cars are allowed, parking is along the sand farthest from the water. Then comes the driving lanes, and then the sun-and-surf beach where beachgoers set up chairs, umbrellas, coolers, and sun tents to enjoy their day. In short, everyone has to walk through the driving area to get to the most desirable beach locations. So if you're driving, look out for pedestrians.

And if you are a pedestrian, look out for inattentive, drunk, or distracted drivers, or this trip to the beach could be your last.

Lest you think I exaggerate, a four-year-old child was run over and killed on the New Smyrna beach just a few years ago, the second child killed on the New Smyrna beach that year. Another fatal incident involved a sixteen-year-old tourist. Overall, more than twenty beachgoers have been mowed down since 2000. Most of these accidents involve cars driven by lifeguards, beach patrols, police, and other officials, not tourists. But on an average beach weekend, there will be thousands of cars lining the beach and thousands of kids romping in the sun. Parents and drivers have an obligation to keep the two separated.

Given the hazards, why is driving on the beach allowed at all? First, it has *always* been allowed and has always been a part of Old Florida culture. Volusia County (where both Daytona Beach and New Smyrna Beach are located) also realizes substantial revenue from beach driving. In recent years, the annual revenues from beach driving passes have been around $4 million. If beach driving were not allowed, the county and its towns would have to make more nearby parking available, and that costs money rather than making it. So why change anything, even if an occasional tourist gets hurt?

There is, of course, constant pressure from New Floridians to ban beach driving in the state altogether. Barely a year goes by when Volusia County officials don't take up some version of a beach-driving ban. The antis have slowly nibbled away at the practice. At one time, there were forty-seven miles of Volusia County beach where driving was allowed and today there are only about sixteen miles left. Arguments against the practice range from safety concerns to environmentalism to promoting more beach development, all the sorts of things New Floridians would worry about. Arguments in favor are that beach driving is a tradition, a draw for tourists, and an inalienable Old Florida right. One proponent put it this way: "Not supporting the wishes of your people can only be compared with the ruthless rule of King George and be met with the same commitment of resistance." Beach driving, in short, is something Old Floridians are serious about.

SPRING BREAK

Many people first experience Florida beaches during their college spring break, since for most of the nation east of the Mississippi, "spring break" and "Florida beaches" have been almost synonymous for decades. In the past, Fort Lauderdale was the quintessential destination, but in the last several decades, beaches all over the state have been overrun with college kids from late February to mid-April.

Florida's beach cities have a love-hate relationship with spring breakers. The love comes from the revenue spring break brings in. Local bars, eateries, motels, and other commercial enterprises often earn half their annual revenues during spring break. The hate comes from the drunkenness, rowdiness, and general debauchery that college kids bring. Wet T-shirt contests (which originated in Spain, not in Florida) are common wherever there is a hose, along with "best bikini" competitions, all-female nude coleslaw wrestling, beer-chugging contests, roaring beach fires, and more. Some once-favorite spring break destinations, for example, Fort Lauderdale and Panama City Beach, have attempted to tame the rowdiness by passing and enforcing strict antialcohol laws, but that has served mainly to drive spring breakers to beaches such as Daytona, Fort Myers, or Key West, where the attitude is more laissez-faire.

Daytona Beach has been designated the number-one spring break destination by numerous listing and rating organizations. The Daytona Beach tourist "season" starts with "Speedweeks," nine days of racing events at the Daytona International Speedway that culminate with the Daytona 500 in mid-February, an event attended by a quarter million people. College spring breakers start showing up shortly thereafter. Estimates of the spring break crowd are unreliable because college kids will sleep on the beach or in motels eight or ten to a room, so an accurate count is impossible. But spring breakers in Daytona alone must surely number in the hundreds of thousands. The *comparative* size of the spring break crowd is indexed by the number of arrests made by local police, and by that standard spring break 2016 was the largest in more than a decade—464 college kids were arrested and 125 fake IDs were confiscated in March alone.

Then sometime in mid-March, Daytona hosts Bike Week, a ten-day motorcycle rally and festival that is thought to draw a half million people. Here too, accurate estimates are impossible. The key indicator of the Bike Week crowd used by some is the number of motorcyclists killed or injured in biker accidents. In 2016, the death toll was fifteen, the largest number so far this century. In 2018, however, only two deaths were reported. A second and no tamer motorcycle rally at Daytona is Biketoberfest, a four-day event held in mid-October.

Just as Bike Week winds down and the spring break crowds are starting to thin out, Daytona hosts its annual Black College Reunion, spring break for African American college students. Black College Reunion is traditionally held over the three-day weekend of the annual football game between Bethune-Cookman (located in Daytona) and Florida A&M, two historically black institutions. At its peak, Black College Reunion brought a hundred thousand people into the city and $150 million into the coffers of local businesses, but both attendance and revenues have since fallen. Hanging out on the beach and cruising the main drag through town (International Speedway Boulevard) are favorite activities, but sex and "dressing to impress" are also well up on the list.

Around the start of summer (summer usually comes to Florida in April) up to the July Fourth weekend and the summer race at Daytona, Daytona Beach settles down into a fairly quiet coastal city with very heavy beach crowds on the weekends. But the summer race brings another quarter million people into the city, along with more drunkenness and rowdy behavior, and ditto Biketoberfest in the fall.

For three or four months of the year, Daytona is a happening place— full of visitors, with campgrounds and motels bloated, motorcycles roaring up and down the main drag, cash registers ringing, and beer flowing abundantly. For the rest of the year, it is a sleepy little town along Florida's east coast, blessed (as all of Florida) with plenty of sunshine and beachfront, but where the most exciting thing that might happen is that someone will get bitten by a shark. The town's politics are defined by the inevitable tensions between the "party, party, party" atmosphere of Speedweeks, Bike Week, and spring break *versus* the desire of most residents to live in a small, quiet, laid-back coastal village. Should driving on the beach be outlawed? Should the town "get tough" on underage drinking? What can be done about the massive traffic jams on race days? Should the wet T-shirt contests be banned? Daytona locals look with much disfavor on the bawdy drunkenness of these various springtime events, but none gainsay their importance to the local economy.

In 2016, a controversy broke out in Daytona over a new gun range that opened near the intersection of I-95 and International Speedway Boulevard. Alcohol is widely available all around the range, and customers can rent guns if they wish. Orlando, about sixty miles away, had a couple of incidents where morose people got liquored up, went to a nearby gun range, rented a firearm, and blew their brains all over the ceiling. So citizens of Daytona were understandably concerned. But the range opened anyway—another beachfront victory of the Old Florida over the New.

By the way, there is no such place as "Daytona" per se. There was an official municipal jurisdiction called Daytona up to 1926, when the town was absorbed by the contiguous town of Daytona Beach, an early effort at municipal consolidation. Today, the place is named Daytona Beach, much of which is not on or even very near the beach. What is popularly thought to be Daytona is that twenty-three-mile stretch of uninterrupted white sand beach. The northern anchor is Ormond Beach, where the first beach racing happened, then as you head south along Highway A1A, you come upon Holly Hill, Daytona Beach, Daytona Beach Shores, South Daytona, Port Orange, Wilbur-by-the-Sea, and finally Ponce Inlet. The entire stretch is known colloquially if somewhat inaccurately as Daytona Beach.

JIMMY BUFFETT

No one has more successfully marketed Florida beach culture to America than Jimmy Buffett, considered the founder and foremost practitioner of trop rock. Now in his seventies, Buffett was born in Pascagoula, Mississippi, grew up in Mobile, and moved to Key West in the early 1970s, at which point he adopted his beachcomber persona and began writing songs and releasing albums that celebrated beach life: *A White Sport Coat and a*

Pink Crustacean (1973) and the instant party hit "Why Don't We Get Drunk (And Screw)," along with dozens of others. Buffett standards covered by hundreds of Jimmy Buffett imitators are "Margaritaville" (after his Key West bar) and "Cheeseburger in Paradise" (after his favorite beach food).

The entire Jimmy Buffett oeuvre is a celebration of the beach. He specializes in easygoing tunes ("ear candy") that urge the listener to escape the humdrum of everyday life in favor of warm breezes and gentle surf, whiz up a frozen drink in the blender, kick back, and enjoy the party. Since the early 1970s, Buffett has portrayed himself and his band as "pirates" (pirate imagery and symbolism are very popular all over Florida), complete with the obligatory parrot on the shoulder, so his fans call themselves Parrotheads and show up at concerts in full pirate regalia.

Buffett currently owns homes in Palm Beach, Beverly Hills, in the Hamptons on Long Island, and on the Caribbean island of Saint Barts. He sold his Key West home in 1998 for about a million bucks. At the time, he was known as the Prince of Key West. He tries to live the life his songs celebrate although these days he is more a multimillion-dollar businessman than a laid-back beach bum. He owns a couple of seaplanes, a sailboat, and a Citation II jet. In short, he's a beach bum that's done pretty well for himself. The multibillionaire investor and namesake Warren Buffett is a distant cousin, and Jimmy's own vast business empire includes a string of Jimmy Buffett stores, an expanding network of Margaritaville Cafes and Cheeseburger in Paradise bars, numerous Margaritaville hotels, casinos, and vacation clubs, several novels, memoirs, and children's books, a best-selling autobiography (*A Pirate Looks at Fifty*), and much more. He is constantly on tour. He is also the founder of the Singing for Change Foundation, the honorary director of Greenpeace, a member of the Cousteau Society, and the chairman of the Save the Manatee Club of Florida. Jimmy takes the protection of our open waters seriously.

Buffett met his second wife in a Key West bar when she was spring-breaking from the University of South Carolina. The Eagles played at their wedding reception. Many of his albums make reference to his tropical beach roots: *Coconut Telegraph; One Particular Harbour; Riddles in the Sand; Floridays; Off to See the Lizard; Boats, Beaches, Bars & Ballads; Beach House on the Moon*, and others. He is, by any standard, Florida's number-one beach balladeer. Who else would even be in the running? Joey Fatone? David Cassidy? Pat Boone? Pitbull?

Perhaps inevitably, Buffett's latest business venture is a senior-oriented fifty-five-plus Margaritaville-themed retirement community in Daytona known as Latitude Margaritaville. (Locals called it The Villages East.) The $1 billion project, which has now opened a few models and a sales center, will provide nearly seven thousand new homes and feature golf-car-friendly streets and garages, a fitness center, arts programs, a private club, a band shell for outdoor concerts, and various beach-themed dining options. A second Latitude Margaritaville, currently being developed in Hilton Head, South Carolina, will occupy some twenty-eight hundred acres and will sport a nearly three-hundred-thousand-square-foot retail center. After all, the Parrotheads are as old as Jimmy himself. Why not make a last big chunk of Margaritaville moola off adoring fans?

PONCE INLET

Ponce Inlet is the last town you come to as you drive south on the barrier island of Daytona Beach. The first European settler in the town was the Italian Bartola Pacetti, who built a house there out of driftwood in 1842. A lighthouse at the mouth of the inlet was built in 1887 and remains in place today. Until 1928, the inlet was known as Mosquito Inlet.

Ponce Inlet largely escapes the craziness that besets the other communities on the barrier island by a very simple expedient. The town's beach side is dominated by luxurious high-rise vacation condos, very limited public beach access, and very few amenities (showers, toilets, concession stands) for beachgoers. If you find yourself in Ponce Inlet and need something to do, your best bet is to wander over to Florida's tallest lighthouse, scale the 203 steps, and enjoy the spectacular ocean view.

My research institute, the Institute for Social and Behavioral Sciences at the University of Central Florida, was commissioned a few years ago to study the quality of life in little Ponce Inlet. People there are very satisfied but worry that further development might threaten the quiet, small-town "feel." It is a struggle shared by beach communities all over the state, whether to retain the ambience of a small coastal village or give in to the tourists and snowbirds, let development run rampant, and make a bunch of money. The discerning reader will instantly see these as choices between Old Florida and New. Along Florida's east coast, it is hard to find communities that have successfully balanced these competing objectives.

FLORIDA'S NUDE BEACHES

Pasco County north of Tampa is known as the nudist capital of the world. If clothing-optional sunbathing is your thing, Florida is definitely *the* place to be. Pasco County alone sports some fourteen nudist resorts, clothing-optional clubs, and nude beaches—a naturalist's delight. And there are numerous nude beaches elsewhere in the state. Only the Pasco County nude beaches are officially recognized and sanctioned as such, but nudists will find a friendly "grin and bare it" attitude in many places. Here you can kayak, swim, sunbathe, fish, canoe, ride horses, play tennis, hike, and play shuffleboard naked as a jaybird.

Haulover Beach is located between Miami and Fort Lauderdale and is the oldest and best-known nude beach in the state. Haulover is always listed among the top-ten nude beaches in the world and draws an international clientele. There are public restrooms for showers and shedding your clothes and plenty of parking very near the beach itself. The beach promotes itself as "family friendly."

Blind Creek Beach is in Fort Pierce. Locals and the police are very tolerant of naked frolicking in the sand and surf. But beware: Blind Creek is a "primitive beach," meaning no showers, restrooms, or other amenities. No lifeguards, either. Here you get naked at your own risk.

The Cape Canaveral National Seashore is a breathtakingly beautiful stretch of ocean front that belongs to the federal government and is therefore exempt from local antinudity ordinances. With the full blessing of the feds and the Volusia County government, you can get naked and sunbathe at two places on the seashore: Apollo Beach at the northern end of the park, and Playalinda at the southern end. But do be advised that part of the southern end of the park belongs to Brevard County and nudity is prohibited there. So be sure you are safely inside the Volusia County portion of the park before peeling off your clothes.

DOG BEACHES

Anyone who has taken a dog near water knows that our canine friends enjoy a romp in the surf as much as most humans do, so dog owners will be comforted to know that many Florida beaches are dog-friendly (meaning basically that dogs are allowed and can run off leash at least in some areas). Haulover Beach, the nudist beach near Miami, is also dog-friendly, and visitors will find similar dog beaches along the Panhandle, at Saint Pete Beach, in Venice, Jupiter, Fort Myers, the Keys, Miami, and elsewhere. The best dog beach in Florida is the Fort De Soto Dog Beach Park in Saint Petersburg. The park has fenced-in areas for both large and small dogs, and dogs are allowed anywhere in the park if they are on a six-foot leash. But there is also a Paw Playground beach area where dogs can run off the leash. The park features canine showers to cool Fido off on hot summer days, plenty of hoses, and lots of doggy drinking fountains.

Florida dog lovers maintain a website with up-to-date information on where dogs are welcome and where they are only allowed, with links to specific beach websites. The site lists about twenty-five beaches in Florida as "dog-friendly." For more: www.dogfriendly.com.

Dogs, nudists, spring breakers, Parrotheads, bikers, brides and grooms, NASCAR fans, Spanish explorers, and people in general all seem to resonate equally to the words of the Austrian poet Rainer Maria Rilke: "When anxious, uneasy and bad thoughts come, I go to the sea, and the sea drowns them out with its great wide sounds, cleanses me with its noise, and imposes a rhythm upon everything in me that is bewildered and confused." It's where Old Florida goes to get its groove back.

9

FLY ME TO THE MOON

THE FLORIDA AEROSPACE INDUSTRY

ON JULY 24, 1950, the nascent National Aeronautics and Space Administration (NASA) launched a retrofitted two-stage German V-2 rocket called Bumper 8 on a 150-mile journey out over the Atlantic. This marked the beginning of the program of space exploration at Cape Canaveral. Earlier Bumper flights had been launched from White Sands, New Mexico, and the competition among several sites to house NASA's space exploration program was intense. But in the end, Cape Canaveral won out mainly because it was far away from population centers though readily accessible by road, sea, and air, and also because the Florida weather could be counted on to provide ample clear-day launch windows. The aerospace industry has been part and parcel of Florida culture ever since and has been embraced equally by Old and New Florida.

That first Bumper payload was small and designed mainly to test various rocket systems. But through a series of fits and starts, triumphs and disasters, within two decades NASA was flying astronauts from Florida's east coast to the moon and back, one of the most spectacular achievements in human history.

The very early history of the space program was largely devoted to military and security matters. The Germans had demonstrated the effectiveness of rockets as weapons in World War II, and it was obvious that the United States would need to develop a rocket-based weapons system quickly.

The German rocket scientist Wernher von Braun secretly defected to the United States after the war and became a leading figure in the American program. To get von Braun into the country with the security clearances he would need, US intelligence officials fabricated his employment history and erased all evidence of his deep connections to Hitler's Nazi Party. In short, the technical genius behind America's nascent space program was an illegal Nazi immigrant.

America's first *manned* space program was Project Mercury, which ran from 1959 to 1963. The so-called Space Race had begun on October 4, 1957, the day the Soviets launched their Sputnik 1 satellite and proved to the world that the United States had lost whatever technological edge it formerly held. In response, President Kennedy announced on May 25, 1961, that America would regain and demonstrate its technological superiority over the Soviets by landing a man on the moon before the end of the decade. Cape Canaveral became an important Cold War battleground.

The first step in landing someone on the moon was getting a human being into space and eventually in orbit around Earth, and those were the missions of the Mercury program. The seven Mercury astronauts were announced to the nation with much fanfare on April 9, 1959. Of the original seven, John Glenn is best known, lived the longest, and was eventually an influential senator from Ohio. America's then most famous and most daring test pilot, Chuck Yeager, was not chosen because he was not a college graduate and did not project the image of the astronaut corps NASA wanted. He later referred derisively to the Mercury astronauts as "Spam in a can."

After numerous tests with unmanned capsules, NASA shot its first astronaut into space on May 5, 1961. Alan Shepard was at the helm. A second manned launch came less than three months later, with Virgil "Gus" Grissom in the capsule. The successful Shepard and Grissom missions, both launched from Cape Canaveral, convinced NASA that a human could be shot into space and come back alive, and that set the stage for putting an American into Earth orbit. That happened on February 20, 1962. The first American to orbit Earth was Glenn. Unfortunately, Glenn's flight came 314 days after the Soviet's Yuri Gagarin orbited Earth, so the Soviets were still ahead.

Alan Shepard, the first American in space, was also the oldest man to walk on the moon. This was on the Apollo 11 mission. Shepard was the only one of the original seven Mercury astronauts to do so. Years later, he was asked in an interview what went through his mind, sitting atop an Apollo 14 rocket getting ready to blast off into space. "It's a very sobering feeling," he said, "to be up in space and realize that one's safety factor was determined by the lowest bidder on a government contract."

Project Mercury launched three more manned space missions, concluded in 1963 after the successful flights of its fourth, fifth, and sixth missions, and was replaced by Project Gemini (which started in 1961 and concluded in 1966). The main objectives of this second manned spaceflight program were to develop the space travel, docking, and launch routines that the Apollo mission would need to get astronauts to the moon and back. Two unmanned flights were conducted in 1964–65, followed by ten manned flights in 1965 and 1966. The key accomplishments were largely technical: the demonstration that fuel cells could be used to generate electricity, that humans could be in space for at least eight days (the minimum required to get to the moon and back), and that a lunar capsule could successfully dock with a mother ship in space. To the average American, the truly spectacular successes of Gemini were Edward White's first space walk in 1965 and Buzz Aldrin's demonstration that a human could do useful work outside a spacecraft without succumbing to exhaustion or worse.

The Mercury and Gemini projects set the stage for the Apollo program, the program that would fulfill Kennedy's dream to put an American on the moon and to get there before the Russians. Apollo was NASA's major space-exploration program from 1963 to 1972; everything else the agency was doing in those years was in support of the moon-landing missions. Numerous unmanned Apollo flights tested various components of the rocketry and the flight and docking protocols. The first big step was to demonstrate that it was possible to rocket a manned spacecraft to the moon and back again. This was accomplished by Apollo 8 in December 1968 and then again by Apollo 10 in May 1969. With all systems "go," the big one— Apollo 11, the flight to the surface of the moon and back—launched on July 16, 1969, reached the lunar surface on July 20, stayed there for about twenty-two hours, then returned safely to Earth on July 24, 160 days ahead of JFK's target deadline. Clearly, we had surged ahead of the Soviets at last.

Five more missions landed on the moon between 1969 and 1972; a sixth was the ill-fated Apollo 13 mission. "Houston, we have a problem" is what is most remembered about this mission, but the actual quotation was "Okay, Houston, I believe we've had a problem here." In all, twelve US astronauts walked on the lunar surface, ten active members of the US Navy or Air Force and two civilians (Neil Armstrong and Harrison Schmitt, the latter a geologist).

Getting to the moon came at a high price, both monetary and human. On January 27, 1967, Gus Grissom, Edward White, and Roger Chaffee burned to death when an uncontrolled fire swept through their Apollo 1 cabin, the first of twenty-four Americans to perish (as of 2018) in the effort to conquer space. If you ever find yourself in Central Florida, a trip out to the Kennedy Space Center Visitor Complex is well worth the effort. It is "the only place on Earth where you can tour launch areas, meet a veteran astronaut, see giant rockets, train in spaceflight simulators, and even view a launch!"—if one happens to be scheduled. It is also the site of the Space Mirror Memorial, part of the Astronauts Memorial, NASA's monument to the men and women who died in the American space program—a moving and poignant reminder that everything worth doing comes at some cost.

Once we had the moon landing in our back pocket and the unquestioned technological edge in manned space exploration, what next? The answer was the Space Transportation System, or STS, more commonly known as the Space Shuttle. The STS program ran from 1972 until its termination in 2011. The shuttle was the first reusable space vehicle and was essential to the International Space Station project, the first component of which was launched into space on the shuttle in 1998.

In all, the shuttle(s) flew 135 missions, mostly ferrying food, equipment, supplies, new modules, and scientific experiments to the Space Station. There were four shuttle vehicles active at any one time, but six were built and five flew missions. The Space Station, a massive international collaboration among the USA, Canada, Japan, Russia, and the European Space Agency, is the largest artificial Earth satellite ever built, and under the right condition can be easily seen with the human eye as it passes overhead.

The two STS missions most people remember are the 51st mission, when the shuttle *Challenger* broke apart shortly after launch killing all seven of the crew, and the 113th, when the shuttle *Columbia* disintegrated during reentry over California, also killing the crew of seven. Both disasters caused long hiatuses in shuttle launches, while investigations were undertaken and problems fixed. The last shuttle launch, the 135th, left Earth on July 8, 2011, and after that the US Space Shuttle was no more. An era in the culture of Florida had ended, and practically no one was happy about it.

For the better part of seven decades, watching rockets launch from Cape Canaveral has been a major tourist attraction, a favorite activity of locals, and a taken-for-granted part of Florida life. Few experiences in this lifetime are as awe-inspiring as watching a rocket launch not more than five miles from the launch site. When NASA lights the fuse on these babies, the solid rocket boosters blast the payload into space with several million pounds of thrust. Words cannot adequately describe the sight, sound, and feel of one of these events—like the Grand Canyon and oral sex, it must be experienced to be appreciated.

Back when we lived in Orlando, Chris and I could watch these rocket launches from our driveway some fifty miles away, even in the middle of the day. And traveling to Cape Canaveral to watch the shuttles return to Earth was always a special treat. The shuttle would announce its arrival with the trademark double sonic boom—*Boom, BOOM!!*—and shortly thereafter you could see the bright silvery craft dropping from the sky. Space enthusiasm in the state has dimmed somewhat since the final return of the Space Shuttle on July 21, 2011, but even now, there are traffic jams on the access roads whenever a launch is scheduled. If you are within five miles of the launch site, the sky lights up, the ground rumbles, the crowds cheer, and waves of unrepentant patriotism surge through your body. And all this from an otherwise largely insignificant little town on Florida's east coast.

American astronauts have always been depicted in the media and in NASA's official publications as clean-cut, square-jawed patriots and heroes, and while their feats are certainly amazing, nothing that begins or ends in Florida is without its share of weirdness. There was, for example, Alan Shepard's famous golf shot on the moon. Shepard had managed to smuggle a makeshift six iron onto Apollo 14 and tee up a shot on the lunar surface. In the moon's lighter gravity, his six-iron shot rivaled the best the pros could do on earth. He remains the only person ever to have hit a golf ball on the moon. The makeshift club used for the purpose can be viewed today at the US Golf Association Museum in Far Hills, New Jersey.

Astronaut John Young was also something of a cutup. Young was the commander of the Apollo 16 lunar mission (April 1972) and is one of the twelve men who have walked on the moon. And while he was not the only astronaut to develop a serious case of flatulence while on duty, he was certainly the only one whose gastrointestinal discomfort was broadcast live to the entire world:

> YOUNG: I have the farts again. I got 'em again, Charlie. I haven't eaten this much citrus fruit in twenty years! And I tell you one thing . . . in another twelve fucking days, I ain't never eating any more. I put 'em up over the . . . right up in here. They ain't there? Oh, shit.
> CHARLIE (GROUND COMMAND IN HOUSTON): Orion? Houston.
> YOUNG: Yes, sir.
> CHARLIE: Okay, John, we have a hot mike.

The incident touched off a small furor in the Sunshine State. Then governor Reubin Askew was miffed at Young's insinuation that Florida's oranges were somehow the source of his intestinal gas. The irony in Young's very public flatulence attack is that in the early stages of the manned spaceflight program, flatulence was a major safety concern. It is impossible to belch in zero gravity and almost impossible not to fart in the very low air pressure in a space capsule. A lot of intestinal methane being "leaked" into an oxygen-enriched environment could create a potentially explosive situation. Therefore, much research was done capturing and analyzing the composition of astronaut flatulence and adjusting diets accordingly.

Severe flatulence was not the only thing Young carried into space. During Gemini 3's orbits around Earth, Young pulled a corned-beef sandwich out of his space suit and began eating it. His copilot, Gus Grissom, also had a bite but quickly stuffed the sandwich into a pocket when the cabin began to fill with crumbs. Regular space food has a special coating to prevent just this sort of thing, but not Young's corned beef on rye. The concern was that the crumbs would eventually drift into high-tech electrical panels and gum up the works with potentially fatal consequences. Congress saw fit to express its displeasure, not so much because of the safety hazard but because it created the impression that American astronauts were brown-bagging it in space.

Probably the weirdest space story of all is the giant urine icicle that formed on the Space Shuttle *Discovery* during its maiden mission in 1984. As those who have seen the movie *Apollo 13* will remember, peeing in space is pretty straightforward. Basically, you relieve yourself into an onboard tank, and the urine is then ejected through a nozzle into space, where it instantly freezes, vaporizes, and explodes into a mesmerizing urine cloud. The nozzle on *Discovery* had somehow clogged so that urine dribbled rather than sprayed out, and before anyone noticed, a giant thirty-pound pee icicle had formed on the side of the shuttle. Since the icicle might break off during reentry, damage the delicate heat shield, and cause the incineration of the crew, something had to be done. Rotating the craft so the pee icicle faced the sun had no effect. Sending a man out to chip it off seemed unnecessarily hazardous. So the space arm was used to grab the icicle and break it loose. A new urine nozzle was quickly developed and deployed on all subsequent shuttle flights.

ROCKET SCIENCE

"It ain't rocket science!" is a cliché often used to describe any endeavor or solution that is deceptively simple and straightforward—that is, the sort of thing any idiot ought to be able to figure out, as opposed to rocket science, which is assumed to require deep, complex, higher-ordered brainpower. Evidently, rocket science stands somewhere near the top in its demand for advanced intellectual prowess, right up there with the frequently voiced alternative, brain surgery.

Or does it? The basic scientific principle underlying rocket science is Newton's third law of motion, commonly given as "For every action, there is an equal and opposite reaction." The three laws of motion have been part and parcel of scientific discourse since 1687 and are covered in high school physics. Their mastery, in short, does not seem to require advanced intellectual capacity.

Workable rockets were known to the Chinese by about AD 1200, and their potential application to astronautics was understood by the beginning of the twentieth century. You can buy one in any hobbyist's shop, and many teenagers and big kids shoot them off every Fourth of July. Granted, engineering a rocket big enough to reach outer space and figuring out how to stabilize its flight, steer it to the correct destination, communicate with it, and the like are by no means passing trivialities. Still, the rudiments of rocket science are not metaphysical mysteries penetrable only by those with 160+ IQs.

The world's largest collection of rocket scientists is probably over at the Kennedy Space Center. Officials in the jurisdictions that abut the space center were scared to death about what would happen to the local economy once the Space Shuttle was phased out. NASA anticipated shedding some three thousand to four thousand jobs in the span of two years once the Space Shuttle fleet was retired. Earlier estimates ranged upward to eight thousand rocket-science jobs lost. And in fact, NASA had programs in place since at least 2005 to figure out how to sustain its workforce and to develop "career paths" for space scientists and engineers once the Space Shuttle program was gone. A simple question: Why do we need federal retention bonuses and expensive job-retraining programs to avoid mass unemployment among Space Shuttle scientists and engineers? Aren't NASA's rocket scientists smart enough to figure this out on their own?

P

PART THREE

PEOPLE
AND
POLITICS

10

THE THREE STATES OF FLORIDA

CRACKER CULTURE, NEW HAVANA, AND THE I-4 CORRIDOR

FLORIDA IS NOT one state but three. Whether the criteria are political, social, or cultural, North, Central, and South Florida are three very different places with very different outlooks, origins, cultures, and ways of life. Basically, North Florida is Old Florida, Central Florida is New Florida, and South Florida is New Havana. Let me explain.

NORTH FLORIDA: CRACKER COUNTRY

North Florida is the southern terminus of the true South. Many Central Floridians refer to North Florida as "South Georgia," the home of Florida crackers and their culture. To paraphrase Jeff Foxworthy, if your family's roots in Florida go back earlier than, say, 1950, you may be a cracker. The term is not always pejorative, either. Many Georgians and Floridians proudly self-identify as crackers, particularly if their family history goes back a half century or more.

The term "cracker" is often said to refer to the "crack" of the cattle herder's whip. This is the History Channel's theory on the origin of the word, and is also the theory advanced by the Florida Historical Society. And while it is true that Florida cowmen herded cattle by whip and dog rather than by lasso, the term may have derived instead from the Middle English word *craic,* meaning a braggart. That is clearly the meaning of the term as it appears in Shakespeare's play *King John* (written in 1595): "What cracker is this . . . that deafes our ears / With this abundance of superfluous breath?" In contemporary Gaelic, *craic* is still used to refer to a vain, boastful person. The Shakespeare play predates cattle herding in Florida by a few centuries.

Other theories have argued that "cracker" is a variation on the Spanish word *cuáquero,* meaning "Quaker." In the colonial era, the Catholic Spanish referred to all Protestants derisively as "Quakers," so "cracker" was intended as a slur on the Protestant Scots-Irish settlers of the region. Still another guess is that the word derives from "cracking" (grinding) corn to make corn flour. There is no serious etymological evidence favoring either of these interpretations, or for that matter, strongly supporting any alternative theory, either. No one knows for sure where "cracker" as a reference to poor southern whites came from.

Until it became known as the Peach State, Georgia was known as the Cracker State. Whether the term is a compliment or a disparagement depends on context. When the African American relatives of Trayvon Martin refer to his killer as a "redneck cracker," "cracker" is synonymous with "bigot" or "racist." And if a Yankee calls a long-haired country boy from North Florida a "cracker," "cracker" is synonymous with "ignorant" or "backward." But if two cattle herders from Kissimmee are in the bar having a few beers and refer to each other as "crackers," it is a term of endearment.

Mike Miller's essay on the Florida cracker ("Florida Cracker: Smile When You Call Me a Cracker, Stranger!") sets out the following standards. A proper cracker:

- Has a family history that predates the huge explosion in Florida's population after the Second World War
- Is self-reliant ("When modern civilization collapses, the Florida cracker will be hunting, fishing, trapping and growing his own food while the rest of us will be standing in line at the government-owned grocery store with our ration stamps.")
- Is white, was raised in a rural setting, and self-identifies as a southerner (usually meaning that there is a Confederate battle flag displayed on the cracker's pickup truck)

Real crackers also eat cooter (a soft-shell turtle), grits, chitlins (pig intestines cleaned and deep-fat fried), greens, fried alligator tail meat, hominy (white corn soaked in lye and then boiled), and piney woods rooters (feral hogs that crackers love to hunt), along with occasional roadkill (as described in a later chapter) and pretty much anything else from Ernest Mickler's *White Trash Cooking* cookbook. Cracker politics are antiestablishment, anti-big-government, anti-welfare-state conservatism. North Florida has been reliably Republican since the big realignment in 1968 (when white southerners abandoned the Democratic Party and began voting Republican).

If you were looking for the precise spot where the South ends and something else begins, it would be the country-western bar and nightclub in Sanford, Florida, known as The Barn. South of The Barn, you are back in regular America. The Barn is symbolic of cracker culture: sixteen thousand square feet of space, seven separate bars, thirty-four TVs, live country-western music (most nights), line dancing, a mechanical bull, Ladies Night every Saturday, a reliably large number of foxy, nubile GRITS (Girls Raised in the South), and a phalanx of pool tables where the locals test their skills at eight-ball. Performers such as Garth Brooks and Blake Shelton played The Barn before they were established country-western stars, and the huge neon sign out front, which features a dancing cowboy and cowgirl, has been nominated by the Sanford city commissioners as a historic landmark. "Historic items like this [the neon sign] are important in retaining a community's cultural identity," according to Christine Dalton, who serves as Sanford's historic-preservation officer. "They tell something about a community."

You get a bunch of crackers liquored up, and that often spells trouble, especially when the drinking is over and the crowd spills out into the parking lot. In 2014, Sanford police were dispatched to The Barn about seven hundred times and had to break up seventy parking lot altercations. There's been at least one parking-lot shooting in recent years.

The largest city in North Florida, indeed in all of Florida, is Jacksonville, home to the Lynyrd Skynyrd band, the inventors of so-called "southern rock" music. (As befits the capital city of cracker Florida, Jacksonville was originally named "Cow Ford" because it was a place where the region's abundant cattle herds could ford the Saint Johns River.) The band's most famous tune is "Sweet Home Alabama," but other hits on the Lynyrd Skynyrd playlist include "Simple Man," "Saturday Night Special," "Swamp Music," "Gimme Back My Bullets," "Whiskey Rock-a-Roller," and a number of other cracker anthems that celebrate southern working-class culture. The band suffered a devastating setback in 1977 when a plane crash killed three of the original band members, including founder Ronnie Van Zant, and since the band re-formed in 1987, four more of its members have died. Yet the group soldiered on, toured regularly until 2018, and continued to release albums (nearly fifty all told). "Sweet Home Alabama" has allegedly been downloaded as a cell-phone ring-tone more than two million times.

The band's name, incidentally, is a corruption of Leonard Skinner, a physical-education teacher at the Robert E. Lee High School, where the three founding members of the band were once students. Skinner, it is said, was notorious for his aggressive enforcement of the school's prohibition of long hair on boys. At least one of the band's founders, Gary Rossington, dropped out of high school because he was tired of being hassled about his long hair. In 2006, the revived Lynyrd Skynyrd band was inducted into the Rock & Roll Hall of Fame.

Other reasonably well-known southern rock bands that originated in Jacksonville include Molly Hatchet ("Flirtin' with Disaster," "Whiskey Man"), the Allman Brothers Band ("Ramblin' Man," "Midnight Rider"), .38 Special ("Wild-Eyed Southern Boys," "Rough Housin'"), and Blackfoot ("Left Turn on a Red Light," "Road Fever"). As the names and titles indicate, Jacksonville's brand of southern rock is all about drinking too much, driving too fast, horsing around with firearms, and similar indiscretions.

Jacksonville is named for Andrew Jackson, the first military governor of the Territory of Florida and later seventh president of the United States. As military governor, Jackson gained national renown for waging a brutal, murderous war against Native Americans in the First Seminole War. Entire villages were burned to the ground, homes were destroyed, and natives slaughtered. Congressional resolutions condemned Jackson's actions, but the disapproval of Congress did not prevent Jackson from being elected president in 1828. His popularity is indexed by the large number of American cities named in his honor. Cities named Jackson or Jacksonville can be found in Alabama, Georgia, Kentucky, Louisiana, Mississippi, Michigan,

Missouri, New Hampshire, New Jersey, Ohio, South Carolina, Tennessee, Illinois, North Carolina, Texas, and Virginia. Even more states have counties or townships named in Old Hickory's honor.

Early in the twentieth century, Jacksonville was a more important movie location than Hollywood (indeed, all of Florida was more important to the early film industry than anything in California). In the 1910s, the town was known as the Winter Film Capital of the World. Of the many early films shot at least in part in Jacksonville, the best known is *Creature from the Black Lagoon*. (The water scenes of that movie were shot in Silver Springs.) Several dozen silent movies were also shot in Jacksonville.

The Beatles were scheduled to perform at Jacksonville's Gator Bowl on September 11, 1964, at the peak of American Beatlemania, just nine months after the band's first appearance on *The Ed Sullivan Show*. The Jacksonville concert was booked early in 1964, before the Civil Rights Act of 1964 was enacted. Thus, at the time of the booking, racial segregation was still the law of the land in Florida, and facility management informed the Beatles that the audience would be racially segregated. The Beatles, John Lennon in particular, said they would not perform before a segregated audience. But by the time the concert rolled around in September, the Civil Rights Act had been passed and signed into law, so racial segregation was no longer legal.

A bigger issue for the concert was Hurricane Dora, which blew through North Florida on September 10, the day before the concert was scheduled. Dora came ashore near Saint Augustine as a Category 3 storm, but Jacksonville was the most severely impacted with more than 150,000 households without power and a fifth of the phone lines out of service. Riverine flooding of areas along the Saint Johns River added to the misery. The Beatles were scheduled to fly into Jacksonville from Montreal on September 8, but because of the weather, their flight was diverted to Key West, some five hundred miles away. They eventually made their way to Jacksonville just hours before the concert was to begin. Thousands of fans with tickets were unable to make it because of the loss of power and flooding, but nearly twenty thousand fans showed up. On the day of the concert, winds were still gusting up to 40 mph, so Ringo's drum set was nailed to the stage.

Among its other claims to fame, Jacksonville hosts the annual "World's Largest Outdoor Cocktail Party," the annual football game pitting the University of Florida Gators against the University of Georgia Bulldogs—one of the very few college rivalries still played on neutral turf. Since Jacksonville is only about 70 miles from Gainesville but 338 miles from Athens, one might think that Florida fans would vastly outnumber Georgia fans at this annual event. Not so. In the minds of many, the University of Florida is the hoity-toity elitist university in the state, and their allegiances are with Florida State University in Tallahassee instead. And in North Florida, if you are not a Florida State fan, you are as likely to follow Georgia (or Alabama) as to follow the University of Florida. So the fan bases of the two teams are pretty equal in and around Jacksonville.

The moniker "World's Largest Outdoor Cocktail Party" was used by the City of Jacksonville as the official event name until 1988, when too many cocktails and too much beer sloshed over into a series of drunken outbursts at the game and elsewhere. Thereafter, the city did what it could to restrict excessive fan drinking, although this is not easy when you are dealing with college students from cracker backgrounds.

A posting on the website Quora asked, "What is Jacksonville, FL, known for?" "Bridges, parks, and beaches" was Dave Gano's answer. When it was first opened, the graceful Dames Point Bridge was the longest cable-anchored concrete bridge in the world, rising some 175 feet over the Saint Johns River. Jacksonville also boasts the nation's largest urban public parks system (eighty thousand acres of parks in about 335 locations), and the Jacksonville beaches are as lovely as any in the state. On the other hand, David Fitzgerald tells Quora only that Jacksonville is "a great place to be *from*." In the 1970s, the city's motto was "The Bold New City of the South," but the motto was more boastful than accurate. Atlanta and Charlotte can make much stronger claims. Another Jacksonville distinction is that what is now the Burger King global chain of fast-food restaurants was founded as Insta-Burger King in Jacksonville in 1953.

For most of Florida's history, the state's population was concentrated in North Florida, since with the partial exception of the coasts, the interior of the state was considered unfit for human habitation. As a result, the state was largely run by the so-called Pork Chop Gang, a group of about twenty

North Florida cracker Democrats, all from rural areas, who dominated the state legislature and whose principal political ambition was to maintain racial segregation. In addition to running the state and opposing all efforts at desegregation, the Pork Chop Gang also waged a nine-year battle to identify and remove homosexuals from the state's university system. By the time they were done, some three dozen professors and deans had been dismissed. The reign of the Pork Chop Gang was finally terminated by the new state constitution of 1968, which ended half a century of malapportionment that gave rural North Florida far more political clout than the region deserved. The new constitution also eliminated mandatory school segregation. Since 1968, political power in the state has come to be more concentrated in the urbanized areas of Central and South Florida and less so in the largely rural North Florida.

SOUTH FLORIDA: THE NEW HAVANA

For thousands of years prior to the arrival of the Europeans, southeast Florida was inhabited by various tribes of the Tequesta people. One of these tribes, the Mayaimi, eventually gave the city of Miami its name. Evidence of human habitation in the region goes back about ten thousand years. The Tequesta were strictly hunter-gatherers, in that no evidence of agriculture can be found in the region prior to the European incursion.

The Tequesta were responsible for building the so-called Miami Circle, one of the oldest indigenous archaeological sites in Florida. The Miami Circle is located in what is now downtown Miami and was discovered in 1998 during a mandated archaeological field survey of what was to be the site of a luxury condominium complex. What the survey unearthed were twenty-four holes cut into the underlying limestone that formed a perfect circle thirty-eight feet in diameter. Excavation also turned up a wealth of archaeological artifacts ranging from stone axes to human teeth to the charcoal remains of ancient campfires.

What purpose the Miami Circle served for the Tequesta remains a matter of controversy. One early suggestion was that the holes were intended to hold poles that in turn supported a cone-shaped building of some sort. To others, the twenty-four holes suggested some sort of horological (timekeeping) function. One archaeologist from the University of Florida suggested that the circle was just a sink for sewage from an adjacent sewage tank. Despite efforts to go ahead with the planned condo development, perhaps by relocating the Miami Circle to some other site, the state of Florida stepped up in 1999, purchased the land for $26.7 million, and converted the area to the Miami Circle at Brickell Point Site, which was listed on the National Register of Historic Places in 2002 (and then declared as National Historical Landmark in 2009).

The first known European landing in the area around Biscayne Bay was by Pedro Menéndez de Avilés in 1566, the same man who founded Saint Augustine. The first European settlement in the region was a Jesuit mission established in 1567 and abandoned in 1569. The first *permanent* Spanish settlement in what is now Miami was not founded until 1743, by which time most of the Tequesta had been killed off in internecine battles with other tribes or by European diseases such as smallpox.

By 1920, the Miami population had swollen to nearly thirty thousand people. In the early 1920s, Miami authorities allowed gambling and were notoriously lax about Prohibition, so northerners poured in by the thousands. According to one estimate, the Miami population doubled between 1920 and 1923. But then the bubble burst: transportation systems were not adequate to handle the increased flow of people and goods, land was scarce and increasingly expensive, unemployment was on the increase, the cost of living was soaring, and the Great Miami Hurricane of 1926 practically finished the city off. The Great Hurricane was followed by the Great Depression, and the future of South Florida looked grim.

Miami Beach had been opened to development when a bridge to the barrier island was completed in 1913, and in the middle of the Great Depression, the Art Deco Historic District of Miami Beach was developed. Even in the Depression, there were enough people of means to sustain a lively tourist economy on Miami Beach, and the district thrived despite tough economic times everywhere else.

Franklin Delano Roosevelt was elected to the presidency in 1932. In those days, formal inauguration of a new president was held in March, not in January, so on February 15, 1933, FDR was still the president-*elect* when the Italian anarcho-syndicalist Giuseppe Zangara opened fire in Miami's Bayfront Park, killing Chicago mayor Anton Cermak and narrowly missing Roosevelt. Zangara was arrested on the spot, tried for the murder of Cermak, found guilty, and was executed on March 20, 1933, barely a month after the Cermak assassination. Today, the average elapsed time between capital conviction and execution in Florida's "death row" (the nation's second largest) is almost fifteen years.

The first Jewish people came to Florida early in the nineteenth century. By the twentieth century, Florida was a very popular Jewish retirement destination. Today, there are more than a half million Jewish people living in the three counties of southeast Florida: Broward, Miami-Dade, and Palm Beach; and nearly a million statewide. Even today, the retired Jewish lady from Palm Beach is a prominent cultural stereotype. Cities such as Boca Raton have Jewish percentages as high as 67 percent, nearly all of whom are fifty-five and older. Miami has the second-largest Jewish population of any city in the nation. (New York City is first.) Indicative of their increasing numbers and political power, the city of Miami elected a Jewish mayor (Abe Aronowitz) in 1952.

The beginning of the end of Jewish prominence in South Florida can be dated to January 1, 1959, when the Cuban dictator Fulgencio Batista fled Cuba for the Dominican Republic with about $300 million and ceded the Cuban government to Fidel Castro. Batista loyalists, anti-Communists, and pro-American Cubans fled the island nation in droves, and many landed in South Florida. In the fifteen years following Batista's overthrow, some half a million Cubans resettled in Miami; another 400,000 have come between 1980 and 2012 (125,000 in the Mariel boatlift alone). Today, the Cuban population of greater Miami exceeds 1.2 million. And that is just in Miami. Every city in Florida has a perceptible and sometimes quite large Cuban community. The effect of Cuban immigration (and subsequent fertility) is to have remade Miami and its surrounds into Spanish-speaking cities.

Tensions between Cuban immigrants and native Miamians date to the very first wave of Cuban exiles. Many African American Miamians were upset that Cuban immigrants were taking their jobs; the school system was likewise strained by having to educate thousands of Spanish-speaking children. It also seemed likely that Miami would be "ground zero" in an American-led effort to oust the Castro regime (as in the failed Bay of Pigs invasion in 1961) and that such an effort might mark the onset of World War III. But soon enough it was obvious that Castro was not going away and that the Cubans were in South Florida for the long haul.

So while North Florida is predominantly white working-class crackers who drink beer and eat fried alligator, South Florida is predominantly middle-class Hispanics who eat *ropa vieja* (shredded beef stewed with to-matoes) and fried *plátanos* and sip icy mojitos on the beach. Jacksonville is Lynyrd Skynyrd tunes blasting over the pickup-truck radio; Miami is Tito Puente–style music by the Pepe Montes Trio in classy Cuban-themed jazz cafés.

The Cuban community in Miami has successfully assimilated into America, and American culture has readily assimilated Cuban influences in return. Most contemporary Cuban Americans are perfectly bilingual and speak Spanish from preference rather than necessity. Some third- and fourth-generation Cuban American children speak no Spanish at all. Large Cuban concentrations are found in Texas and California as well as Flor-ida. Every US city of any size has an array of Cuban restaurants. Dishes such as black beans, *ropa vieja,* and many others have entered the Ameri-can culinary mainstream. And these days, a bartender who can't whip up a classic Cuban mojito is not worth his salt.

One well-known Cuban American politician, Mel Martínez, was born in Cuba, came to the United States in 1962, settled in the Orlando area, and subsequently served as the secretary of the Department of Housing and Urban Development from 2001 to 2003 and as a United States senator from 2005 to 2009. Another well-known Cuban American politician is Marco Rubio, former candidate for US president and currently serving his second term as the junior senator from Florida. Rubio was born in Florida of Cuban parents, went to Tarkio College in Missouri for one year on a football scholarship, and holds a degree in political science from the University of Florida. He once claimed that his parents fled Cuba when Castro came to power, but in fact they left Cuba for economic reasons in 1956, three years before the revolution.

The biggest Miami-Cuban news so far this century was the Elián

González affair in 2000. Six-year-old Elián had been rescued from waters near the Miami coast and soon became the center of an international controversy involving the governments of Cuba and the United States. The affair began when Elián's mother, Elizabeth Rodríguez, attempted to escape from Cuba with her young son and new boyfriend. She drowned in the attempt (one of tens of thousands of Cubans who perished trying to sail on makeshift rafts to the United States), but her son Elián was rescued and turned over to maternal relatives living in Miami, who wanted to keep Elián in the United States. His father demanded that Elián be returned to his care in Cuba. A protracted legal battle ensued, which ended when the federal district court held that only the father had the right to petition for asylum, a decision that was upheld by the US Court of Appeals for the Eleventh Circuit. Once the Supreme Court refused to rehear the case, federal authorities had no choice but to return the boy to Cuba, a move that was intensely unpopular in the Miami-Cuban community (and indeed, unpopular throughout America), since it seemed to condemn the boy to life in a Communist dictatorship rather than in the land of the free.

As of December 2018, Elián is a young man of twenty-five. He joined the Young Communist Union of Cuba in 2008 and began military school in Cuba at age fifteen. He considered Castro a personal friend until Fidel's death in 2016. He describes his time in the United States as "very sad times for me" and sees the efforts of his maternal relatives as an attempt to deny his nationality and culture. In 2016, he received a degree in industrial engineering from the University of Matanzas, and at his graduation he vowed "to fight from whatever trench the revolution demands." Many US Cubans still look on the court of appeals decision as a treasonous betrayal of the Cuban American community.

The Twitter feed #onlyinMiami chronicles the weird and wonderful stuff that happens in the southern part of the state and consists entirely of photos with terse commentary. Recent posts include photos of a store clerk with a button on his apron that reads I SPEAK ENGLISH, miscellaneous items of women's undergarments found hanging in the most improbable places, wild pigs rooting up suburban landscapes, electric mobility scooters festooned with Christmas decorations, overweight men walking around downtown in nothing but Speedos, an iguana lashed to a flatbed trailer, a coffin attached to the roof of a station wagon, and a screen shot from a Miami Beach weather report headlined SEVERE WEATHER ALERT! reporting a current temperature of 74 degrees, partly cloudy skies, and humidity at 79 percent.

South Florida politics is a curious mixture of Democratic urban counties and Republican rural counties. The urban area of Miami–Fort Lauderdale–Palm Beach–Hollywood has been reliably Democratic in presidential elections for several decades, whereas the more rural counties west of the Miami conurbation are more conservative and Republican. The Miami media market has a very sizable ethnic minority population, a lot of retired people, and a large contingent of Jewish voters, so the region is generally pro-Israel, pro-Medicare, pro–Social Security, and pro–welfare/social justice—thus, Democratic. The rest of South Florida consists mainly of moderate and progressive Republicans, many of them transplants from the Midwest and socially tolerant but fiscally conservative. Even given the deeply anti-Castro and anti-Communist sentiments of the Cuban exile community, South Florida usually winds up in the Democratic column in national political contests.

CENTRAL FLORIDA: THE I-4 CORRIDOR

Central Florida consists of the relatively sparsely populated stretch of land from The Barn in Sanford south to the Everglades. The region is defined socially and politically by the I-4 corridor, which runs from Tampa in the west to Daytona Beach in the east and runs through Orlando, the capital city of Central Florida. Central Florida is the state's melting pot. There are sizable populations of Cubans, Puerto Ricans, Africans, and Asians in all the region's major cities, vast retirement complexes along the Gulf Coast (especially Citrus and Pasco Counties) and outside of Orlando (The Villages), a fair number of white working-class crackers, some heavy industry, a lot of citrus, and, of course, the Space Coast along the eastern perimeter.

With mostly Republican counties lying to the north and heavily Democratic Miami lying to the south, Central Florida is the swing area in general elections and is often taken to be the state's bellwether. Florida, in turn, is a national bellwether. In the twenty-one presidential elections held in the United States from 1936 to 2016, the winner in Florida was also the winner nationally in nineteen. The only exceptions: In 1960 Florida went for Nixon whereas Kennedy won nationally, and in 1992 Florida wanted to reelect George H. W. Bush to a second term whereas the national vote was for Bill Clinton. So the road to the White House indeed runs along the I-4 corridor.

The I-4 corridor is culturally diverse. Its attractions run the gamut from the fabulous Salvador Dalí Museum in Saint Petersburg to Walt Disney World in Orlando to the Daytona International Speedway on Florida's east coast. You could visit all three in a weekend.

The Dalí Museum in Saint Pete houses the second-largest collection of Dalí works anywhere in the world. (The largest is the Dalí Theater-Museum created by Dalí himself in his hometown of Figueres, Spain.) The museum began as the private collection of Reynolds and Eleanor Morse, who lived in Cleveland, Ohio. In 1971, the collection was moved out of their private residence and into a museum. Later in the 1970s, federal tax law changed and the Morses were required to declare the total current value of their art collection for tax purposes. With more than 2,000 Dalí works in the collection, the taxes owed on it far exceeded the Morses' entire net worth, so they began looking for a museum—any museum—to which they could donate it all. They insisted that the collection be maintained in the whole, and that, plus other stipulations, made it difficult to locate an acceptable museum. Finally, about 1980, a group of Saint Petersburg investors came up with a proposal that satisfied all conditions and enough money to make it happen. And that is how a spectacular collection of Dalí's works ended up in Florida. Dalí himself never set foot in the Sunshine State.

A story I have heard more than once is that Dalí intended to will his collection of paintings, prints, and sculptures to Saint Petersburg in Russia, whose Hermitage Museum houses one of the finest art collections in the world. It would make sense for an artist of Dalí's caliber and persona to engineer a memorial to his genius in a museum such as the Hermitage. On the other hand, confusing a small city on the west coast of Florida with the home of the Russian czars strains credulity, and, in fact, the story is baseless, a pure concoction. The collection was amassed by a Cleveland industrialist and his wife and forced into Florida by an unfavorable federal tax law. Not too romantic, but true.

The center of Central Florida is Orlando, which styles itself as "The City Beautiful" mainly because of the lovely and iconic Lake Eola in its very heart. The Orlando area is home to more than a dozen theme parks as well as the University of Central Florida, where I taught from 2001 until 2017.

There are four or five different versions of how Orlando got its name. The area around present-day Orlando was originally known as Fort Gatlin, a US artillery encampment built during the Second Seminole War. The first permanent nonmilitary settlers in the area were the brothers Isaac and Aaron Jernigan, so for a while, the town was known as Jernigan. The town was renamed Orlando in 1857 because Aaron Jernigan had fallen into disfavor for his vicious conduct of war against the Native Americans and for a murder he and his sons allegedly committed. But why *Orlando* as the alternative?

One theory is that the town was named for an Orlando Reeves, a soldier who was killed by Native Americans in an attack during the Second Seminole War. Another story is that an ox-herder named Orlando was passing through on his way to Tampa, died, and was buried in a grave on the banks of Lake Eola. (The grave is still there on the southeastern bank.) Still a third story involves a cattle rancher and sugar farmer named Orlando Rees whose sugar fields were burned by the Seminoles in 1835 and who vigorously pursued the Seminoles for years thereafter. A final theory is that the town was named after Orlando, the protagonist in Shakespeare's play *As You Like It*.

This latter theory is vouched for by Judge Donald Cheney, the one-time chairman of the Orange County Historical Society, whose father John Moses Cheney was a major figure in Orlando history from his arrival in 1885. The elder Cheney was an associate of one James Speer, the man who originally proposed "Orlando" as the town's name. Speer was an admirer of Shakespeare's plays and anxious to honor the Bard. Consistent with this story, a major street in Orlando is named Rosalind, the same name as the heroine of *As You Like It*. Which of these theories is the correct one is anybody's guess, although the theory of Shakespearian origins has grown in popularity.

The Golden Age in Orlando history was the final quarter of the nineteenth century, when Orlando emerged as the hub of the burgeoning citrus industry. But the Great Freeze of 1894–95 caused the bulk of the industry to shift southward, and while there are still a number of orange groves in Orange County, most of the citrus industry lies elsewhere. From 1900 to 1970, Orlando was a small town with a largely agrarian regional economy based on citrus, cotton, and cattle. Then came Disney.

In 1871, an Ohio native named Matthias Day bought a two-thousand-acre chunk of Florida swampland on the west bank of the Halifax River for purposes of real estate development. Florida real estate was not the hot-ticket item then that it is today, and all that Day himself managed to build on the site was a small hotel. A year later, nearly bankrupt, he sold the land to Thomas Saunders, a Washington-based landscape gardener. To memorialize Day's vision for the property, Saunders named his estate *Daytona*. Today, Daytona is a small city (population of about 66,000) on Florida's east coast—largely unremarkable except for its gorgeous white sand beaches and the speedway, features that attract millions of visitors annually.

Dr. Sara Strickhouser (a former PhD student and frequent coauthor of mine) was born and raised in Daytona, and when I told her I was writing on Daytona history, she shared the following thoughts:

Despite my Daytona nativity, I just can't get interested in racing. I can't think of any friends or family from the area interested in racing either. The races were always just an excuse to go out, take a cooler, and get drunk at a big public event.

The 500 and the Pepsi 400 are such spectacles. My parents aren't race fans, but they had their honeymoon in February 1980, the day after their wedding, at the Daytona 500. Imagine "honeymooning" at the Daytona 500! But that's the NASCAR of the 80s—the Days of Thunder *Daytona. Daytona and racing in the 80s seemed really neat and exciting; there always seemed to be a feeling of hope and potential in the city.*

But the Daytona where I grew up in the 1990s and 2000s seemed to just struggle, always: a struggle with declining tourism every year, increasing poverty, crime, unemployment, and homelessness, and perpetual struggle between the needs of the tourists versus the needs of residents. As a local, I also know if you are a resident of Daytona Beach, you are mostly poor, transient, or . . . no, that's it . . . just poor or transient or both. The place is kind of a hellhole, truthfully.

Strickhouser's comments underscore a recurring theme in the struggle between Old and New Florida: namely, is Florida for Floridians or for the hundred million tourists who come here each year? Orlando profits immensely from the tourism generated by Disney World, but the result has been a labor economy dominated by low-wage jobs in the service sector. Daytona surely profits from NASCAR racing, spring break, and Bike Week, but during these events the city is practically unlivable for locals. This struggle plays out daily all over the state, but nowhere more visibly than along the I-4 corridor.

A UCF vice president wrote a column in the campus magazine titled "Orlando—We're No More Weird than Anywhere Else." The author, Tom Cavanagh, acknowledged that Orlando seems at times to harbor an outsize share of the total state weirdness—Casey Anthony, George Zimmerman, pet pythons that strangle children, wild bears that attack housewives, and, much more. From time to time, the region is wracked by deadly hurricanes and, more than once, whole trailer parks and condo developments have been swallowed up by giant sinkholes. Then there was the Pulse nightclub shooting in June 2016, where Islamic radicalism, homophobia, and hatred of Hispanics coalesced to produce fifty-eight wounded and fifty dead. But, hey, "We're no more weird than anywhere else." Only in Florida would an enthusiast mount such a defense.

THE HANGING CHAD AND RELATED MYSTERIES
OF FLORIDA POLITICS

OF THE MANY elections in which the Florida outcome was important in determining the presidency, none is more memorable than the "hanging chad" election of 2000, an election decided by 537 votes. And even this result turned on an intensive recount (two of them, in fact) and a Supreme Court decision that awarded the presidency to George W. Bush.

Although opinions vary, many commentators believe that the 2000 election was stolen from Al Gore and given to George Bush by the Republican Party of Florida. At the time, the leader of the Republicans in Florida was then-governor Jeb Bush, George's younger brother and himself a failed candidate for president later, in 2016. All key statewide posts, including—importantly—the secretary of state, were controlled by Republicans, as was the state legislature. The entirety of Florida's power structure was firmly in Republican hands.

When the election dust settled, the Florida outcome was determined by the United States Supreme Court on a 5–4 vote in favor of Bush. Gore ended up with the majority of the popular vote nationwide and, at least according to an analysis by *The Miami Herald*, would have won Florida by about twenty-three thousand votes had the hand recount been allowed to proceed. But the recount was halted by the Supreme Court decision and, indeed, the strategy of Bush supporters all along was to prevent a recount from going forward until the Supreme Court could weigh in. The late Judge

Antonin Scalia, appointed to the Court by Ronald Reagan in 1986, cast the decisive vote that gave the presidency to Bush.

Between election night (November 7, 2000) and the Supreme Court decision thirty-five days later (December 12), Florida Republicans led by W's brother Jeb did everything they could to create the impression that W had won the election. Secretary of State Katherine Harris certified Bush as the winner even as the vote count was still being challenged legally. This helped to create an impression of inevitability. It has also been documented that both Jeb and W made calls on election night to their cousin John Ellis, an advisor to the Fox News "decision desk," urging Fox News to call the election for Bush, which it did at 2:16 A.M. (NBC News had called the Florida election for Gore earlier in the evening and then reversed its decision and later followed the Fox News lead.) Buzzflash editor Mark Karlin has noted, "Jeb Bush wasn't just the governor of Florida in 2000; he was a key orchestrator and strategist in the theft of the Florida election on behalf of his brother. It was Jeb who teed up the ball and let Antonin Scalia hit it into the stands on behalf of George W. Bush." Karlin also reports a remark from Nixon strategist Keven Phillips, who said that "the Bush family has only excelled at two things: corporate cronyism and stealing elections." That is probably a bit harsh for a family that has given us two presidents (and don't count Jeb out yet: he is only in his sixties), but the conclusion that the 2000 Florida outcome was stolen is not hyperbole.

HANGING CHADS

The most memorable weirdness of the 2000 election in Florida were the so-called hanging chads. While most states had long since gone to fully electronic voting machines (or just continued to use reliable paper ballots), Florida was still using Votomatic punch-card ballots in some districts, which required voters to punch out little circular boxes with a stylus to register their vote preferences. If the chad was fully punched out, there was no ambiguity about whether a vote had been cast or for whom. But many of the punch-card ballots had chads that were still attached, leading to four possibilities:

Chad is attached to the ballot at only one corner: This is the "hanging chad."

Chad is attached to the ballot at two corners: These are "swinging chads."

Chad is attached at three corners: the "tri-chad."

Chad is attached at all four corners but is dimpled, indicating a vote preference (maybe!): these are "pregnant," "fat," or "dimpled" chads.

When the recount began, it became clear that each of the Votomatic punch-card ballots would need to be inspected by hand to see if the chad was still attached, and if so, attached at how many points. A further issue: At what point does a hanging, swinging, or pregnant chad cease to be ambiguous and become countable as an actual vote? The two-corner standard was eventually adopted: if the chad was hanging by one corner or swinging by two, it could be counted, but if it was still attached at three or all four corners, it was rejected as an invalid ballot. By this standard, the recounted vote favored Bush by 363 votes. If all hanging and swinging chads were declared invalid and only fully removed chad ballots were counted, the recount favored Gore by 3 votes.

Hanging and swinging chads led to the recount spectacle of poll watchers with a magnifying glass in one hand and a punch-card ballot in the other trying to determine what kind of chad they were looking at and whether it could be counted as a valid vote or not. That the leadership of the free world hung in the balance has to be counted as one of Florida's weirdest political moments.

Following the spectacle of 2000, most Florida counties bought new voting machines for subsequent election cycles. But an NPR story about the Florida 2016 election pointed out that all these "new" machines are now sixteen years old, far beyond the anticipated lifetime of most modern electronic gadgets. It was reported that one Florida county had to buy spare parts off eBay to repair their broken machines.

In 2002, a little-known act called the Help America Vote Act was passed specifically to assist states like Florida in phasing out punch-card ballots in favor of entirely electronic voting systems. This resolved most of punched-ballot problems but opened up a Pandora's box of cybersecurity issues, vulnerability to malware, and hacked voting machines potentially changing the vote outcome. Can anyone state with complete certainty even today that America and not Russian hackers elected Donald Trump president? Most of the "modern" voting machines presently in use run on Windows XP or Windows 2000, and Microsoft did not issue a security patch for that operating system between 2014 and 2017, dates spanning the 2016 presidential election.

THE RECOUNT(S)

Election night 2000 was chaotic. Everyone in the political-news business wants to be first to call the outcome and does so based on early returns and exit polling, both of which can be (and have often proven to be) misleading. In 2016, for example, exit polling showed Hillary Clinton winning four swing states that ended up in the Donald Trump column once all the votes were counted. In the 2000 election, the early returns and exit polls seemed to show a Gore victory, and Florida was called for Gore (by NBC and CBS) about an hour after the polls closed. But part of the heavily Republican Florida Panhandle lies in the central time zone, and when those returns started coming in, the networks reversed themselves and said Florida was "too close to call." Later, the networks called it for Bush but had to reverse that as well, so by midnight, it was still "too close to call." At one point in the evening, Gore even called W to concede and then retracted his concession.

The first "official" election-night results showed Bush the winner by about eighteen hundred votes. That narrow margin triggered an automatic machine recount under Florida law. The machine recount took place the next day and showed a margin for Bush of about nine hundred votes. By that point, it was also clear that the Florida result would determine the outcome nationwide. The Gore team demanded a hand recount in critical swing districts; W's legal team in turn sued to prevent the hand recount from going forward. As the hand recount began, numerous irregularities surfaced, including the hanging chad business and a great deal more. But all further recounting efforts were halted with the Supreme Court decision on December 12 that ceded the presidency to Bush.

IRREGULARITIES

The political chicanery surrounding the election had begun months before Election Day. With the apparent blessing of Governor Bush, Secretary of State Katherine Harris had performed a preelection purge of the voting registration rolls that kicked tens of thousands of alleged felons out of the Florida electorate. About sixty thousand voters were purged, almost all of them African Americans who would have voted for Gore with high probability. In some cases, more black voters were purged than there were black people in the county. Gore supporters objected that many had no felony record and thus had every right to vote, but in Florida, Republicans have gotten used to doing whatever they want. Harris and her predecessor had contracted with an outfit called DBT Online, a contractor allied with the Republican Party (according to the Sarasota *Herald-Tribune*) to prepare a purge list, at a cost to the state of $4.3 million. The owner of DBT Online, ChoicePoint, was sued by the NAACP for violations of the Voting Rights Act of 1965, a suit that ChoicePoint elected to settle.

Then there were the so-called Palm Beach "butterfly ballots" (see page 120), on which presidential candidates were listed side by side across two adjacent pages. It is completely clear how to vote for Bush: you punch the top hole. Many voters then appeared to reason that a vote for Gore could be cast by punching the second hole. But no: a punch in the second hole cast a vote for Pat Buchanan. A vote for Gore required a punch-out of the *third* hole. Evidently because of the confusion, Buchanan received far more Palm Beach votes than anticipated and said on the *Today* show, "When I took one look at that ballot on election night . . . it's very . . . easy for me to see how someone could have voted for me in the belief they voted for Al Gore."

A worse complication arising from the butterfly ballot was the evident belief of many voters that the presidential election balloting was on page one and some other race was on page two, because nineteen thousand voters cast two votes for president and thereby invalidated their ballots. Ballot spoilage in the 1996 election only added up to three thousand votes. An analysis published in the *American Political Science Review* concluded that the voting errors caused by the butterfly ballot cost Gore the election.

A similar problem occurred in Duval County (Jacksonville), where the "caterpillar ballot" also had presidential candidates spread over two pages. Instructions printed on the ballot told voters to "vote every page," with the result that many people invalidated their ballots by voting for two different presidential candidates. And there was a clear racial gradient in the invalidated ballots. African Americans comprised about 11 percent of the Florida electorate but a bit more than half the uncounted ballots. Such was the conclusion of the US Commission on Civil Rights.

A postelection study by the National Opinion Research Center examined about 175,000 ballots from across the state, with a focus on the "overvotes," that is, the ballots that contained two different votes for president. Of the overvotes examined, it was determined that about three-quarters were votes for Gore and a minor party candidate, with the remainder being votes for Bush and a minor party candidate. Given that the statewide margin was only 537 votes and that 3 percent of the ballots cast were invalid because of overvoting, the voting errors introduced by confusing

THE PALM BEACH BUTTERFLY BALLOT

ballots and overvoting may well have cost Gore the election. University of Pennsylvania researcher Steve Freeman concluded that a complete hand recount would have given the election to Gore.

Any capable history of the 2000 Florida election will discuss numerous other voting irregularities, including the major networks "calling" the race for Gore ten minutes before the polls closed in the western (central time zone) counties; the fact that several counties distributed sample ballots that differed from the real ballots; and the numerous allegations of voter intimidation, recount disruptions, illegally registered voters, and invalid votes from Americans living overseas, including members of the US military. Most (but not all) of these political chicaneries worked to the advantage of candidate Bush. Even those who doubt that a recount would have changed the outcome can agree that the 2000 Florida election was among the most sordid and bizarre in the nation's political history.

WATERGATE

A quarter century before the 2000 election was the scandal known as Watergate, described by many as the biggest political scandal in the nation's history. (Some give the nod to Warren G. Harding's Teapot Dome Scandal, instead.) With the passing of time, many may have forgotten the Florida connection to the Watergate scandal, but the connection was certainly there. The scandal unfolded with the attempted break-in (and wiretapping) of the Democratic National Committee headquarters at the Watergate Hotel in Washington, DC, in June 1972. Security guard Frank Wills noted on a routine inspection that some of the latches to the building's doors had been taped open, so he removed the tape and thought nothing further about it until he returned an hour later and noticed that the latches had been re-taped. Police entered the DNC headquarters and arrested five burglars: Virgilio Gonzalez, Bernard Barker, James McCord, Eugenio Martínez, and Frank Sturgis. All but McCord were anti-Castro political operatives and Bay of Pigs veterans who were living in and around Miami and had been recruited by McCord or E. Howard Hunt to assist with the dirty works of Nixon's "plumbers."

Barker had been born in Cuba of a Cuban mother and Russian father, served the United States in the Second World War, then returned to Cuba after the war to work for Batista's secret police. Along with thousands of others, he fled Cuba when Castro came to power. After completing his Watergate prison sentence, he worked as a building inspector for the city of Miami.

Gonzalez too was born in Cuba and moved to Miami after Fidel's revolution, where he was a prominent figure in the anti-Castro movement. There is some speculation that Gonzalez was somehow involved in the Kennedy assassination (as was Barker), although this has never been proven. Martínez was also a Cuban émigré who was active in the Miami anti-Castro community.

Frank Sturgis was an American citizen who served in the US military, moved to Miami in 1957, and then became a gunrunner for Fidel Castro's revolutionary forces. It is said that he trained Che Guevara in the art of guerrilla warfare. He was sent by Castro to Miami in June 1959 to negotiate with American gambling interests, defected a month later, and joined the anti-Castro exiles.

McCord was a former CIA operative who had also worked for the FBI and was serving as the security coordinator for the Committee for the Re-election of the President, Nixon's chief 1972 campaign organization. He is the only one of the five with no apparent Florida connections.

Another Watergate principal was the elusive E. Howard Hunt, an intelligence officer and sometime spy novelist. Hunt was also one of Nixon's "plumbers," and while he was born in New York, he was living in Biscayne Park, Florida (a Miami suburb), at the time of Watergate and died of pneumonia in a Miami hospital. And speaking of Nixon, it was during a trip to Disney World on November 17, 1973, that he gave his now-infamous "I am not a crook" speech.

THE IRAN-CONTRA AFFAIR

"Irangate" broke as a political scandal in 1985–86 during Ronald Reagan's administration. The scandal was that various US operatives, including Colonel Oliver North, were conducting secret arms sales to Iran, even though Iran was under a US arms embargo at the time, and were using the proceeds to fund and arm the anti-Ortega Contras in Nicaragua. Any aid to the Contras had been prohibited by an act of Congress, so the Iran-Contra dealings were in direct defiance of Congress.

A key player in the deal was a pro-Contra operative named Tom Posey, who was a chief organizer of the arms shipments. Officially, Posey was the head of an Alabama-based outfit called Civilian Materiel Assistance, but privately, he was rabidly anti-Communist and a fervent Contra supporter. He was targeted in 1988 by a federal grand jury in Jacksonville and charged with gunrunning, drug smuggling, plotting assassinations, and various other violations of the US Neutrality Acts. These charges were later dropped. One of Posey's key US supporters and contacts was allegedly Jeb Bush, who was also involved with numerous other anti-Castro Cuban Americans in the United States, including Armando Codina (with whom Bush formed a business partnership), Camilo Padreda (a Cuban intelligence officer under the Batista regime, who was later convicted of defrauding HUD out of millions of dollars), Miguel Recarey (an associate of crime boss Santo Trafficante), and several others.

2016

When the 2016 campaign season opened, two full-time Floridians and one part-timer were in the hunt for the Republican presidential nomination: former governor Jeb Bush (declared to be the front-runner the very day he formally announced); the state's junior senator, Marco Rubio; and Donald J. Trump. Trump savaged Jeb as a "low-energy kind of guy" and blew off Rubio with the derisive moniker "Little Marco." Bush left the race after a stinging defeat by Trump in the South Carolina primary; Rubio put all his chips on his home state but went belly-up. He said ruefully, "While it is clear that we are on the right side this year, we were not on the winning side." In the general election, Trump won Florida handily, even though the state voted for Obama in both 2008 and 2012.

It would be hard for any state to top the weirdness of someone like Donald Trump heading the Republican ticket, and for once, Florida didn't even try. Early voting, voting by mail, and absentee voting sent the Florida turnout to an all-time high, with 9.4 million votes cast. Oh sure, there was the Trump supporter in Palm Beach County who got miffed and pepper-sprayed a vocal Clintonite, a couple of Broward County poll workers who were dismissed for actively intimidating voters, and a hand-ful of ballot problems, voting-machine malfunctions, and scanner jams. But nothing obviously illegal or nefarious was reported anywhere in the state; Florida in 2016 was weird for appearing to be so normal.

The state's most influential Trump supporter was Governor Rick Scott, widely regarded as a shoo-in for a post in Trump's cabinet but rebuffed after a much-publicized visit to Trump Tower. Florida history does not lack for controversial, unfit, or flagrantly incompetent governors: the Prohibition-ist, antiblack, anti-Catholic, anti-Jewish Sidney Catts, elected in 1916, is one example; Civil War governor John Milton, who killed himself while in office rather than participate in the reunification of North and South, is another. But Florida people from the author Carl Hiaasen to retired politi-cal scientist Darryl Paulson to members of the Transport Workers Union of America have concluded that Rick Scott is the worst of the bunch.

I mentioned earlier Scott's sordid history as CEO of Columbia/Hospital Corporation of America. As governor, he has slashed spending on educa-tion and health care to make room for tax cuts for corporations and his superrich friends; spent more than a million public dollars defending himself and several staff members against lawsuits for violating the state's sunshine laws (state laws about conducting public affairs out in the open); demanded that welfare recipients be drug-tested (only to find that the cost of testing exceeded the money the state would have realized in cutting off benefits to the tiny percentage who tested positive); engineered a law allow-ing state agencies to randomly drug-test their employees; and proposed purging the liberal arts and humanities from the state university system on the grounds that psychology, sociology, and anthropology majors made no significant contribution to the state's economic well-being.

One Scott broadside singled out psychology as the state's most popular but least useful degree, which prompted a statewide response from happily employed former psychology majors. Undaunted, Scott turned his gaze on anthropology. "We don't need a lot more anthropologists in the state," Scott said. "It's a great degree if people want to get it, but we don't need them here. I want to spend our dollars giving people science, technology, engineering, and math degrees. That's what our kids need to focus all their time and attention on, those types of degrees, so when they get out of school, they can get a job." Ironically, Scott's daughter, Jordan Kandah, has a degree in anthropology from the College of William & Mary.

Scott has been reliably on the far right of contemporary Republican politics for his entire tenure as governor. He refused to expand Medicaid under the Affordable Care Act, depriving more than half a million Floridians of health insurance. He signed an anti–Planned Parenthood bill and another bill imposing severe restrictions on the state's abortion clinics. He tried to build new golf courses in state parks while cutting the state's education budget by 10 percent. He proposed eliminating state support for two historically black colleges and universities. He also banned the term "climate change" from state offices and is regarded by Florida environmentalists and the *Tampa Bay Times* as an "environmental disaster." The organization Friends of the Everglades calls Scott "the worst governor in modern Florida history."

12

THE FLORIDA HALL OF FAME AND SHAME

EVERY STATE BOASTS a list of citizens who are unforgettable for one or another reason, and Florida is no exception. In my research for this book, I have come across a number of Floridians of whom I had never heard or that I had heard of but did not know about their Florida connections or their often astonishing chicaneries and accomplishments. Some are historical prominences; others are near contemporaries; all qualify as the state's first, best, wildest, most memorable, or most treasonous.

There is no overarching theme to the material in this chapter, just a collection of fun or interesting anecdotes that seemed too juicy to leave out of the book. I am certain a similar listing could be conjured up for every state. But when you start reading and writing about Florida, you eventually come to wonder where the real estate con games began or how the Florida cattle industry got started or what the earliest examples of political incompetence and corruption were. These were the kinds of questions that, in the pursuit, turned up the following Florida Hall of Fame and Shame. For ease of presentation, I have organized my list more or less chronologically.

FLORIDA'S FIRST REAL ESTATE CON MAN

Jesse Fish was a colonial-era swindler, merchant, and property tycoon who was the original Florida real estate crook. At one time, Fish had land and property holdings in and around Saint Augustine that were exceeded only by those of the Spanish Crown. (My information on Fish comes from Robert Gold's paper, "That Infamous Floridian, Jesse Fish," *Florida Historical Quarterly* 52, no. 1 [July 1973].) Fish was part legitimate businessman and part schemer, contraband merchant, and slaver. Most of the African slaves who came into Florida during Spanish rule were registered through Fish. On the legitimate business side, he operated a cargo shipping company that plied the waters between Saint Augustine and New York City. In 1738, the Spanish banished all Englishmen from Saint Augustine except for young Fish, who was necessary in order to obtain flour and meat from Yankee ports.

Fish's foray into Saint Augustine real estate came once Florida was ceded to the British in 1763. Virtually the entire Spanish population of the city emigrated to Cuba or elsewhere in "New Spain." The British gave the Spaniards eighteen months to dispose of their real property, but few buyers were available. Through a series of mostly illegal machinations, nearly 200 Spanish estates in the area were conveyed to Fish. Over the next decade, 138 of these estates were transferred to other owners. Fish's records of these transactions survive to this day and show numerous instances of the same properties being traded multiple times, exorbitant fees assessed on the transactions, bogus repairs and other charges levied on the sale, and related scurrilous items. Interestingly, there is no evidence in these accounts that any of the Spanish owners were ever paid anything.

MOST TREASONOUS HISTORICAL FIGURE

Lewis Powell (aka Lewis Payne, Lewis Paine) was born in Alabama, fought for the South in the Civil War, and was wounded at Gettysburg. His family moved to Florida in 1859, and when the war broke out, he made his way to Jasper, Florida, and enlisted. His antipathy toward the North was evident in his practice of carrying the skull of a Union soldier to use as an ashtray. Early in 1865, he made the acquaintance of John Wilkes Booth, and together they hatched a plot to kidnap and assassinate President Lincoln, Vice President Johnson, and Secretary of State William H. Seward. Booth was to kill Lincoln, Powell would take out Seward, and a third conspirator, George Atzerodt, was to slay the vice president. Of the three, only Booth succeeded, although Powell managed to inflict numerous serious wounds on Seward and his entourage. Powell was later captured along with a number of other coconspirators and hanged on July 7, 1865, less than three months after the assassination attempt.

The bizarre story of Lewis Powell, however, does not end with his execution but with the history of his remains. After their deaths, Powell and the three others who were hanged with him were buried in a mass grave at the site of the executions in Washington. Atzerodt was one of the three, David Herold was another (Herold's crime was that he led Powell to Seward's home), and the third was Mary Surratt, the first woman executed by the federal government. (Surrat's small boarding house was where the conspirators met.)

During the next twenty years, Powell's remains were removed and reburied at several different sites. In 1885, his skull (identified by the broken jawbone that Powell had suffered as a child) was found as specimen no. 2244 in the Army Medical Museum at Ford's Theatre, where Lincoln had been assassinated. Thirteen years later, the skull was given to the Smithsonian's Anthropology Department (probably not for use as an ashtray!). In 1991, the Smithsonian found the skull among a large number of Native American remains, identified it as Powell's by the marking "P 2244" inside the skull, contacted known relatives, and agreed to release the skull to be buried alongside the grave of his mother in Geneva, Florida, a small town northeast of Orlando. Whatever happened to the rest of Powell is unknown, but you can visit his grave at the Geneva Cemetery.

FIRST CATTLE BARON

Ziba King was a Confederate soldier who walked from war-torn Georgia to Florida with five dollars in his pocket. By 1868, he had accumulated enough capital to open a Tampa-area dry goods store, and in about 1870, he moved to the Arcadia area and acquired a 160-acre homestead and a few head of cattle. Forty years later, he owned a herd of fifty thousand beef cattle, the largest herd in Florida and a tenth of the state's entire cattle inventory. Along the way, he was also appointed as a judge and named as president of the First National Bank of Arcadia. The cattle industry he helped found was a mainstay of the Florida economy until about 1970.

MOST FAMOUS CRACKER COWBOY

As a big-time cattle baron, Ziba King was forever in need of cowboys, and his favorite was Morgan Bonaparte "Bone" Mizell. Bone Mizell was born in 1863 in Desoto County and died in 1921 "with his boots on," passed out in a train depot waiting for King to wire him some money. Bone's fame derives not so much from his prodigious drinking (the cause of death on his death certificate is listed as "Moonshine—went to sleep and did not wake up"); nor his skills as a cowman and whip wielder (one account claims that Bone could "gracefully flick a fly off a cow's rump with his 18-foot bullwhip, never raising a hair on the poor dumb beast"); nor his uproarious trips to local bordellos and county lockups (he once got off on a cattle-rustling charge when he pointed out that he had rustled plenty of cattle for the judge in the case); nor his frequent drunken antics (he often rode his horse right into the saloon); nor his gaunt six-foot-five frame. He became the most famous cracker cowboy ever when the celebrated artist of the American West, Frederic Remington, traveled to Florida and chose Bone as the model in his painting, *A Cracker Cowboy,* the best known in a series of Remington paintings of Florida cowmen, all of which appeared as illustrations in *Harper's Magazine* in August 1895.

MOST FORWARD-THINKING DOCTOR

Dr. John Gorrie was born in the West Indies, was of Scottish descent, grew up in South Carolina, went to medical school in New York State, and moved in 1833 to Apalachicola, a region on the Gulf Coast best known for its sublime oysters. He was a specialist in tropical diseases and believed that "bad air" caused malaria and other diseases. His theory was that good air, by which he meant cool air, might cure disease. One approach was to suspend tubs of ice in medical wards and use fans to blow air over the ice, providing bedridden yellow fever patients below with some relief. But ice had to be cut from northern lakes in the winter, stored, and transported to Florida, so it was expensive and scarce. Gorrie was enough of a scientist to understand that if a compressed gas was allowed to suddenly expand, a cooling effect would result, and in 1842 or thereabouts, he invented and deployed an imperfect but workable cooling machine. A few years and a number of refinements later, Gorrie was awarded a US patent in 1851 for the invention of mechanical refrigeration and air-conditioning. The Florida we know today owes as much to John Gorrie as to any other person.

MOST SHORTSIGHTED GOVERNOR

The nineteenth governor of Florida was a river pilot, Napoleon Bonaparte Broward, for whom Broward County (Fort Lauderdale) is named. Born in 1857 in Jacksonville, Broward was orphaned at age twelve, worked as a farmhand, logger, steamboat roustabout, steamboat captain, and finally steamboat owner before beginning his political career as sheriff of Duval County (1888). In succession, he was elected to the Jacksonville City Council (1895), then to the Florida House of Representatives (1900), and finally to the governor's office (served 1905–09).

As governor, Broward's most dubious accomplishment was embarking on a plan to drain the Everglades to create more land for agriculture. In fairness, neither he nor many other people at the time appreciated the role the Everglades played in the state's ecology. As far as he could see, the

Everglades were useless swampland, just as Chicago had been less than a century before. The project was highly controversial. One newspaper charged, "The treasury will be drained before the Everglades." Despite opposition, the project continued for nearly a century, until the Comprehensive Everglades Restoration Plan was authorized by Congress in 2000 and Florida embarked on a thirty-to-fifty-year, $10 billion effort to undo the damage that Broward initiated. Broward's drainage project obviously did far more harm than good, but it also helped establish the state citrus industry as a going economic enterprise.

THE ORIGINAL FLORIDA HIGHWAYMAN

Cars and roads to drive them on were essential in the development of modern Florida. Among the many early Floridians who were involved in highways and real estate development, none looms larger than Carl Graham Fisher, who was to Florida highways what Henry Flagler was to its railroads. Fisher was a native Hoosier born in 1874. Like many other early auto pioneers, he came up in the bicycle business but soon developed an interest in gasoline-powered "horseless carriages." He was friends with Barney Oldfield, and the two of them opened the Fisher Automobile Company in Indianapolis in about 1904, thought to be the first automobile dealership ever opened in the United States. Fisher was also the prime mover behind the building of the Indianapolis Motor Speedway.

The successes of his auto dealership, his speedway, and other commercial ventures made Fisher a wealthy man, and he soon turned his attention and energy to the main obstacle to further growth of the automobile industry in the United States, bad roads. Indeed, "bad" is hardly adequate. In the first decade of the twentieth century, most of the nation's roads were little more than rutted dirt cattle paths. Even gravel roads were rare. Fisher wrote in a letter to a friend, "The highways of America are built chiefly of politics, whereas the proper material is crushed rock or concrete." So in 1912, Fisher hatched a plan to build a transcontinental highway running from New York City to California. That road, later known as the Lincoln Highway, opened along much of its route in 1913 but was not completed until the 1920s. Once completed, it ran from Times Square to Lincoln Park in San Francisco, passed through thirteen states, and traversed some 3,142 miles.

While the Lincoln Highway project was under way, Fisher turned his attention to a Florida project that involved draining a lot of mangrove swampland and building a city in its place. That city was Miami Beach. Fisher and his wife, Jane, first visited the area in 1912. The couple was attacked by giant swarms of mosquitoes, and Jane saw no future for the swamp, but Carl was more visionary. According to an essay by the Indiana Historical Society, he told his wife, "Look, honey, I'm going to build a city here! A city like magic, like romantic places you read and dream about, but never see."

Fisher was convinced that Miami Beach would be a perfect winter destination for people from the Midwest, but getting people from Indiana, Ohio, and Michigan all the way to the southern tip of Florida would require another massive road-building effort. Even as the drainage and construction in South Florida continued, Fisher wrote a letter in 1914 to the governor of Indiana proposing that an interstate highway be built from Chicago to Miami. A meeting of governors of the affected states was held in Chattanooga in early 1915, and the governors enthusiastically endorsed the plan. Construction on what came to be known as the Dixie Highway began at once and continued until 1927. Most of the stretch from Indianapolis to Miami Beach was opened in 1916. Fisher is thus considered not only the founder of Miami Beach but the father of motorized tourism in the Sunshine State.

THE INVENTOR OF COMMERCIAL AIR TRAVEL

Juan Trippe was a New Jersey–born World War I naval aviator who practically invented the commercial airline industry when he founded Pan American Airways in Florida in 1925. Trippe's interest in flying was stimulated by watching Wilbur Wright pilot an airplane around the Statue of Liberty in 1909. His airline Pan Am was the unofficial American flag carrier from its founding until the company collapsed in 1991. Pan Am's first flight

(October 19, 1927) went from Key West to Havana, and the airline was soon providing service to cities around the Caribbean and the United States. Trippe also introduced tourist-class service to Europe, opened commercial air service from the United States to Asia, and was instrumental in persuading Boeing to engineer and build the Boeing 747, at the time the largest commercial passenger aircraft in the world. As much as any man, Trippe democratized air travel for everyday people. He was also an important player in Florida's space industry, having built part of the network of stations that tracked rockets launched from Cape Canaveral.

MOST PROGRESSIVE AND BELOVED POLITICIAN

Claude Pepper was an influential voice on the political left from his initial special election to the US Senate in 1936 until his death as a member of the US House of Representatives in 1989. Like many others of liberal persuasion in the 1930s and 1940s, he was seduced by Soviet-style Communism but later become an ardent anti-Communist and an articulate defender of the rights of common folk, most of all African Americans. He was a classic New Dealer and a mentor to people such as Hubert Humphrey, Henry Wallace, and even the young Jack Kennedy. He was an early white southern champion of civil rights.

Pepper led a "Dump Truman" campaign at the 1948 Democratic National Convention, and in retaliation, Truman summoned George Smathers, at the time a member of the House of Representatives, to a 1950 White House meeting and implored Smathers to "beat that son-of-a-bitch Claude Pepper." Smathers ran a classic red-baiting campaign, including circulating a pamphlet entitled "The Red Record of Senator Claude Pepper." Pepper lost, and his political career went into eclipse until he ran for and was elected to the House of Representatives in 1962 (one of only three former senators in modern times to serve a subsequent term in the House).

The most famous "episode" in the Smathers-Pepper 1950 senatorial contest never happened. An alleged Smathers diatribe against Pepper has been quoted hundreds of times as a classic of political pettifoggery: "Are you aware," Smathers is quoted as saying, "that Claude Pepper is known all over Washington as a shameless extrovert? Not only that, but this man is reliably reported to practice nepotism with his sister-in-law and he has a sister who was once a thespian in wicked New York. Worst of all, it is an established fact that Mr. Pepper, before his marriage, habitually practiced celibacy." These exact words were attributed to Smathers in an April 1950 issue of *Time* magazine and have been repeated hundreds of times since. But Smathers never said them, and even the original *Time* article describes the account as a "yarn."

FLORIDA'S FIRST NASCAR SUPERSTAR

Auto racing at Daytona Beach dates to 1902, and France's NASCAR racing association was founded in 1947, but NASCAR's first real superstar was probably Edward Glenn Roberts, a native Floridian. Better known as "Fireball," Roberts was born in Tavares (in Central Florida, not far from Orlando) in 1929, began racing on the Daytona Beach road course in 1947, and died on July 2, 1964, from burns suffered in a massive crash at the Charlotte Motor Speedway in May. In his NASCAR career, Roberts amassed thirty-three victories and remains one of a very few drivers to have won both the Daytona 500 and the Firecracker 250 (the summer race at Daytona) in the same year. Fireball is the stuff of many legends, but the best known is the story of his death. He and several other drivers crashed in the World 600, and Roberts was burned horribly. He was sent to a nearby Charlotte hospital in critical condition, hung on for six weeks, then died of sepsis and pneumonia. At the funeral, one of Fireball's relatives was heard to remark, "Want to hear about bad taste? Glenn gets burned to death and the mortuary sends the family a smoked ham! That's the goddamn South for you."

"THE VOICE OF A NEW GENERATION"

Florida has given the nation not one but two voices of new generations. One is the novelist Jack Kerouac, the voice of the "beat generation." Kerouac, although born in Lowell, Massachusetts, moved to Orlando in 1957, just as his novel *On the Road* was being published. He died from chronic alcohol abuse in Saint Petersburg at the age of forty-seven. Even at that, he outlived another "voice of a new generation," Jim Morrison of the rock band The Doors. Morrison was born in Melbourne in 1943 and by 1967, his band had become one of the most popular rock groups in the world. By July 1971, he was dead, one of a long list of pop musicians to expire at age twenty-seven. (Janis Joplin, Jimi Hendrix, Kurt Cobain, and Amy Winehouse are some of the better-known others.)

BEST-KNOWN WASHED-UP RIGHT-WING CROONER

The singer Pat Boone was born in 1934 in Jacksonville and is still alive today. Boone, who may or may not be distantly related to the pioneer icon Daniel Boone, depending on whose genealogy you believe, was the second best-selling recording artist of the late 1950s, outdone only by Elvis. Boone also had a popular television series (*The Pat Boone Chevy Showroom*), starred in several movies (including *Journey to the Center of the Earth* in 1959, a personal childhood favorite), has authored numerous inspirational and religious books, and was inducted into the Gospel Music Hall of Fame in 2003.

Lately, Boone has been noteworthy mostly because of his fanatical right-wing political views. In August 2009, he published an article likening liberalism to cancer, was an early and vocal supporter of the birther movement, regularly alleged that Obama was fluent in Arabic, and has compared gay-rights protests to terrorist attacks.

BEST-KNOWN BANDIT

Burt Reynolds was born in Lansing, Michigan, in 1936, but his family moved to Riviera Beach (near Palm Beach) in 1946. He was a football star at Palm Beach High School and went to Florida State University on a football scholarship, but his football (and college) career ended with injuries suffered in the first game of his sophomore season. He dropped out of school hoping to find a career as a policeman or parole officer and was taking classes at a local junior college when his English professor urged him to try out for a play the professor was producing. Reynolds's performance won a Florida State Drama Award and a scholarship to a summer stock theater outfit in Hyde Park, New York.

Reynolds beat around the New York theater scene for several years, landing occasional film and television spots. His breakout role was as Lewis Medlock in the 1972 John Boorman classic *Deliverance*, a visceral and disturbing portrayal of the people and mentality of the Deep South. Probably his best-known film role was as the Bandit in *Smokey and the Bandit* and its two sequels. (Jackie Gleason, a Florida resident from 1964 until his death in 1987, was Smokey.)

MOST LAID-BACK TELEVISED ART INSTRUCTOR

Bob Ross was the star of the how-to-paint show *The Joy of Painting*, a PBS staple even now, more than two decades after his death. If you are not sure who Bob Ross is, his biography is entitled *Happy Clouds, Happy Trees: The Bob Ross Phenomenon*, by Kristin Congdon, Doug Blandy, and Danny Coeyman, on whose account I rely.

Ross was born in Daytona Beach in 1942, left school in ninth grade, lost part of a finger to a carpentry project when he was just a boy, joined the US Air Force at age eighteen, where he served as a drill sergeant for twenty years, was stationed in Alaska (Alaska landscapes are the obvious inspiration behind many of his paintings), and taught himself how to paint while in the service by watching a how-to-paint television show. The supercalm, ultra-comforting persona for which he is notable was developed, he once said, because his time as a drill sergeant had convinced him he never wanted to yell at anyone again. His other trademark, an exuberantly frizzy hairdo, arose when he realized that if he permed his hair, he wouldn't need to get it cut as often.

Ross's painting studio was the basement of his home in Orlando (notable mostly because very few houses in Orlando have basements). A one-time neighbor described him as "one of the kindest people I knew." From childhood, he was always caring for animals and kept squirrels as pets in his home, one of whom ("Pea-Pod") would often peek out of his shirt pocket while he was painting. No one knows how many paintings he did in his lifetime, but reliable sources put the number somewhere near thirty thousand. He often donated paintings he did on his TV show to local public-broadcasting fundraising efforts.

MOST DEMENTED SERIAL MURDERER

Florida's all-round sickest serial murderer was undoubtedly Ted Bundy, put to death by electrocution in January 1989 at the age of forty-two. Bundy had a disturbed childhood. His true father has never been identified but was probably his mother's father. He was raised by grandparents: the grandfather was a tyrannical bigot who frequently and loudly expressed his loathing of Jews, blacks, Catholics, and Italians; beat his wife; and tortured animals, including the family dog; the grandmother was regularly treated for depression by electroconvulsive therapy.

No one knows for sure how many women Bundy tortured, raped, and murdered, but many put the number far higher than the thirty or so murders Bundy is known to have committed. In various death row interviews, Bundy claimed as many as 130 killings, beginning when he was just fourteen. His murderous path through life began in Washington State and included murders in Oregon, Utah, Idaho, California, Colorado, and finally Florida. All of his victims were young white women, and all were sexually assaulted before, during, or after they had been slain.

Bundy's murders were brazen and sick. Frequently, he would revisit the death scene even as the police investigation was under way. He often feigned injury or disability to lure women into trusting him, then took them to secluded locations where they were raped and killed. He is known to have decapitated at least a dozen of his victims and to have kept the severed heads in his apartment as souvenirs. He also frequently revisited death scenes weeks or months later to have sex with the decomposing corpses.

Bundy's murderous path across the United States ended when he was captured in Florida in 1978, where he was given three death sentences in two separate trials. One conviction came when the prosecution showed that the bite marks on the buttocks of one of the victims matched Bundy's dentition perfectly.

FIRST FEMALE MASS MURDERER—NOT!

Aileen Wuornos was born in Michigan in 1956. Her early life was a horror. Her father (whom she never met) killed himself while in prison on a child molestation charge. She was then abandoned by her mother at age four and went to live with her grandparents. Her grandmother proved to be an abusive alcoholic, and her grandfather routinely "had his way" with her. In later life she also admitted to having had sex with her brother. She became sexually active at about age eleven, trading sexual favors for drugs, food, and cigarettes. A rape by a friend of the grandfather left her pregnant at age fourteen. By the time she was twenty, Wuornos was living in Florida, had been arrested on a variety of charges ranging from assault to disorderly conduct, and was turning tricks to get by.

From late 1989 to fall 1990, Wuornos murdered at least six and possibly seven men along various Central Florida highways. All of them were apparently soliciting sex when Wuornos shot them. She was convicted of multiple murders in January 1992, was sentenced to death, and spent ten years on death row until her eventual execution by lethal injection in October 2002.

Wuornos is frequently depicted in the media as "America's first female serial killer," but this is not true. The first female serial killer in the United States was probably Lavinia Fisher (1792 or 1793–1820), who along with her husband murdered dozens of men in their Charleston, South Carolina, hotel, for whatever cash and goods the victims possessed. As she was about to be hanged for her crimes, Fisher jumped from the gallows and hanged herself—technically a suicide, not an execution. A precise count of her victims has never been made public but surely exceeded Wuornos's six or seven. Wuornos was not even the first female serial killer to be executed for her crimes in Florida. Four years before Wuornos, the state executed Judy Buenoano (aka Judias Welty) for the murders of her husband, her son, her fiancé, and a boyfriend.

MOST FAMOUS HARLEY-DAVIDSON ENTHUSIAST

While Florida is only middling in per capita ownership of motorcycles (it ranked twenty-fourth in 2011), motorcycle culture is evident throughout the state, from Bike Week in Daytona in the spring to the Saint Pete Beach BikeFest in November. Florida's year-round warm weather and lack of a helmet law mean that motorcyclists can let their freak flags fly pretty much any weekend they want. Many suburbs are assaulted every Saturday morning by the blast of Harley-Davidson exhaust pipes, as retired accountants and schoolteachers fire up their Electra Glides, tie on their bandanas, don their fading leathers, and cycle around the neighborhoods pretending to be twenty again.

The archetype of the aging Harley-Davidson enthusiast and an icon of Florida motorcycle culture was Bruce Rossmeyer, late of Ormond Beach, owner of a dozen or so Harley dealerships in Florida and four other states and one of the largest Harley-Davidson dealers in the nation. His successful business empire left him free to ride in motorcycle events all over the world, and he was on his way to an event in Thermopolis, Wyoming, when a pickup truck made a left turn into Rossmeyer and his Harley. He was declared dead at the scene at age sixty-six.

MOST SUCCESSFUL HIGH SCHOOL DROPOUT

Kentucky-born Johnny Depp settled with his family in Florida when Depp was seven years old. The family bounced around Florida before landing in Miramar (near Miami), and once his parents divorced, Depp dropped out of high school to pursue a career as a rock musician. His effort to return to school was rebuffed by the principal, who apparently felt that he had a better chance of succeeding as a rock star than as a high school student.

Depp's musical career was a nonstarter. He moved to Los Angeles and supported himself working numerous odd jobs. A turning point was a chance meeting with Nicolas Cage, who urged Depp to pursue an acting career. His first film role was a bit part in *A Nightmare on Elm Street.* By the late 1980s, he was a TV "teen idol" for his role in the television series *21 Jump Street.* Then in 1990, he rose to movie stardom in the Tim Burton film *Edward Scissorhands* and ever since has enjoyed a reputation as one of America's most talented and versatile actors.

Today, Depp is best known to moviegoers as Captain Jack Sparrow in the *Pirates of the Caribbean* franchise, a role that has netted Depp hundreds of millions of dollars, a great deal of which has been frittered away on his extravagant lifestyle—a 156-foot yacht with a monthly maintenance cost of $350,000, a vast collection of classic guitars, dozens of pricey residences (including a private four-island property in the Bahamas and an entire hamlet in the south of France), his collection of expensive and quixotic art, and numerous other items of conspicuous consumption. One persistent rumor is that Depp spends $30,000 a month on wine. Not bad for a high school dropout from Miramar.

On the other hand, Depp has evidently been in a deep financial crisis since 2017, when rumors of an impending bankruptcy first circulated. Today, the yacht, several of the properties, and a miscellany of other personal goods are for sale and his staff of forty (total payroll: $300,000 a month) has been pared. He is currently suing his former business managers on the grounds that they mismanaged his funds. His managers say that his extravagances are to blame.

NATIONAL HIDE-AND-SEEK CHAMPION, 1999

One Florida-born (Merritt Island, 1966) murderer who plea-bargained his way out of a death sentence is Eric Robert Rudolph, the "Olympic Park Bomber," who killed one person and injured 111 when he detonated a bomb in Atlanta, Georgia, during the 1996 Olympic Games to protest, he said, the Games' "global socialism agenda." Between 1996 and 1998, Rudolph was responsible for a string of bombings targeted at gay communities and abortion clinics. In 1998, he headed off into the woods of western North Carolina and spent five years as one of the FBI's Ten Most Wanted Fugitives.

I spent six weeks in a cabin in the Nantahala Gorge in the fall of 1999, and everywhere I went, there were reminders that Rudolph was hiding out somewhere in the North Carolina mountains. Every gas station, gift shop, and convenience store sported a poster announcing a million-dollar reward for information leading to his arrest, and yet despite this he remained at large, living off the land, successfully evading a massive federal manhunt for more than two years. No one doubted that he had been abetted in this evasion by local people who admired his pluck, politics, and righteous defiance of the feds. One rough-looking fellow at an Andrews gas station even sported a T-shirt that read ERIC ROBERT RUDOLPH: WESTERN NORTH CAROLINA HIDE-AND-SEEK CHAMPION, 1998–1999. He was arrested in Murphy, North Carolina, in 2003, and in 2005 he agreed to a plea bargain that traded the death penalty for four life sentences.

MOST FAMOUS THEORETICAL PHYSICIST

John Archibald Wheeler was born in Jacksonville in 1911, was educated at Johns Hopkins University, published his first scientific paper at the age of nineteen, completed his doctorate at age twenty-two, studied in Copenhagen under Niels Bohr, and went on to become one of America's premier theoretical physicists. In 1941, Wheeler was asked by Arthur Compton to join the Manhattan Project, the top secret US scientific effort to build an atomic weapon, and Wheeler made numerous major contributions to that effort. After the Manhattan Project work was completed, he returned to Princeton University, where he continued to teach basic physics to freshman and sophomores and to supervise many PhD dissertations, among them the dissertations of Richard Feynman, Kip Thorne, and several others of equivalent stature. He was also a marvelous science popularizer who was adept at explaining deep scientific concepts in terms laypeople could understand. His 1994 book *At Home in the Universe* remains one of the finest examples of popular science writing ever produced.

BEST-KNOWN WAR HERO (OR SHOULD BE)

More than a thousand Floridians died in the Second World War, among them Tampa's Ernest "Boots" Thomas, Jr. Boots was the leader of the six Marines pictured in Joe Rosenthal's famous photograph as they raised the American flag on Mount Suribachi during the Battle of Iwo Jima. The flag raising was on February 23, 1945, and Thomas was awarded the Navy Cross for his heroism—posthumously, since he was killed on March 3 by enemy rifle fire. One week shy of his twenty-first birthday at the time of death, he was buried on Iwo Jima in the Fifth Marine Division cemetery, then exhumed and reburied in Monticello, near Tallahassee.

FIRST CIVIL RIGHTS MARTYR

Possibly the most important development immediately following the Second World War was President Truman's Executive Order 9981 that abolished racial discrimination in the US Armed Forces. Ironically, it was the military—not the schools, not public transportation, not the churches—that first banned racial discrimination. And if white and black men could stand shoulder to shoulder to fight Nazis or Communists, then surely they could eat at the same lunch counters, go to the same schools, or sit beside one another on the bus.

History reminds us that it was a long, arduous, and at times violent struggle to get to these obvious conclusions. Among many who made the ultimate sacrifice in the cause of civil rights stands Harry Tyson Moore, an African American man born in Suwannee County (near Lake City in northern Florida). Moore founded the first branch of the NAACP in Brevard County in 1934, was instrumental in increasing African American voter registration to the point at which Florida had the largest black electorate of any state in the South, and he worked to get black teachers equal pay in the schools. In 1946, he and his wife Harriette were fired from their public school jobs because of their civil rights activism, and on Christmas night in 1951, their home in Mims was bombed and the two were killed. No suspects were ever arrested, and it was not until forensic work was done in 2005–06 that the probable killers were identified as four members of the local Ku Klux Klan, all long dead by the time the investigation was completed. The Moores were the first members of the NAACP to be murdered for their civil rights activism, and in a book on their murders, Harry Moore is described as America's first civil-rights martyr by Ben Green in his book *Before His Time: The Untold Story of Harry T. Moore*. Alas, they were by no means the last to die in the cause of civil rights, not in Florida and not elsewhere in the nation, either.

PART FOUR

THE NATURAL ENVIRONMENT, IF YOU WANT TO CALL IT THAT

13

STORMY WEATHER

WHAT PEOPLE SAY they like most about living in the Sunshine State is the weather, yet for half the year—June 1 to November 30—it is hurricane season, where the hot, humid days of summer and fall are punctuated with cyclonic storms of almost indescribable ferocity. At these times, the weather is a potent and sometimes lethal adversary.

All of the eastern Atlantic coast and the Gulf Coast is at risk, of course, everything from Bangor, Maine, all the way around to Brownsville, Texas. Florida has more than six hundred miles of exposure on the Atlantic side and another eight hundred miles of exposure on the Gulf Coast side, so we are more vulnerable to hurricanes than any other state.

Hurricanes have swept across the Florida peninsula for millions of years, but only for the last century have there been lots of people and property in the way. In 1900, the entire population of the state was a little over a half million people and most of the peninsula south of the Panhandle was un-inhabited. But by 1920, the state's population had nearly doubled and hurricane vulnerability had increased, as evidenced by the Key West Hurricane of September 1919. The 1919 storm, one of the deadliest in history, crossed the Florida Keys on its way to Texas and was responsible for about eight hundred deaths, many of them passengers and crew on the ten ships that were lost at sea.

In the United States, hurricanes were not routinely given names until

1953; the exclusive use of women's names for the purpose ended in 1978. So hurricanes occurring before 1953 are usually identified by where they came ashore or where they did the most damage.

Another massive early-twentieth-century storm was the Great Miami Hurricane of September 1926, which devastated most of greater Miami and left nearly four hundred people dead. Resort hotels along Miami Beach were converted to temporary hospitals and morgues to treat the injured and tend to the dead. Hundreds of homes were leveled and hundreds more were damaged beyond repair. Looting broke out in the aftermath, martial law was declared, and three hundred special-duty policemen were sworn in to restore order. Even today, the hurricane is considered the fatal blow to the 1920s economic boom in South Florida and caused many banks and companies to fail, a harbinger of the Great Depression.

Soon thereafter was the so-called Okeechobee Hurricane of September 1928. This hurricane passed over Puerto Rico as a Category 5 storm and had weakened somewhat when it slammed into Palm Beach. Still, packing winds of 145 mph, the hurricane pushed up a storm surge in Lake Okeechobee that caused water to pour out of the lake and into the surrounding communities. Hundreds of square miles were flooded at depths as high as 20 feet. Some twenty-five hundred or more people drowned in the flooding, most of them African American migrant workers who were denied even a proper burial because the few available caskets were reserved for whites.

Both the Greater Miami and Okeechobee hurricanes resulted in significant improvements in local building codes and greater efforts at flood control. Among other things, these storms ushered in the one-story concrete block Florida home, a staple of vernacular residential architecture ever since.

A few of Florida's twentieth-century hurricanes were important political events, just as Katrina was in 2005. The Florida Keys Labor Day hurricane of September 1935 was a Category 5 storm that killed at least 408 people in the Keys. Particularly hard hit were three veterans' work camps on Windley and Matecumbe Keys, camps that had been established to employ veterans to complete the Overseas Highway that would connect Key West with the mainland. The camps were controversial since they had evidently been created to move the so-called Bonus Army of World War I vets as far away from Washington, DC, as possible. (The Bonus Army— perhaps nearly fifty thousand veterans, family members, and supporters, many of them out of work and destitute because of the Great Depression— marched in DC in the summer of 1932 demanding cash payment of their service "bonuses.") Storm surge as high as 20 feet swept over the low-lying islands, destroying everything. Some have said that this was the most intense hurricane ever to strike the United States, with maximum wind speeds close to 200 mph. People who lived through the storm said the winds were so strong that blowing sand literally shredded clothing from victims' bodies.

American author Ernest Hemingway moved to Key West in 1928 and was living there when the 1935 storm hit. Of the 408 confirmed dead, about 260 were veterans, and to someone with Hemingway's political views, these deaths were scandalous. In an essay for *The New Masses*, Hemingway commented that "wealthy people . . . do not come to the Florida Keys in hurricane months. . . . But veterans, especially the bonus-marching variety of veterans, are not property. They are only human beings; unsuccessful human beings; . . . and all they have to lose is their lives." Hemingway further derided the "coolie labor" the government had forced on these men, the miserable wage they were being paid ("a top wage of $45 a month"), and the obvious effort to isolate the veteran protest movement. The author demanded an answer to the question "Who sent nearly a thousand war veterans . . . to live in frame shacks on the Florida Keys in hurricane months?"

The mother of all Florida hurricanes, "The Big One," was Hurricane Andrew in August 1992. Andrew killed 44 people and inflicted some $25 billion in property damages in Florida alone. (The Bahamas and Louisiana also suffered, but they were minor compared to the devastation in Florida.) Within just Dade County (now Miami-Dade), nearly twenty-six thousand homes were destroyed and another hundred thousand suffered major damage. Homestead (outside of Miami) suffered a direct hit, and virtually all of the city's large mobile home inventory was destroyed. Looting was widespread, and the federal response to the hurricane became an issue in the 1992 presidential campaign. Democrats from then-governor

Lawton Chiles to presidential candidate Bill Clinton accused President George H. W. Bush of reacting too slowly to assist in Florida's recovery, not unlike the criticisms leveled against his son in the aftermath of Katrina (or against Donald Trump in the aftermath of Maria). Nonetheless, Bush Sr. carried Florida in the November 1992 election by more than one hundred thousand votes.

When we think of hurricane impacts, we usually think about their impacts on humans, but other species are also disrupted. Andrew smashed into the Miami MetroZoo (now Zoo Miami) and unleashed a number of non-native species that have since taken up various ecological niches in the state's ecosystem. Hurricane Andrew resulted in the introduction of the Burmese python into the Everglades, where perhaps as many as a hundred thousand of the reptiles now live. Also introduced into the Florida ecosystem by Andrew's destruction were the African sacred ibis and several species of monkeys, which escaped research labs and are now a feral presence in South Florida.

Hurricane Wilma in October 2005 crossed through the migratory paths of several species of birds, notably the chimney swift, which migrates annually from Canada to the Yucatan Peninsula and beyond. Wilma's strong winds carried the swifts as far east as western Europe, with unusual sightings of swifts in Portugal's Azore Islands and Spain's Canary Islands off the coast of Africa. A 2006 survey in Quebec suggested that the storm had reduced the population of chimney swifts by half, and apparently the species has yet to recover.

Beyond the sheer physical destruction, Hurricane Andrew had major social, political, and economic impacts on the state. The storm caused the bankruptcies of eleven insurance companies, and nearly a million Floridians lost their homeowners' coverage. Coverage has been expensive and hard to get ever since. Most policies since Andrew have very high hurricane deductibles. The hurricane rider on my current policy exempts the first ten thousand dollars in hurricane damage from coverage, and this is by no means unusual. Also, many homeowners whose insurance policies paid up used the funds to relocate elsewhere. The total population loss in Dade County in the year following the storm amounted to about thirty-two thousand people.

HURRICANES, PREPAREDNESS, AND BUILDING CODES

While most of the major hurricanes that struck Florida at least since the 1950s occasioned some renewed attention to hurricane preparedness and the development of hurricane-proof building standards, the attention was mostly local, not regional or statewide. In much of the South and certainly in Florida prior to about 1970, zoning and building codes were largely dismissed as Communist plots that threatened property rights. For most of the twentieth century (and not just in Florida), if you owned a piece of land, the law said you could build pretty much anything you wanted on it, by whatever means and material at your disposal; building codes and standards and zoning laws, to the extent they existed at all, were very much a matter of local control. So while a hurricane-stricken city in one location might decide to implement a wind-safety standard for new construction, an equally vulnerable community twenty miles on down the coast might decide not to. Building standards were a patchwork of local regulations.

Hurricanes in South Florida in the 1940s and 1950s led to the development of the South Florida Building Code, which was adopted by Broward and Dade Counties in 1957. Based on the so-called Uniform Building Code in use in most of the western and some of the northern states at the time, the South Florida code was intended specifically to make structures strong enough to withstand hurricane-force winds. The document was revolutionary in that it was the first building code based on wind-loading engineering designs and on a specific formula to calculate loadings from hurricane winds, taking both the wind speed and height above ground into account. (The "wind load" is simply the force on a structure resulting from the impact of wind.) But this code was adopted in only two South Florida counties (Dade and Broward), and in Broward, it was not mandatory for all jurisdictions until 1976.

Hurricanes of the 1960s and 1970s led to the development of the state minimum building code, which, as the term implies, was intended to establish *minimum* standards, not maximally safe standards. Still, a 1974 law requiring local adoption and enforcement of the minimum code was a big step forward in developing statewide standards and breaking the control of local jurisdictions on their building codes.

A key issue in all discussions of building codes up to 1993 was the composition of local appeals boards and how the members of those boards would be selected. This was a struggle pitting technocrats who represented the engineering, architectural, and related professions against Florida's "good old boys" who were accustomed to running local governments and telling people what to do—a classic Old vs. New Florida confrontation. To accommodate all interests, the local boards were often improbably large, with byzantine rules about who could vote and who couldn't and how new representatives would be chosen.

Prior to 1993, then, there were at least some "hurricane protection" measures built into the local building codes of some Florida jurisdictions, but while they may have been appropriate to the construction practices of the time, they were designed reactively and only took new construction techniques into account after big hurricanes revealed major failures. Systematic review and upgrading of building codes statewide awaited the destruction caused by Andrew.

When Andrew struck South Florida in the fall of 1992, what was considered at the time to be the best hurricane-safe building code in the United States, the South Florida Building Code, was exposed as a complete failure. Many of the 150,000 homes that were destroyed or suffered major storm damage from Andrew had been built well after the South Florida Building Code had been implemented, and those had generally fared no better than structures built earlier. A long series of lawsuits against the state ensued, and in response, then-governor Lawton Chiles established the Florida Building Codes Study Commission with the charge to review and assess all the building codes then on the books and make recommendations for changes. The result was the Uniform Florida Building Code enacted in 2000 and implemented everywhere in Florida by 2002.

Scarcely any aspect of home building was ignored by the new code, right down to the proper procedure for nailing asphalt shingles into plywood roofs. Gable ends of structures were required to have additional bracing to prevent collapse. Wood-frame walls were required to be braced with a complete layer of plywood subsheathing. Roof joists and wall-to-wall and wall-to-foundation intersections were to be strengthened with metal connectors, effectively making the structure a single complete unit (as opposed to multiple components simply nailed together). And there were enhanced nailing requirements for roof shingles and other building components.

The Florida hurricanes of 2004 and 2005 showed that the 2002 building standards prevented most catastrophic structural failures, but some building components continued to fail. The blue tarps covering many roofs throughout the state subsequent to the 2004 hurricanes attested to the continuing failure of roof coverings in hurricane-force winds. A lot of vinyl siding was also blown away; windows, entry doors, and garage doors also tended to fail; and many of the state's ubiquitous aluminum pool enclosures (known locally as lanais) were reduced to piles of rubble. Thus, a number of new building requirements have been implemented since 2004, but until Irma in 2017, no large storm had come along to test them. Despite the shortcomings, building damage from the 2004 hurricanes was dramatically lower for structures built since 2002 than for older structures, and the property damage from Irma was fairly minimal.

Readiness has been improved in other ways, too, as a result of the 2004 drubbing. Back then, hurricane news arrived mainly via radio and television, but now the state has an extensive social media platform that will send text alerts to every cell phone within range of Florida cell phone antennas. The power companies have also invested heavily in hardening the grid, clearing overhanging vegetation, installing monitors, and upgrading poles, transformers, and other equipment. Many local jurisdictions have embarked on a program of undergrounding their utilities, a pricey but highly effective measure. Because of the 2004 power outages, which lasted as long as a week in some areas, gas stations with eight or more pumps are now required to have emergency generators; many smaller stations and most grocery stores now have them, too. So posthurricane access to food, water, and fuel is not as problematic as it used to be. There is also a frenzy of hurricane-readiness reporting at the start of each hurricane season, and homeowners are urged to stock up on essentials "just in case."

By any measure, Floridians are safer from hurricanes now than ever before. Advances in meteorology often give people weeks to evacuate or prepare; evacuations are well planned and relatively orderly; those who decide to "shelter in place" do so in structures demonstrably safer than they were even a few decades ago. These days, no one is caught off guard by an approaching storm. Much the opposite seems to be true: the days and days of hurricane warnings and media coverage prior to the arrival of a big storm seem to create a "cry wolf" boredom, almost a sense of disbelief, most of all when the storm fails to live up to the dire prestorm admonitions (as was the case for Hurricane Irma). Still, for all the advances in meteorology, preparedness, and safer building codes, it is hard to drive up and down the coastal areas of the state and not be reminded of Tim Dorsey's stark conclusion in *Florida Roadkill,* that here "we have The New Florida, underplanned, overbuilt and ripe for a killer hurricane that'll knock that giant geodesic dome at Epcot down the turnpike like a golf ball. . . ."

14

MONKEYS, SHARKS, BEARS, GATORS, AND SNAKES

SACRED IBISES AND feral monkeys may sound pretty harmless, but in fact they are not. The sacred ibis is native to sub-Saharan Africa. The big birds entered the Florida ecosystem when five of them escaped from Miami MetroZoo during Hurricane Andrew and their numbers gradually increased in South Florida and the Everglades (although the population has since been eliminated as the result of an aggressive state eradication campaign). They will eat virtually anything and are one of only a few birds that prey on the eggs and nestlings of other birds, including gulls, terns, cormorants, pelicans, and gannets. Several of these are imperiled species, and predation by the sacred ibis was considered a cause of mortality.

A population of feral rhesus macaques has existed along the Silver River in Silver Springs since 1938, when tour operator Colonel Tooey released a number of the primates to enhance his Jungle Cruise tour. (A popular local legend, that several other macaques were released during the filming of the movie *Tarzan Finds a Son!* is false, as no macaques were used in the filming). Several other monkey species, for example, the common squirrel monkey, the vervet monkey, and a few others, were released by Hurricane Andrew (or through other sources) and have established breeding populations around the state. The famous Mystery Monkey of Tampa Bay, a thirty-pound macaque living in and around Saint Petersburg, was captured and placed in a zoo in 2012. He was one of about a thousand feral monkeys that were captured as of 2013, seven hundred of which tested positive for the Herpes B virus. Accordingly, the monkeys are considered by wildlife officials to be a possible public health threat, although one can only speculate about the methods of transmission.

However harmful the sacred ibises and feral monkeys might be, their threat to human life is pretty minimal compared to the state's unfriendly native fauna: specifically, sharks, bears, alligators, and snakes. Florida has always been the shark-bite capital of the United States. One Florida county, Volusia County, accounts for more than a third of the thousand or so shark attacks that have occurred in Florida since records were first kept in the late nineteenth century. The county's New Smyrna Beach, just south of Daytona Beach, is notorious for shark bites, and in at least one source is listed as the third most dangerous beach in the world. In September 2016, three different surfers on New Smyrna Beach were attacked by sharks in a single three-hour period. The same day, a surfer at Indian Harbor Beach, about seventy-five miles south of New Smyrna Beach, was also bitten. *Surfline* magazine describes Volusia County as "one of the sharkiest places on earth." But shark attacks have been reported in all the state's coastal waters.

The year 2016 set a record for shark-human interactions, with 32 recorded shark bites between March 4 and December 27. As in all years, the vast majority of these "shark attacks" were unprovoked and nonlethal. Since records were first kept (there are some records that go back to 1845), 83 percent of all shark "incidents" in the state were unprovoked; of the unprovoked attacks, 96 percent were nonfatal. In fact, the last fatal shark attack to have occurred in Florida was on February 3, 2010, when thirty-eight-year-old kitesurfer Stephen Howard Schafer was surrounded by sharks and bitten multiple times while in the water a quarter-mile offshore. Prior to Schafer's unfortunate demise, the previous fatal attack in Florida had been in 2005, when a fourteen-year-old Louisiana girl was attacked while swimming off the Florida Panhandle. Globally, we average maybe four or five fatal shark attacks a year, although there were thirteen worldwide in 2011 and ten in 2013.

Most shark attacks are about as serious as a dog bite. Given the size and power of the average Atlantic or Gulf Coast shark, one can assume that most of these bites are motivated more by curiosity than by hunger or lethal intentions. Still, it is not unusual for bite victims to come up missing fingers, toes, and limbs. In 2001, an eight-year-old boy had his arm ripped off by a shark while swimming near Pensacola; in 2005, a sixteen-year-old boy had his leg almost fully severed in a shark attack near Pensacola; and nearly every year, there are attack victims whose limbs remain attached but are missing large chunks of flesh and have wounds that require hundreds of stitches to close.

The University of Florida Museum of Natural History has a web page where the comparative risk of death by shark attack is analyzed. This museum is the national repository for shark-bite data and the keeper of the International Shark Attack File, so its data are highly credible. Their web page (floridamuseum.ufl.edu/shark-attacks/) enumerates eighteen "things more likely to kill you than sharks." You are, for example, twice as likely to die from an alligator bite than a shark attack, twice as likely to be killed by a bear, 50 times more likely to be killed by lightning, 1,000 times more likely to die in a bicycling accident, 132 times more likely to drown at the beach, and 390 times more likely to be killed in a boating accident. Still, if you are enjoying Florida's coastal waters and notice a large, dark, torpedo-shaped fish coming your way, get out of the water. There is little consolation in knowing you are at greater risk from a lightning bolt when a six-foot bull shark is gnawing at your leg.

Florida's black-bear population has also been in the news for its now-regular appearances in suburban backyards. The bears have suffered habitat loss amounting to twenty acres per *hour* due to suburban development for the last several years and have compensated by reclaiming the suburbs as their new habitat. Although bear sightings have been reported all over the state, there are significant clusters near Tallahassee, north of Orlando in the Ocala National Forest, and in South Florida along the southwestern coast. The big bears have been found lumbering through the developments of suburban Longwood and Winter Springs, in rural Mount Dora, even in downtown Orlando two or three blocks from City Hall and on the campus of the University of Central Florida.

Once considered a threatened species that nearly disappeared in the 1970s, the Florida black bear, aided by aggressive conservation efforts, has made a stunning comeback—so much so that the Florida Fish and Wildlife Conservation Commission (FWC) authorized a very controversial black bear hunt in 2015, the first legal bear hunt in the Sunshine State since 1994. In commenting on the state-sanctioned hunt, Carl Hiaasen posed the kind of question that can only be asked in Florida: "What's the point of saving a native creature from extinction if we can't start shooting the darn things again?" That, Hiaasen said, is the "unspoken philosophy" of the FWC, "which after two decades of protecting the black bear has decided that the time has come to open fire." One can grant the irony and still acknowledge that culling the herd is a common and well-understood principle of wildlife management, and while bear hunters in 2015 may well have outnumbered the bears, only about three hundred bears were taken out of a total population of three or four thousand. The hunt was very unpopular, and a 2016 repeat was canceled because of public opposition.

In 2017, about a dozen animal-welfare groups petitioned to have the Florida black bear placed on the Federal Endangered Species list, but the US Fish and Wildlife Service denied the request because there are more black bears roaming around Florida today than at any time in the past century. Besides, the bear is already a protected species under Florida law. The ruling was positive news to the FWC, which sees the Florida black bear comeback as a huge success story and a tribute to the state's conservation efforts.

At least one Florida county, Seminole, has responded to the bear-human interaction problem by passing bear-friendly ordinances, chief of which is the requirement for bear-resistant trash cans. While Florida black bears are omnivores, they show a striking preference for the contents of suburban garbage cans. Thus, using bear-proof trash cans is a principal means of keeping the creatures out of the neighborhoods. Related measures are not keeping pet food outdoors where bears can get at it, limiting or eliminating bird feeders (which bears are adept at raiding), keeping ripe fruit and vegetables from home gardens picked so bears are not attracted, and regular and thorough cleaning of outdoor grills. (Apparently, the odor of char-grilled meat is irresistible.)

Black bears look cute and cuddly, and every time a big bear wanders through suburbia, large crowds of onlookers materialize. But bears are perceptive and intelligent creatures that quickly learn to associate food with people, at which point they can only be controlled by euthanasia. They are also large creatures, males averaging about three hundred pounds. So in confrontations with humans or pets, the bears usually come out on top. On the other hand, they stand no chance against automobiles. Car encounters are the bears' number-one cause of death in Florida.

National Geographic reported in 2014 that "black bear attacks are on the rise in Florida." The precipitating event that caught the magazine's attention was a bear attack on a Seminole County woman. The woman had seen as many as five bears rooting through her trash cans, and when she went into the garage to investigate, a bear bit her on the head and dragged her outdoors.

To explain the increase in bear attacks, the *National Geographic* article mentioned two factors: more bears and more humans. As noted, the bear population has made a remarkable recovery since the 1970s, and of course Florida's suburbanization and population growth continue apace. The inevitable result is more interaction between the two species. These days, "bear calls" to the FWC number more than six thousand annually.

Florida began keeping statistics on bear-human interactions in 1976. Despite the large and increasing number of these interactions, few are injurious and even fewer are fatal (less than one per year on average). In contrast, there are more than two hundred bears run over and killed by cars each year. So the lethality ratio (human killing of bears versus bear killings of humans) is well more than 200:1. In 2015, when bears were legally hunted for the first time in two decades, the ratio exceeded 500:1. So bears are not nearly as dangerous to us as we are to them. That having been said, a recent bear-car collision in . left one bear and three humans dead and four more humans seriously injured.

It is often mistakenly asserted that bears come into suburbia foraging for food because they have run out of "natural" food. This is not so. The woodland areas of Florida have natural bear food in abundance. But bears are smart enough to be lazy: there is no naturally occurring source of bear food that has anywhere near the concentrated caloric content of an average American garbage can. They don't come into the neighborhoods because their natural food sources are scarce but because suburban food sources are abundant and calorie-rich.

Bears are hibernating animals, so their quest for food is most intense in the few months before they hibernate and right after their hibernation ends. In between, the average Florida black bear will consume about five thousand calories a day (about twice the daily human caloric intake). As hibernation approaches, the caloric intake will shoot up to more than twenty thousand calories a day, bears will spend up to eighteen hours a day foraging for food, and they are not at all particular about what they eat.

Bears are a greater threat to dogs than to humans, in Florida and elsewhere. Instances of bears attacking and harming pet dogs are common and have been reported from the Florida Panhandle to Orange City on Florida's east coast to inland Orlando to Golden Gate near Naples.

The bear situation in Central Florida was the topic of a lengthy 2014 article in the *Orlando Sentinel*. The piece opened, "They lumber down the street as if they owned the place—and who are we to argue?" As a major international tourist destination, Orlando can scarcely afford to have bears "lumbering down the streets," but perhaps the *Sentinel* can be forgiven a bit of journalistic excess. After all, the Orlando zip code area 32779 has led the state in "bear calls" every year since 2008. "They may dig for leftovers in a neighbor's garbage, then deposit that same meal in your backyard. [Bear poop is always mentioned as one of the creature's most annoying traits.] They'll steal the dog's food, pick fruit trees clean and, if given half a chance, sneak into your garage to sample the steaks in the freezer. Maybe top it off with a few pints of Häagen-Dazs. They're also known to enjoy a beer or two—or 18—then sleep them off in someone's driveway."

Granted, bears have been spotted in Orlando area trees, trash cans, porches, and even swimming pools, where they have been known to shred screened-in pool enclosures. They have been observed wrestling with one another in peoples' yards, stealing Halloween candy, breaking into cars, attacking pets, killing chickens, even raiding home freezers. And they are very good at scaring the bejesus out of homeowners. But for all that, at least so far, the bears remain more a nuisance than a threat and various bear-proofing measures keep the nuisance to a minimum.

The FWC has an outstanding website dealing with all aspects of the

Florida brown bear (most of the factual information in the preceding discussion is taken from their web page). Among the many entries is a passage telling you what to do if you encounter a bear at close range:

> Remain standing upright. Speak to the bear in a calm, assertive voice. Back up slowly toward a secure area, be sure you are leaving the bear a clear escape route. Avoid direct eye contact—bears and other animals may view this as aggressive behavior. Stop and hold your ground if your movement away seems to irritate instead of calm the bear.

Or you can just run like hell and hope the critter loses interest!

Alligators are everywhere in Florida. Any open body of water will be home to one or more of the large prehistoric reptiles. They turn up in the water hazards of golf courses, in the retention ponds of suburban developments, even occasionally in backyard swimming pools. There are thought to be about 1.3 million gators in Florida, about one for every sixteen persons, and there are very few Floridians who have not seen a gator in the wild. Serious unprovoked gator attacks have increased along with the state's population, but fatal attacks remain rare. Still, more than twenty people have been killed by gators in the state since 1973 and about four hundred gator bites have been reported in the same period. The state averages about eight or nine serious unprovoked gator bites each year.

The most recent gator tragedy in the state involved two-year-old Lane Graves and his family, the toddler who was grabbed and bitten by an alligator at Disney World on June 14, 2016. Disney World was certainly not "The Happiest Place on Earth" that day for poor Lane and his parents, who announced about a month after the attack that they would not be suing Disney after all. The terms of the settlement were not disclosed, but local personal-injury attorneys were certain the case was worth something in the tens of millions. Lane's parents used some of the settlement money to establish a foundation created in the child's memory. In the aftermath it was revealed that Disney had captured and killed some 240 nuisance gators from its vast acreage since Disney World opened in 1971.

Alligators (and crocodiles) have the strongest bites of any animals on earth. A large gator can bite with about three thousand pounds of force per square inch. Even the mighty lion only bites with about a thousand pounds of force; humans weigh in at a paltry two hundred pounds of force. Thus, tales of humans wriggling loose from a committed alligator bite are almost certainly false, for example, that of the ten-year-old Florida girl who claimed that she was able to pry an alligator off her left leg. According to experts at Florida State University, this was "very unlikely." "If that alligator wanted to hold on, not much could have stopped it."

There is no end to the bizarre Florida gator stories. One of my favorites concerns the twenty-one-year-old Lakeland man who ran into a lake to avoid capture by the police. A waiting gator bit off three-quarters of his left forearm. There was also a burglary suspect in South Florida who attempted to elude capture by jumping into a pond with signs posted: DANGER: LIVE ALLIGATORS! The suspect was killed by one of them. Then there was sixty-nine-year-old Sandra Fristi, a resident of the Tampa Bay area, who got up from her computer, went into the kitchen for a break, and encountered an eight-footer. The gator had pushed through Fristi's screen door, strolled through the living room, down a hallway, and into the kitchen. In the same vein, in 2016, a Plant City man called 911 when he discovered that a nine-footer had climbed the stairs to his front door and was trying to get in.

There were fatal gator attacks in Florida in 1973, 1977, 1978, 1984, 1985, 1987, 1988, 1993, 1997, 2001, 2003, 2004, 2005, 2006, 2007, 2015, and 2016. We don't get a fatal attack every year, but we do get them most years, and in some years we get more than one. Floridians who have died from alligator attacks range in age from two to eighty-one. The eighty-one-year-old was Robert Steele, who was out walking his dog by a Sanibel canal when an eleven-foot gator attacked and bit off his leg. Police think he was trying to protect his dog when his leg got in the way. Steele bled to death before help could be summoned.

The largest gator on record in Florida measured fourteen feet three inches from snout to tail and weighed in at 654 pounds. A shorter but heavier gator was just under fourteen feet but weighed 1,043 pounds. In 2016, two hunters reported killing a gator near Okeechobee that they

said was nearly fifteen feet long but the measurement was not confirmed. The monster gators are always males. Female gators are shorter and
lighter. The largest female ever recorded was 10 feet long and weighed
over 300 pounds.

One of the first natural histories of the American alligator, *The Alligator's Life History,* was published in 1935 by Edward Avery McIlhenny, son
of Edmund McIlhenny, the inventor of Tabasco brand hot pepper sauce.
In the book, McIlhenny claims to have cavorted in Louisiana lakes and
rivers with alligators as long as twenty feet and also claims to have killed
an alligator that measured nineteen feet—some five feet longer than the
longest Florida gator on record. Is it possible that Louisiana gators are just
that much bigger than Florida gators? Or that gators back in the 1930s grew
much bigger than gators these days? Or do we conclude instead that old
Ned McIlhenny, like storytellers everywhere, was not above embellishing
his story for dramatic effect?

McIlhenny's analysis of the gut contents of gators he killed did firmly
establish that the American alligator will eat practically anything: fish,
frogs, birds, turtles, snakes, cats, dogs, pigs, small deer, rodents, goats, and
even other gators. Large gators regularly snack on little gators; indeed,
gator cannibalism wipes out about a tenth of each year's crop. What any particular gator eats depends on what is available in its environment, and if
that happens to include Fido, you can kiss Fido goodbye. Alligator prey is
typically swallowed whole and digested by stomach acids that are as strong
as lemon juice. Most prey items are completely digested within twenty-four
hours. (In addition to meat, gators will also eat fruit when it is available.)

No account of Florida's alligators would be complete without some comment on the immense concrete gators often featured in old Florida tourist
attractions. The record is the 220-foot-long "Swampy" at the Jungle Adven-
tures alligator park on Highway 50 near Christmas. There was also a
124-foot-long concrete gator at the now-defunct Jungleland Zoo in Kissimmee, which held a Land Rover in its mouth. But the most famous of the
state's ersatz cement alligators is the gaping mouth that greets visitors to
Gatorland, a photo of which appears in the beginning of this book.

Herpetologists have identified about fifty species of snakes that inhabit
various parts of Florida, including all of the nation's venomous snakes: cop-

perheads, cottonmouths, coral snakes, and three different rattler species (the canebrake rattler, the eastern diamondback, and the pygmy rattler, all highly venomous). All these are indigenous species, and I'll confine my comments to them. Invasive snake species, in particular the green anaconda and the Burmese python ("the snake that's eating Florida"), are discussed later.

Snakebites in Florida are common. More than three hundred of them occur each year, and those are just bites from venomous species that are called in to poison control. Most are not serious but a few are. Shands Hospital at the University of Florida sees at least one snakebite case a week during the summer months and has seen as many as three cases in a single day. Most snakebites occur when people are trying to kill or capture the animals and are therefore self-defensive bites.

Nationally, there are seven or eight thousand snakebite cases each year, of which less than a half dozen or so are fatal. In most cases, a snakebite is about as painful and about as serious as being stung by a wasp. Since the 1940s, when records were first kept, there have only been seven fatal snakebites in Florida, most recently four-year-old Brayden Bullard, bitten in 2014 by a rattlesnake in his family garden while he was planting watermelons. Poor Brayden hung on for about two weeks after the bite but then succumbed. In 2006, Inocenio Hernandez-Hernandez of Bonita Springs died from the bite of an eastern coral snake. And in 2005, Joe Guidry, the Putnam County fire marshal, died of a rattlesnake bite. He shot at the snake, the snake slithered under a shed, and Guidry was bitten as he reached under the shed to extricate the rattler. Another fatal rattlesnake bite occurred in Lakewood in 2000. There were no fatal snakebites in Florida in the 1990s but a twenty-two-year-old Ocala man died of a eastern diamondback rattler bite in 1989. Snakebite fatalities were also reported in 1955 and 1943.

In 2016, CBS News reported that nationally, snakebite cases were "on the rise" and that Florida was a prime location for these encounters. The study was based on snakebite cases involving children, of which there are more than thirteen hundred each year. Snakebites of kids have been reported in all fifty states and the District of Columbia, but Florida and Texas account for about a quarter of the total. About two-thirds of the bites involve boys. A surprising number involve kids wearing flip-flops and playing in high grass. The increasing number of snakebites nationally was attributed to extensive encroachment by humans on the snakes' natural habitat.

Most snakebites are the result of backyard encounters between homeowners seeking to rid themselves of snakes and snakes that want to stay. But a surprising number of them take place in nurseries and garden centers. In 2006, a pigmy rattler bit a woman at an Ocala home-improvement store. She was moving plants around in the Lowe's garden center when a pigmy rattler took offense. A number of similar incidents have been reported at Walmart and Home Depot stores. Most garden-center bites involve the pigmy rattler because they are usually only about a foot long and sit in tight coils that are not easy to detect.

Snakes seem to make Florida people do stupid things. Consider the Bostwick guy who had a little too much to drink, pulled an eastern diamondback out of its cage, and tried to kiss it, evidently to impress his drinking buddies. The rattler bit the man on the tongue and sent him to the hospital in critical condition. Or the six-year-old Kendall boy who captured a coral snake and was tossing it back and forth with a friend when the snake took offense and bit. Or the Sebring woman who allowed her pet snake to bite her one-year-old daughter as a way to introduce the child to snakes and "teach her a lesson." It was, she said, a "teaching opportunity." The woman, Chantelle St. Laurent, videotaped the entire episode and posted the video to her Facebook account.

Snakes will also bite cats and dogs if cornered or threatened, and these bites are as unpleasant for Fido as they would be for you or me. Alas, there appear to be no statistics on snakebites of species other than humans, but one Florida vet with twenty-two years of experience handling snakebite cases at the UF veterinary school estimates about a 20 percent fatality rate for dogs bitten by the eastern diamondback.

Specialists in the treatment of human snakebites joke that a snakebite is the product of testosterone and alcohol (one of the world's most lethal mixtures). "Snakes don't go after people for a meal," said one. "They're biting in self-defense." Luckily, even serious bites by venomous snakes are rarely fatal, in part because antivenins are very effective and widely available. The critical issue in these cases is how quickly the victim gets care.

Neither testosterone nor alcohol were involved when Sneads resident Frank Shelfer was bitten four times in a row by an eastern diamondback when he attempted to put a stick on his woodpile. Authorities speculate that he inadvertently stepped on the critter. Shelfer was helicoptered to a nearby hospital in critical condition with four bite wounds on his left ankle and foot. The poor man was bitten just after he had gone outside to get a breath of fresh air for the first time since gall bladder surgery the previous Friday.

Theresa May, the post-Brexit prime minister of the United Kingdom, once said, "Like Indiana Jones, I don't like snakes—though that might lead some to ask why I'm in politics." Unlike the prolific and deadly political snakes that have thrived on both sides of the Atlantic, the vast majority of snakes are harmless if unthreatened and quite helpful in keeping mice, rat, cockroach, and other pest populations under control. Ophidiophobia, the fear of snakes, is widespread but usually not justified. "Politicophobia," the fear or dislike of politicians, is rampant, understandable, and entirely justified.

15

ROADKILL

THE NORTH CAROLINA sociologist John Shelton Reed once said that you knew you were in the South when most of the roadkill was armadillos. The ability to identify roadkill after days of decomposition in the hot sun and incessant nibbling by the ever-present buzzards and vultures is a mark of the true southerner. Where I grew up (Indiana), roadkill specimens were described as "sail cats," a reference to the resemblance of flattened, desiccated critters to Frisbees. Another common euphemism is "highway pizza." While the topic may strike some as offensive, roadkill is an integral part of Florida's natural environment.

Roadkill may seem a lighthearted topic, and I will treat it as such, but death by automobile is a serious issue for many wild species. Wildlife biologists guess, for example, that there are fewer than 250 Florida panthers left, but as many as twenty-three of these beautiful cats are killed by cars each year, along with more than a couple hundred bears and God knows how many deer, raccoons, dogs, cats, porcupines, and other species. Matthew Aresco, a wildlife biologist, says, "In general, roadways across the U.S. have a tremendous negative impact on wildlife populations from very small animals like frogs and salamanders all the way up to large carnivores like bears and panthers." In the eastern Florida Panhandle, death by car is thought to have been responsible at least in part for the extinction of the eastern indigo snake. So roadkill is another example of the lethal bending of the natural world to satisfy human will.

The critters do extract a measure of revenge. There are an estimated 1.5 million wildlife-vehicle collisions in the United States each year serious enough to warrant an insurance report. About 200 people die in these collisions annually, another 29,000 are injured, and property damage runs to more than a billion dollars. Deer-car collisions are especially lethal to both deer and humans, so much so that the timid white-tailed deer is now responsible for more human deaths than alligators, sharks, bears, snakes, and all species of insect combined. As a cause of human mortality, the white-tailed deer is our most lethal species.

An article in *Newsweek* magazine posed the fundamental roadkill question: "Is It OK to Eat Roadkill?" The story appeared in *Newsweek* online on June 23, 2017, and reported that according to the Humane Society of America, the roadkill toll on American highways is about a million critters *per day.* Most of the dead are small creatures such as squirrels, rabbits, possums, and armadillos, and the vast majority of these collisions are not serious enough to generate an insurance claim. The most common large creature killed by cars is the deer, but here in Florida, there are also bears, panthers, and alligators in the yearly kill. So the daily toll leaves literally millions of pounds of fresh meat just lying there on the highway. Why should such an abundance of protein go to waste?

Of course, roadkill doesn't really go to waste. It forms an ecological niche into which a number of species fit. Buzzards and vultures subsist almost entirely on dead creatures and are often seen dragging roadkill carcasses off to the side of the road to be eaten in comparative safety. But eagles, crows, ravens, and even hawks will also sample roadkill from time to time, as will foxes, possums, and a variety of carnivorous insects. A rotting carcass is also ideal habitat for maggots. Florida drivers are sometimes astonished at how quickly even a relatively large dead carcass disappears from the roadside. One day there is a crushed pit bull off to the side of the road and the next day it is gone.

But what about food for humans? Could roadkill become a staple protein source in the average American diet?

Most people squirm when pondering this question and are squeamish about eating small mammals that have been run over by cars. This overlooks that at one time, rabbits, squirrels, and even raccoons and possums were common fare on the American table. A few classic dishes such as Kentucky burgoo or Brunswick stew demand squirrel or rabbit even today, and sometimes this demand is satisfied with road-killed animals. Really, does it matter that the rabbit in your Brunswick stew was run over by a car or shotgunned in a nearby field? And why are we happy to eat some mammals (cows, pigs, lambs) but not others (rabbits, squirrels, horses)?

One advocate for eating roadkill—sort of—is PETA, People for the Ethical Treatment of Animals. Here is their official statement on the matter:

> If people must eat animal carcasses, roadkill is a superior option to the neatly shrink-wrapped plastic packages of meat in the supermarket. Eating roadkill is healthier for the consumer than meat laden with antibiotics, hormones, and growth stimulants, as most meat is today. It is also more humane in that animals killed on the road were not castrated, dehorned, or debeaked without anesthesia, did not suffer the trauma and misery of transportation in a crowded truck in all weather extremes, and did not hear the screams and smell the fear of the animals ahead of them on the slaughter line. Perhaps the animals never knew what hit them.

Penn State philosopher Donald Bruckner has taken this logic a step further to argue that vegetarians who subscribe to the principle of reducing intentional harm to animals are morally *obligated* to eat roadkill since the more unconventionally sourced animal protein we consume, the fewer cows, pigs, lambs, turkeys, and chickens will be slaughtered. As he says, "picking up road-killed animals does not harm any animals. Road-killed animals are already dead."

None of this is hypothetical, by the way. A key element in the *Newsweek* story is that many states have liberalized their roadkill laws to facilitate human harvest and exploitation. One state featured in the story is Oregon, which enacted Senate Bill 372 that allows motorists to salvage wildlife killed by automobiles. You need a permit to do so in Oregon and several other states, but once you have the permit, you are allowed to recover, possess, use, or transport animals accidentally killed by autos (whether yours or someone else's). Some twenty other states have legislation like this on the books, or so *Newsweek* says.

And here's the Florida angle on the topic: Florida distinguishes itself among the American states by having the nation's most permissive laws concerning roadkill. "Florida: The Roadkill State"—again, not much of a marketing slogan, but descriptive. Unlike the law in many states, if you run over an animal in Florida, it's basically yours to keep (unless it happens to be a protected species, in which case you are required to turn the animal in to the state wildlife service). You don't even need to run over it yourself. If you find a dead animal that is not a protected species, you are free to take it.

Many states (Texas, California, Wisconsin, and maybe twenty or so others) prohibit the taking of roadkill entirely (or with pretty severe restrictions); most of those that allow it require permits. Many states have elaborate rules and regulations about roadkill. In New Jersey, for example, you can keep roadkill only once you obtain a permit from a state trooper; in Illinois, you can keep the kill but only after state officials determine that you are not in arrears on child support; in Wyoming, you can keep large-animal roadkill (deer, moose, elk) only if you have a proper tag from a game warden. In Arizona, roadkill is salvaged by the state and used to feed wolves. In Alaska, roadkill is offered to needy families and charitable organizations. In New York you can keep your roadkill, but only if you can convince the game warden that the animal's death was truly accidental.

But with relatively few and loose restrictions, Florida is practically an all-you-can-eat roadkill state. Help yourselves! Alas, the most desirable roadkill for eating is deer, and Florida ranks almost at the very bottom (forty-seventh) in annual car-deer collisions. But possums, raccoons, and armadillos—we're right up there near the top!

Newsweek cautions, "As with any meat, the practice of eating roadkill carries some safety concerns." I'd say. Even freshly killed wild animals can be riddled with parasites and other diseases that make consumption of their flesh hazardous. But if you believe present-day vegetarian activists, factory-farmed meat is full of poisons, too.

A major concern with liberalized roadkill laws is that hungry motorists might start going out of their way to have "accidental" encounters with wildlife (this is called bumper-hunting). A Clemson University study showed that about 6 percent of all drivers said they would swerve to run over a turtle crossing the road (although one hopes a far larger number would swerve to avoid the turtle), so the concern is not without at least some foundation. But Florida, which has had permissive roadkill laws for years, does not seem to have dramatically more roadkill than other nearby states where roadkill harvest is illegal or requires a permit. So perhaps this concern is without significant foundation.

Vegetarian writer and activist James McWilliams has written an essay called "A Roadkill Revolution." "For those (such as me) who argue that it's ethically unjustifiable to raise and kill sentient animals for food we don't need, but at the same time remain sympathetic to the perceived difficulties of complete abstinence [from meat], the promise of a roadkill revolution is encouraging. When it comes to eating animals, the further we move away from conventional agricultural and hunting practices, and closer we get to a foraging mentality, the better."

The McWilliams essay, by the way, is illustrated with a dead possum lying on the side of the road, apparently awaiting the arrival of the buzzards. The *Newsweek* piece is accompanied by a photo of a badger skull stewed in brown gravy with its brain exposed. Quotes about the cooked product contained in these stories run along the lines of "came out pretty well"—damning with faint praise, for sure. The implicit subtext seems to be "Okay, it's not prime rib, but at least it isn't tofu."

One issue with eating roadkill is that a moving automobile packs about as much force as a civilian is allowed to command. An arrow enters the body with relatively little force and does relatively little damage; a bullet is more forceful and therefore more damaging; but being hit by a speeding car is about the most damaging thing imaginable. An average squirrel, for example, weighs about a pound. The average car is about four thousand pounds. So hitting a squirrel with a car at 60 mph would be like running over a human with an eight-hundred-thousand-pound object traveling at the same speed. Most roadkill will be heavily bruised with shards of broken bone infused throughout the flesh. A road-killed animal is usually pretty squishy, and that makes it hard to salvage the edible parts.

Putrefaction of flesh sets in pretty quickly and even more so if the creature has been turned into meat pulp, so roadkill harvesters must be attentive to the recency of the kill. If the weather is cool and the kill has happened within the previous four or five hours, the meat is probably safe. But the weather in Florida is rarely cool, and just when the animal was killed is often only a guess. In such matters, wise advice is to err on the side of safety.

The best outdoor cook I ever knew was my dad, known to his friends and family as the "Cowboy"—partly because he was raised in Texas, but more because he was everything a cowboy ought to be: a rough-and-tumble guy whose idea of a good time was to go to the Neighborhood Tavern and pick fights with bikers half his age, a foulmouthed old cuss who could build or repair *anything*, a harmonica player who loved sitting up half the night blowing on his mouth harp and telling lies, a guy whose idea of a big breakfast was a triple shot of Calvert and a beer back, and above all, a man whose campfire cooking always drew a crowd. You could be a half mile upriver and the aromas drifting by on the breeze would tell you when the old man had started cooking.

My cousin Bob recounts a camping trip with Cowboy when they came upon a bridge over a small creek. Down on the water, maybe six feet away, was a large snapping turtle sunning himself on a dead log. With one smooth stroke Cowboy unsheathed his hatchet and flung it at the turtle, hitting it blade-first square in the back. There followed a lesson in how to clean a turtle, what parts you could eat and what should be discarded, and, a few hours later, snapping-turtle stew. (I will remind the reader at this point that turtle soup is a luxury item in New Orleans's finest restaurants.) At one time or another, I also saw him knock a squirrel out of a tree with a slingshot and turn it into killer campfire chili, snare-trap a rabbit at two in the afternoon and serve rabbit stew at five, and gut a freshly killed goat and cook the warm bloody offal into something people enjoyed eating.

Cowboy took a child's delight in sneaking things into his dishes that people normally wouldn't eat—squirrel, rabbit, possum, porcupine, even raccoon or muskrat meat. Often enough, these ingredients had been harvested from the side of the road. He'd wait until people were done eating, ask them if they liked it (they always did), then tell them what they had just eaten. There was no "damning with faint praise" for Cowboy's critter stew. This stuff was *good*.

I can't remember a camping trip with the old man that didn't feature critter stew, whether using animals he'd trapped or killed himself or harvesting fresh roadkill. Cowboy crafted his critter stew from just about any small game you could imagine. And he always used the same recipe no matter what kind of critter he had available. Start with a freshly killed, properly dressed critter. "Properly dressed" means that the animal was gutted and bled soon after it was killed. Skin the animal carefully and inspect the flesh closely for buckshot, bits of rock and tire, dirt, maggots, and anything else you wouldn't want to eat. With your sharpest knife, peel the critter's flesh away from its bones and cut the flesh into bite-size chunks, roughly one inch to the side.

Dredge the chunks of meat in well-seasoned flour, using ample salt and pepper in the seasoning. Heat a half inch of oil in the bottom of a heavy stewpot or Dutch oven and cook the floured flesh until golden brown all over. Coarsely chop up some onion and sauté it in the same oil until translucent. Add chopped tomatoes (canned or fresh), a healthy jolt of chili powder (at least a couple of tablespoons), some more salt, and just enough beer to cover everything. Deglaze the stewpot and let the mixture simmer, uncovered, on low heat until the meat is very tender, at least a couple hours and, if you have the time, all day. Check the pot occasionally and add more beer if necessary. You could use water, wine, or broth, I suppose, but on Cowboy's camping trips, it was always beer. Half-empty cans of flat beer left over from the previous evening's drunkfest work perfectly in this application.

When you have about thirty to forty-five minutes to go before it is time to eat, add your veggies to the stewpot. This can be any combination of celery, potatoes, carrots, turnips, parsnips, rutabagas, sweet peppers, zucchini, green beans—whatever you have in the larder or backpack. Cook until the veggies are tender, correct the seasoning, and serve. And don't tell people what's in the stew until they have finished eating.

16

INVASIVE SPECIES

A FEW OF Florida's better-known invasive species—the Burmese python, the monkeys of Central Florida, and so on—have already been discussed. The state's warm climate, abundant vegetation, and ample food sources have allowed a number of other non-native species to establish a foothold, often to the detriment of native flora and fauna. The ubiquitous and iconic green iguana, for example, often found sunning itself along Miami roadways and canals, is not a native species. The animals are descended from escaped pets. As an invasive species, iguanas are legal to hunt, capture, and eat, although few do. Surprisingly, people who have eaten iguana—the reptiles are harvested for food in places like Honduras, Nicaragua, and Mexico—do not say that "they taste like chicken," but are more gamey and fishy than chicken and not particularly pleasant.

An even more common invasive species in Florida is the "wild boar," really a feral domesticated pig that can be found in woodlands all over the state. These animals, which can weigh as much as a couple hundred pounds, roam in packs and can destroy suburban lawns overnight. They are ferocious rooters and extremely destructive of native habitats. The Florida wild swine population is descended from escaped domesticated pigs possibly brought into Florida in the sixteenth century by Hernando de Soto. In short, as the Florida Division of Hunting and Game Management says dryly, "They have been here a long time." They number at about a half million and are found in every Florida county.

Wild pigs are prolific breeders. The average litter is five or six pigs and can be as large as ten. Also, with a gestation period of 115 days, they are capable of two litters per year. Females begin breeding at about one year of age. They are "opportunistic omnivores," which means they will eat almost anything.

Wild pigs are also prized prey for the state's hunters. The only game animals more popular in Florida than wild pigs are deer. According to John Mayer, author of a paper entitled "Wild Pig Attacks on Humans," there are 412 documented attacks of wild pigs on humans worldwide, of which the largest share (24 percent) were in the United States. And of the US attacks, Florida (with 12 percent of the total) ranked second only to Texas (24 percent). "Wild pigs," Dr. Mayer assures us, "do have the potential to be dangerous."

Other common invasive species that haunt the Florida ecosystem include the coyote (which showed up in the 1920s as the last of the red wolves died out); several dozen freshwater fish species, including a number of species of tilapia, the African jewelfish, several species of catfish, and the Asian swamp eel; the Cuban treefrog, the cane toad, and other amphibians; various storks, ibises, ducks, flamingoes, parrots, and geese; the black rat, the Norway rat, the macaque monkeys, nutria, fruit-eating bats, capybara, and the prairie dog; and a few hundred invasive plants, some of which threaten to choke off the state's waterways. Invasive species get to Florida by various means: some hitchhike in on ships and planes, others are dropped by passing birds, are accidentally released from zoos and aquariums, or escape from pens where they were being raised as food.

But the most common route is through escape from or, more often, release by exotic-pet owners. In the decade from 2006 to 2016, more than 260 such "escapes" or releases were reported to authorities, and one assumes that not all cases get reported. In the usual case, the owner has acquired an exotic pet, found that the pet is far more demanding or much larger than originally envisioned, and released the pet into the wild. Most released animals soon die—having been raised by humans, they lack survival skills—but a few survive, find one another, mate, and establish an invasive breeding population. There are hundreds of non-native animal species now extant in Florida that got into the ecosystem through irresponsible pet ownership.

The release of exotic pets into the wild has become such a problem that one county, Broward County just north of Miami, now has an annual Exotic Pet Amnesty Day on which owners of exotic pets can drop them off at the local Fish and Wildlife Conservation Commission office—no questions asked. Other counties have such a day or soon will follow suit.

Pet escapes sometimes turn tragic. In July 2009, two-year-old Shaiunna Hare was strangled to death by an eight-foot Burmese python that was her mother's boyfriend's pet. The undernourished python escaped the boyfriend's terrarium; found, bit, and strangled the child; and was obviously preparing to eat her when the horrific incident was discovered. The mother and boyfriend are now doing time in a Florida prison for aggravated manslaughter. The tagline: the boyfriend's terrarium was only covered with a loosely pinned quilt.

The Shaiunna Hare case received quite a bit of media attention, not just because of the tragic outcome but because the Florida Department of Children and Families investigated the family a few months before the incident and did nothing. Astonishingly, DCF received an investigative report on May 1, 2009, stating that there was a two-year-old girl in the house, along with a large python and a large stash of cocaine, marijuana, Ecstasy, Xanax, and other narcotics that the couple admitted to using and did not intend to stop. DCF decided that Shaiunna was safe and could be left in the home.

The Burmese python, "The Snake That's Eating Florida" (according to *The New York Times*), is surely the state's most notorious invasive species. Native to Southeast Asia, these reptiles have been spotted in the Everglades since the 1980s. But the largest influx was the result of Hurricane Andrew in 1992. Nobody knows for sure just how many pythons now live in Florida. Some estimates are in the hundreds of thousands but tens of thousands is probably closer to the truth. Only a couple of human deaths have been attributed to the snake, but the snakes have devastated the small mammals of the Everglades. Populations of raccoons, possums, rabbits, bobcats, and foxes have all been reduced by 88 to 100 percent by the slithering giants, whose only large predator in the ecosystem is the alligator, and then only rarely.

In an effort to reduce the python population, a hunt was organized in South Florida in 2013, the very first of its kind in the state. Python hunters traipsed through more than a million acres of habitat but netted only 68 reptiles. Despite the small numbers, a similar effort continues to be mounted every year. The 2016 effort, for example, enlisted over a thousand hunters from twenty-nine states but only 106 snakes were captured. All 106 were killed and turned over to researchers in the hopes that analyses of the corpses would provide a clue or two about how to control them. After analyses, the snakes were either destroyed or returned to their captors to be made into wall hangings, boots, wallets, purses, and other snake memorabilia. (Eating python meat is not recommended because of the very high levels of mercury in the snake's flesh.)

In 2017, evidently weary of the results being produced by amateur hunters, the Southwest Florida Water Management District (acronym: SWFWMD, pronounced "swift mud") announced that it would be hiring twenty-five full-time professional snake hunters to spearhead the eradication effort in the Everglades and elsewhere. It is evident that the reptiles are expanding their range. They've turned up in Key Largo and on an island in Miami's Biscayne Bay, which means they are swimming long distances through salty water to find new habitat. SWFWMD wants to kill as many pythons as possible as quickly as possible and is prepared to pay to make that happen. Since 2013, all the hunts combined have produced fewer than a thousand dead snakes from a population numbering at least in the tens of thousands. The water management district thinks that progress against the reptile needs to be quicker. Most wildlife biologists agree.

Another invasive snake species is the green anaconda, the largest snake in the world. The first of these reptilian giants was spotted in the Everglades in 2013, and several others have been spotted since. One has already turned up in a suburban Melbourne neighborhood. The anacondas are native to the Amazon rain forest and can grow to 550 pounds and twenty feet. They are large enough to swallow a human whole. There is a concern that the green anaconda may soon replace the Burmese python as the most serious threat to native species in the Everglades.

I said earlier that alligators were the only predators of the pythons, but this is somewhat misleading. Another invasive species, the imported red fire ant (native to South America), preys on the python population. Pythons lay eggs, and female pythons spend several months each breeding season guarding their nests by wrapping themselves around their eggs. These months of immobility make them vulnerable to the fire ants, who attack in giant swarms with extremely painful stings. A large colony of fire ants is capable of swarming, killing, and eating an adult female python and all her eggs *in a single day*. Thus, the fire ants help limit the python population. Not so the anacondas, who bear live young and do not nest. Also, the anacondas are almost entirely aquatic, which makes them impervious to ants. Whether the anacondas have established a successful breeding population or not is still unknown, and there are informed opinions on both sides. But if they have, that's very bad news.

The Burmese python is one of four python species that have invaded the Florida ecosystem. Also on the list are the Northern African python, the Southern African python, and the reticulated python. Likewise, the green anaconda has been joined by the yellow anaconda, DeSchauensee's anaconda, and the Bolivian, or Beni, anaconda on the list of invasive snakes, along with the boa constrictor. And these are just the invasive *constrictors*. At least forty-six other reptilian species have also invaded, among them the spectacled caiman and the Nile crocodile.

And yet, according to an item in *Time* magazine, only the Burmese python makes it onto the list of the five most destructive invasive species in the Florida Everglades, and the other four are all surprising. Far more destructive and worrisome than any snake, for example, is the giant African land snail, often eight inches long, thirty to forty grams in weight, and incredibly prolific, a creature that literally eats the stucco off houses for the calcium. Aside from the stucco-eating and all-round ickiness, these snails also carry a parasite that can cause meningitis in humans. Native to East Africa, the snails were first brought into Florida as pets (only in Florida!). They spawn at least twice a year and lay up to four hundred eggs at each spawn. Efforts at eradication have proven futile. The snail is known to feed on over five hundred different plant species, some of them crops, so they are considered a significant threat to agriculture. They have thick shells that protect them from most predators and are inactive during the day. You'll hear a lot more about these awful creatures as their range expands northward. For now, the threat is confined mostly to Florida.

Another seemingly harmless but highly destructive invasive species is the Brazilian pepper tree, sometimes called Florida holly. This species, more a shrub than a tree, was introduced into Florida in the nineteenth century as an ornamental plant. It has bright green leaves and bright red berries and is very attractive, but it has also proven to be an aggressive invader that forms a dense twenty-to-thirty-foot-high canopy that shades out other plants. It is the most widespread of all non-native invasive plant species, displaces rare and endangered plants, and encroaches on nesting habitats. It is the dominant plant in about 700,000 acres of Florida. Control costs millions of dollars a year in the Everglades alone.

Yet a third "most destructive" invader is the Cuban treefrog, a large frog first spotted in Miami in 1952 but since observed in about half of Florida's counties. These frogs secrete highly noxious toxins from their skin which limits their vulnerability to predation, and they feed voraciously on native amphibians (toads, other frogs, small lizards, and the like). They probably arrived in Florida as stowaways in shipping crates from the Caribbean and are very well established in the South Florida ecosystem. Breeding populations have been found as far north as Cedar Key and Jacksonville. They are directly responsible for the decimation of native tree frog species such as the squirrel treefrog and the American green tree frog, both of which are rarely spotted these days. Even their tadpoles are superior competitors to other tree-frog tadpoles. The Cuban treefrogs have a high nuisance factor and sometimes chew through electrical power lines, causing local outages.

Finally, we have the cane toad, native to Central and South America and intentionally introduced into Florida as a "natural" control for certain sugarcane pests. Once here, it practically wiped out various native toad species. The cane toad is a large creature, sometimes nearly ten inches long, is very hard to kill, and is now well established throughout South Florida.

Other destructive invaders include the monk parakeet, initially introduced in the 1960s as a pet. The monk parakeet eats fruit and builds condolike communal stick nests that can be as large as a small car. These nests are often built on power poles and electrical substations and often cause power outages and fires that cost millions of dollars a year. Or consider the walking catfish, which can survive out of water for days at a time and can use its leglike fins to propel itself across wet ground into new habitats. The walking catfish is native to Thailand and other parts of Southeast Asia, was imported into Florida in the early 1960s as a potential aquaculture species, and is a voracious consumer of native fishes, crustaceans, and aquatic eggs. In fact, in tough times, the walking catfish will eat just about anything. They are notorious for invading aquaculture tanks and eating every living thing they find.

Then we have the strikingly attractive lionfish, considered the most destructive exotic species living in the coastal waters. The lionfish has venomous spines that deter all predation, are incredibly prolific (they can lay as many as thirty thousand eggs every four days), and have insatiable appetites. They will consume many dozens of organisms in a single feeding, drastically reducing the populations of other fish species and significantly altering delicate offshore reef systems. And when local organisms prove insufficient, the lionfish eat one another.

The lionfish first appeared in Florida's coastal waters in the 1980s and probably got there by being released from someone's aquarium. Efforts at lionfish control, which include doing away with catch and size limits for fishermen, teaching divers how to spearfish for them, and publishing a lionfish cookbook, have been of little avail. The state has also sponsored an annual Lionfish Removal & Awareness Day every spring since 2015. Despite all efforts, "they keep going up in densities, sizes and weights. It's pretty crazy." Or so says Kristen Dahl, who wrote her PhD dissertation on the species.

And it is not just animals who invade. The Brazilian pepper tree (previously discussed) is only one of several hundred non-native, invasive land and aquatic plant species that are rampant in Florida. The key characteristics of invasive plants are that they are highly adaptable to new environments, grow aggressively, and have enormous reproductive capacity. The resulting population explosions can be devastating to native plants, disrupt local ecosystems, and harm animal species whose preferred food sources and habitats are destroyed or pushed out. Invasive aquatic plants are especially problematic because they clog up navigation routes, disrupt boating and other recreational water uses, undermine local efforts at flood control or estuary improvements, and create new mosquito breeding grounds.

Invasive plants arrive through various means. Seeds and plants can escape from nurseries, landscapers, aquariums, and gardeners. Whole plants or viable plant parts can arrive in ballast water from foreign ships. Some invasive species have been brought into Florida by travelers as souvenirs. And sometimes invasive species are introduced on purpose as a way of "improving" a natural area. This is the case with the melaleuca tree, introduced into Florida from Australia as a method to aid in the drying up of the Everglades. Those trees now cover much of the Everglades and continue to be removed aggressively at a huge annual expense. Hydrilla, which infests tens of thousands of acres of Florida waters, was introduced as an aquarium plant but now requires continuous management with herbicides and machines. Hydrilla management costs Floridians millions of dollars a year.

Yet another invasive animal species is the black-hooded parakeet, quite a number of which hang out near my home in Saint Pete Beach. These birds, also known as Nanday parakeets, are native to Brazil, Bolivia, Paraguay, and Argentina, but their striking good looks and brash personalities made them a favorite species in the pet trade, which is how they first came to Florida.

The first of these handsome birds were reported around Miami and Tampa Bay in 1969. These are both large, active port cities and major hubs for the exotic pet industry. So the initial introduction of the species could have come from a shipment of the birds that managed to escape. Alternatively, those first specimens might have been escaped or released pets. Colonies were established in about ten Florida counties by the 1990s and in at least nineteen counties as of 2016, of which ten are known to be breeding colonies.

The black-hooded parakeets are about a foot long with bright electric-green bodies, bluish breasts, and distinctive black hoods over their heads.

They travel in flocks of up to thirty or more individuals and signal their arrival by loud, piercing squawks that guarantee they are heard well before they are seen.

In my neighborhood, as many as twenty or thirty of these birds are regulars at the backyard bird feeder, making frequent noisy visits and scaring off all the other birds as they swoop in to sample the goodies. Yes, they are a non-native species that doesn't really belong in my backyard or anywhere else in Florida. But they are a constant source of amusement, they make me happy, and they don't seem to harm anything, save for scaring off the other birds when they come in for a landing. I'm glad these birds are here, whether they truly "belong" here or not.

Finally, no account of invasive species in Florida would be complete without at least a passing mention of the one species considered by natives to be the most dangerous, prolific, and invasive of all—midwesterners, the people from Indiana, Ohio, Illinois, and Michigan who have flocked to Florida in droves, either as snowbirds, permanent immigrants, or retirees. "Florida" is number thirty-three on Cara Freie's list of "stuff white Midwesterners like," from her book *I Love Ranch Dressing: And Other Stuff White Midwesterners Like.* Parts of the state are populated almost exclusively by ex-midwesterners, and as Freie says, "It's like there is some unwritten White Midwestern Rule that retirement = snowbirding in Florida, usually on 'the gulf side.'" Many midwestern immigrants, like my Uncle Charley and Aunt Mary Ann, end up in trailer parks, where the luxury end of the housing market is "a snazzy doublewide" featuring a Florida Room built into the side, topped off with a two-person, three-wheeled bicycle parked outside.

17

FAMOUS FOODS OF FLORIDA

FLORIDA HAS NEVER been known as a gastronome's paradise. To the extent that there is a genuine "Florida cuisine," it is defined by relatively few dishes: fried gator tail, rock shrimp, key lime pie, conch fritters, and Tang pie. Also distinctively Floridian are the Cuban sandwich, swamp cabbage, stone crabs, grouper sandwiches, citrus marmalades, and the now-famous mojito, essentially a mint julep made with rum instead of bourbon. Here I recount the histories of and give recipes for or links to all these classic Florida dishes.

Fried Gator Tail

The American alligator has been in Florida for thirty million years. Despite habitat loss, the species continues to thrive in Florida wherever open bodies of water can be found, which is just about everywhere. Efforts to get people to eat more alligator have not been very successful, so gator tail remains a very specialized foodstuff. Only the tail meat of a gator is considered fit for human consumption. The usual recipe is as follows:

Ingredients

1 cup buttermilk

1 cup hot sauce

Salt and pepper to taste

1 pound alligator tail meat, cut into one-inch cubes

Flour for dredging the pieces

Oil for frying

1 bottle ranch dressing

Directions

Combine the buttermilk and hot sauce in a bowl. Set up a large plate for dredging. Salt and pepper the gator chunks liberally, dredge in flour, dip in the buttermilk–hot sauce mix, then dredge in flour a second time. Fry the breaded chunks in a deep-fat fryer until golden brown. The gator chunks cook about as fast as breaded shrimp do; that is, they only need a few minutes. Drain on a paper towel, sprinkle with salt, and serve with ranch dressing for dipping.

Some people recommend that gator tail meat be soaked overnight in buttermilk or plain milk to tame the flavor. I've never bothered. Once it is all fried up, gator tail indeed "tastes like chicken," although many say that fried frog legs are a closer comparison.

Gator tail can also be cooked on your charcoal grill. Melt a stick of butter in a large pan and sweat a bunch of onions and garlic in the melted butter. Coat slabs of gator tail with the onions, garlic, and butter, sprinkle liberally with salt and pepper, then it's off to the Weber. Make sure the gator is cooked through (internal temperature of at least 165 degrees). One Oregonian who has tried gator cooked on the ___ says "anybody who don't like that is Communist."

Finally, gator meat makes a fine gumbo. Swap it out pound for pound in any gumbo recipe calling for chicken.

Rock Shrimp

Rock shrimp are a product of Florida waters. They have a hard, spiny shell ("hard as a rock," hence the name) and a taste that is closer to lobster than shrimp. Floridians love the little critters, and most people will tell you that the best rock shrimp around is the broiled rock shrimp served at the Dixie Crossroads restaurant in Titusville, Florida. The restaurant's recipe can be found online: dixiecrossroads.com/recipes.asp. Rock shrimp can also be boiled, roasted in a pan with garlic, served with a spicy cream sauce, or used in virtually any shrimp recipe. Personally, I think rock shrimp are overrated, but Floridians drive for miles to gobble them up at Dixie Crossroads.

Key Lime Pie

The key lime is a particular kind of lime, smaller and more acidic than a conventional lime. It has a unique flavor and is a "must" ingredient in authentic Florida key lime pie. Bottles of key lime juice can sometimes be found in supermarkets and are acceptable in a key lime pie.

There are dozens of recipes for key lime pie, no two identical. Fistfights have broken out over proper key lime pie preparation. Only three points are universally agreed to: (1) Key Lime Pie is never green, but rather a creamy light yellow; (2) real key limes are essential; standard grocery store Persian limes won't do (but frankly, if you used Persian limes, most people wouldn't notice); and (3) whatever else your pie contains, it must at least contain sweetened condensed milk.

In matters of Southern cuisine, *Southern Living* is an authoritative source, and at myrecipes.com/recipe/key-lime-pie you can find their recommended recipe for key lime pie. This key lime pie features a graham-cracker crust, but some locals insist that the graham-cracker crust is an abomination and that a regular pie crust should be used instead. I've tried both and liked them equally. Also, this version is topped with whipped topping but a meringue or real whipped cream works just as well. As always, let your tastes and the ingredients at hand dictate how you proceed.

....

Conch Fritters

Conch (the proper pronunciation is "conk") is any of a variety of sea snails that can be found in the Florida Keys and elsewhere. Key West natives are often called conchs, and Key West itself is sometimes known as the Conch Republic. Conch is used in chowders, sometimes served raw in salads, but is usually eaten in the form of conch fritters. Here is a generic recipe:

Ingredients

1 quart vegetable oil (for frying)
¾ cup all-purpose flour
1 egg
½ cup milk
Cayenne pepper, black pepper, red pepper flakes, salt, and/or seasoning salt, to taste
1 cup chopped conch
½ onion, chopped fine
¼ green bell pepper, chopped fine
¼ yellow bell pepper, chopped fine
¼ red bell pepper, chopped fine
2 stalks celery, chopped fine
2 cloves garlic, minced fine

Directions

Heat the oil in a large pot or deep fryer to 365 degrees. In a bowl, mix the flour, egg, and milk. Season the batter with salt and pepper(s). Mix in the conch meat, onion, chopped peppers, celery, and minced garlic. Carefully drop rounded tablespoons of the conch batter into the hot oil and fry until golden brown, about 5 minutes. Remove the fritters, lightly salt them, and drain them on paper towels. Conch fritters are traditionally served with a rémoulade sauce for dipping (ketchup, mayonnaise, hot sauce, and lemon juice).

Tang Pie

Tang is a fruit-flavored drink mix that became famous when NASA included the product among the provisions of the Mercury and Gemini space missions. Given the association of Tang with the US space program, and the space program's association with Central Florida, Tang pie must be included in any accounting of Florida cuisine.

Ingredients

¾ cup Tang instant breakfast drink powder

1 can sweetened condensed milk

1 container (8 ounces) sour cream (or reduced-fat sour cream)

½ large container (12 ounces) Cool Whip

graham-cracker pie shell (baked according to the label instructions)

orange zest or mint leaves (for garnish)

Directions

Whip together until very smooth and fluffy the Tang, condensed milk, and sour cream. Fold half of the Cool Whip into the mixture. Pour the mixture into the baked graham-cracker pie shell, top with the rest of the Cool Whip, and refrigerate until the mixture sets. Serve cold. Garnish with a sprinkle of Tang, orange zest, or fresh mint leaves. This pie is cool, refreshing, and absolutely scrumptious.

The Cuban Sandwich

A number of Cuban dishes came over to Florida with the anti-Castro exiles and wormed their way into Florida's cuisine. There are Cuban restaurants everywhere that serve more or less authentically Cuban dishes, and most Floridians have their favorites. The mojito has become a very popular cocktail. And the Cuban sandwich now makes an appearance on nearly every greasy-spoon menu in the state.

Trouble is, the Cuban sandwich is not native to Cuba. Most food historians agree that the ham and pork delectation was invented in Ybor City, now a Tampa suburb and originally home to the American cigar industry. Cubans came to Ybor City more than a century ago to roll cigars, and the sandwich was developed to feed them. But some argue that the sandwich originated in Miami, which has been the capital of Cuban America since Fidel's successful revolution. The two versions of the sandwich are not identical. The Tampa version includes salami, but the Miami version does not. Both cities claim to be home to the "authentic" version of the dish.

Some believe that the first Cuban sandwich was created more than five centuries ago by the native Taino of Cuba. (The Taino word for "sacred fire pit," *barabicu,* evolved into the Spanish word *barbacoa* and eventually into the English word "barbecue.") Thus, the Cuban sandwich might be pre-Columbian. In its modern form, however, roast pork and cured ham are essential ingredients, and pigs were not introduced into North America until 1539 by the Spanish explorer Hernando de Soto—near present-day Tampa, incidentally. This fact favors an American and probably Tampa origin of the dish.

With Cuban sandwiches now featured on nearly every restaurant menu in the state, there are many dozens of recipes and variations. Not even the loaf of Cuban bread is constant across all recipes, although that is certainly the preferred option. Here's a basic recipe:

Slice a loaf of Cuban bread lengthwise and slather melted butter on each side. Layer in sliced ham, sliced roast pork, sliced cheese, and sliced dill pickle. Slather one piece of bread with yellow mustard, form a sandwich, and heat through in a panini press. Slice in half diagonally and serve, usually with a side of potato chips and an ice-cold beer.

The above yields the standard Miami version. Add sliced Genoa salami to the mix and you get the Tampa version. While Swiss cheese is preferred in either version, any mild cheese (provolone, cheddar, Gruyère) will do. Plain yellow mustard is standard, but you can use any mustard you like. Ditto the Cuban bread: it's preferred, but any bread that is crisp on the outside and soft on the inside will do. You can replace the pickle with olive salad, cornichons, or pickled peppers (any variety). Sometimes the sandwich is served open-faced (e.g., at the Bazaar on Miami's South Beach), but this is not standard. Another version replaces the ham with chorizo and adds grilled onions. Still another sometimes substitute for the ham is prosciutto. A slather of mayo is acceptable on any version of the dish.

Swamp Cabbage

Except among Florida crackers, "swamp cabbage" is known as hearts of palm. Other euphemisms are "burglar's thigh" and the "lobster of vegetables." The palm in question is the sabal palm, the state tree of Florida and sometimes known as the cabbage palm. You can buy canned hearts of palm in the supermarket, but canning does nothing for the taste or texture. Fresh swamp cabbage is better.

To harvest swamp cabbage, find an immature palm tree and cut it down (but see the note at the top of page 191). The younger and smaller the tree, the sweeter the heart. (Commercially grown trees are harvested at age two years.) Any palm taller than about ten feet will have a bitter heart. Also avoid trees growing too close to water.

With your chain saw, lop off the upper part of the tree where the palm fronds are. Tear back or chop away the stiff outer segments, taking care not to pierce the core, until the glistening white center is exposed—that is the "heart" of the palm. But beware, a ten-foot sabal log will yield only about a quart of heart. Separating the heart from the surrounding outer segments of tree matter is tedious. And, of course, you killed the tree in the process.

On the other hand, the harvested heart is rich in protein, iron, and fiber and has a delicious sweet taste. Internationally, the French are the biggest consumers, which gives a clue about the product's gustatory merit. The heart of the palm can be sliced into "coins" and served raw or in a salad, which is considered a delicacy in both French and cracker culture. Or try the following classic cracker recipe:

> Fry up six slices of slab bacon until crisp. Remove the bacon, crumble it, and add it back into the rendered fat. Add the "cabbage" harvested from a single tree, a cup of water (or chicken broth), and salt and pepper to taste. Simmer covered until the cabbage is tender, which might take three or four hours. Serve as a side veggie with anything.

If you have leftover swamp cabbage, try your hand at Swamp Cabbage Patties:

Ingredients
2 cups cooked swamp cabbage or 2 cans hearts of palm (drained)
1 cup water
½ cup finely chopped onion
1 egg, slightly beaten
Salt
Lots of pepper to taste
Flour
Bacon fat or cooking oil

Directions
Dice the swamp cabbage. Combine with onion, water, egg, salt, and pepper. Add flour a little at a time until you get a stiff, moldable mixture. Heat up a frying pan, add oil, bring up to temperature, then drop spoonsful of the cabbage mixture into the oil. Fry until brown all over, drain, salt, and serve.

Note: Before you head off into the Florida swampland with a hatchet, do know that as the state tree, the sabal palm is a protected species even though it grows like a weed on thousands and thousands of acres. So harvesting swamp cabbage in Florida is now frowned upon (although not, so far as I can tell, illegal). If there is any chance the tree you want to harvest is growing on someone's property, or is somehow protected by the state, be sure to obtain permission before hacking away.

Given the hard work and dubious ethics of hacking down an entire tree for a quart of strange vegetable matter, perhaps you should just stick with canned hearts of palm. Alas, however, that may not be a solution. The principal producers of the commercial product are Brazil, Costa Rica, and Ecuador, and in all three nations, harvesting wild sabal palm has been mostly outlawed because of concerns about deforestation. The product is therefore grown commercially on sabal palm plantations, but there is concern that the world demand is such that wild sabal palms are being poached to keep up. Costa Rica alone exports sixteen million pounds of palm heart annually. So there's no guarantee that the canned hearts of palm in your cupboard were legally harvested.

Stone Crabs

The Florida stone crab is a medium-size crab with outsize claws that is considered a seafood delicacy throughout Florida. The crab grows in Atlantic waters from Connecticut to Belize, eats mostly oysters, mollusks, and small crustaceans, and is prized for its incredibly sweet and fleshy claw meat. One claw is distinctly larger than the other, and that is the claw that is usually harvested. Once the large claw is removed, the live crab is tossed back into the ocean to grow another. The claw regrows in about a year. Catch limits are strictly enforced, and the annual harvest (two to three million crabs) is believed to be sustainable. The Florida stone crab industry has received high marks for responsible fishery management.

You will find stone crabs on the menus of many restaurants, but Joe's Stone Crab restaurant in Miami is Florida's top buyer of the crabs, and you can't really say you have had a complete stone crab experience until you have tucked into a platter of Joe's. The current lunch menu has a platter of large stone crabs (only the claws are served) for $58.96 and a platter of jumbos for $86.95. Worth every penny!

Stone crab claws are boiled in water or simply steamed and typically served with a mustard dipping sauce. The spicy pungent crab boils characteristic of Louisiana crab recipes are not used with stone crabs, whose sweet delicate flavor would be ruined by a peppery boil. The claws need to cook for only five or six minutes and then are ready to serve.

To make a batch of Joe's mustard sauce, combine 1 tablespoon dry mustard, 1 cup mayo, 2 teaspoons of Worcestershire sauce, 1 teaspoon of A.1. sauce, 2 tablespoons light cream, and salt to taste in a mixing bowl and stir well. Chill the sauce and serve.

The Grouper Sandwich

Next to stone crabs and (for some) rock shrimp, fresh grouper is the best eats Florida waters have to offer. There are several subspecies of grouper, and they can be swapped indiscriminately in any grouper recipe. The grouper is a large fish, and it is illegal to harvest most species until they are twenty to twenty-four inches in length. There are also strict bag limits that game wardens enforce aggressively. The FWC prides itself on the responsible management of all of Florida's water species to assure a healthy future for both commercial and recreational fishing. You pay a stiff penalty for taking any specimen that does not meet the minimum-size limits, the grouper certainly included.

Because the supply of grouper is limited, prices can be high: eleven to thirteen dollars per pound for wholesale grouper fillets, twenty-two to twenty-five dollars per pound at retail, and even more if you order grouper in an upscale restaurant. Grouper flesh is lean and moist, with a mild taste and a firm texture. Grouper reminds many people of sea bass. The fish is served in numerous ways, but many people prefer the ubiquitous grouper sandwich—fried boneless grouper fillets on a soft bun, dressed with lettuce and tomato and served with wedges of lemon and a side of coleslaw. Any fried-fish recipe will do. You can also order your grouper broiled or blackened.

Citrus Marmalade

Floridians with backyard citrus trees often find themselves asking, "What are we going to do with all this fruit?!" One thing you can do is make citrus marmalade.

Almost everyone has sampled orange marmalade at some time, either on toast, in a glaze for ham, or in some other application. Well, you can make lemon, lime, or tangelo marmalade the very same way, and it will be every bit as delicious. Indeed, a favorite marmalade is the so-called Three Citrus Marmalade, a basic recipe for which follows.

Alert! Making homemade marmalade can be a tedious and time-consuming process, and there are simpler ways to use up excess citrus. See the recipe for a salty dog at the end of chapter 6 on Florida's orange industry.

Ingredients

5 pounds of ripe fruit (oranges, grapefruits, and lemons are a common combination)

4 cups of water

6 cups of sugar

1–2 teaspoons instant pectin (optional)

3 pint jars with sealable lids, sterilized

Instant-read thermometer

Directions

All citrus comes in three layers: the external "zest," the bitter white "pith" underneath the zest, and then the fruit itself. Working with one piece of fruit at a time, carefully remove the zest, leaving all the white pith behind. Set the zest aside. Then with a sharp serrated knife, remove all the white pith, working over a bowl to catch the juices. Retain the pith in a separate bowl. Then finally cut each section of the fruit away from its surrounding membrane, squeeze out the juice from the membrane, remove all the seeds, and place the seeds and membrane with the pith. You now have a bunch of bright, flavorful citrus zest, a fair amount of citrus juice, a fairly large quantity of sectioned citrus fruit, and a bowl of pith, membrane, and seeds.

Cut the zest into pieces—bigger pieces for a chunky marmalade, smaller pieces for a smoother one. Tie up the pile of membrane, pith, and seeds in a cheesecloth "bag." This is your pectin source. Or throw the stuff away and mix in the instant pectin instead. Combine the zest, fruit, juice, water, sugar and the pectin bag (or instant pectin) in a large heavy pot. Bring it up to 225 degrees, and hold it there for 5 minutes, or until the mixture thickens. Then let it cool, remove the pectin bag (if used), distribute marmalade among the jars, and store in the fridge, where it will last for up to six months. Use the same basic recipe and approach with any combination of backyard citrus.

Mojito

Unlike the Cuban sandwich, which originated in Florida, the mojito is authentically Cuban and has been traced to sixteenth-century Havana. Evidently, the drink is modeled on an earlier concoction known as El Draque, after Sir Francis Drake. Drake had invaded Cuba in the hopes of sacking Havana, but his crew suffered an epidemic of dysentery and scurvy. Drake had heard that there were local remedies for these conditions. So he sent a party ashore to obtain the necessary ingredients: a local rum of sorts, lime, sugarcane juice, and mint. With the exception of soda water, these are exactly the ingredients from which mojitos are made today.

There are many theories about the origins of mojito as the name. *Mojo* is a peppery sauce made in part with lime juice, so that is one possible origin. *Mojadito* is the Spanish word for "a little wet," and that is a second possibility. Mojito historians (remarkably, there are such) seem divided between these possibilities.

The mojito is alleged to have been Ernest Hemingway's favorite drink, and in the 2002 James Bond flick *Die Another Day,* Bond (Pierce Brosnan) uses a mojito to seduce Jinx (played by Halle Berry). Today, the mojito is a trendy rum cocktail, essentially a mint julep made with white rum rather than Kentucky bourbon. Here's an easy-to-make version:

Ingredients

2 tablespoons fresh lime juice

2 heaping teaspoons superfine sugar

1 cup crushed ice, divided

2 sprigs mint leaves

2 ounces white rum

2 ounces club soda

Directions

In a highball glass, stir together fresh lime juice and sugar. Stir vigorously until all the sugar is dissolved. Add ¼ cup of crushed ice. Rub mint leaves around the rim of the glass, then tear them in half and drop them in. Add white rum, another ¾ cup of crushed ice, and a healthy splash of club soda. Stir or shake until thoroughly mixed and icy. Garnish with a mint sprig and serve.

Fussy connoisseurs will want to swap in pure sugarcane juice for the sugar, and a muddled lime-and-mint mixture for the lime juice. White rum makes the drink light and refreshing, but any rum will do. A little googling will also turn up any number of variations: a pear mojito, one made with grapefruit, another with blackberries or mangoes or strawberries, and so on. Up to a point, these things are fine, but after that point, the result ceases to be a mojito and becomes something else.

CRACKER CUISINE AT THE FODDER AND SHINE

The Fodder & Shine was a restaurant in Seminole Heights (near Tampa) that claimed to feature an entirely authentic cracker menu. As owner Greg Baker explained, "This is not a Southern restaurant, it's a Florida restaurant." The menu was intended to preserve the unique cracker cuisine that evolved in Florida (and Georgia) in the century between the 1820s and the Great Depression, back in the days when there were no supermarkets or corner stores, just a few widely spaced trading posts and an occasional boatful of goodies on the river. Back then, people had to make do with what they had. Baker and his partner searched old cookbooks, interviewed people whose roots in Florida went back to the cracker era, asked about the dishes of their grandmothers and great-grandmothers, took notes, and developed something that was as authentic as it could have been nearly a century after the fact. And he contracted with some local farmers to supply the sometimes-unusual ingredients he needed.

With only a few necessary concessions to modernity, Baker came up with a menu that included a few soul-food favorites (fried green tomatoes, chicken pot pie, bacon and greens, charred okra) and a lot of uniquely cracker culinary contributions: cheddar cheese sofkee (a porridge made from fermented rice grits, cheese, cream, and butter), pilau (pronounced per-loo, a rice dish featuring a rice cake, tomato gravy, sautéed shrimp, sausage, onions, peppers, and an egg sunny-side up), grilled cauliflower steaks, smoked mullet and mullet roe, boudin balls, and a cornmeal-cake sandwich featuring fried cornmeal cakes topped with mayonnaise and a slaw made from collard greens, green peppers, scallions, and hot vinegar. The signature dessert was their Turtle Pie Truffle, a mason jar layered with chocolate chip brownies, caramel, whipped-cream-cheese frosting, and toasted pecans. What you would not find anywhere on the Fodder & Shine menu was a Cuban sandwich, key lime pie, rock shrimp, or any other dish I have mentioned in this chapter.

In 2010, the Fodder & Shine was closed and The Refinery opened in its place. All pretense to "authentic" cracker cuisine has disappeared, although there are a couple of appetizers that might keep the spirit of cracker eats alive (a fried chicken biscuit, rabbit and bacon sausage). Elsewhere on the Refinery's dinner menu one finds falafel, an orange flan, fettucine, grilled lamb, and other American standards. Available desserts are ice cream, a coffee-flavored cheesecake, and a chocolate cake. All tasty, I am sure, but not Floridian in any meaningful sense.

18

SOME SPECULATIONS ON FLORIDA'S WEIRDNESS

THERE IS NO shortage of speculation on what makes Florida weird. Writer Steven Rosenfeld has proposed "5 Theories Why Florida Is So Dysfunctional." Commentator Allison Ford has "Four Theories on Why Florida is the Weirdest State," and author Craig Pittman has a nine-reason list. Even *The Huffington Post* has run a piece called "Why Florida Leads the World in Weird." Clearly, explaining Florida's weirdness has become a go-to topic. This chapter sets forth my thoughts and findings on the matter.

To begin, and in fairness, I have uncovered lots of weirdness in places other than Florida. There was a widely reported cannibalism incident in Miami a few years ago involving two homeless men. My first thought was *only in Florida!* But then I found recent incidents of cannibalism in Massachusetts, Maryland, Indiana, and other states, as well as in Canada, England, Pakistan, Russia, South Korea, China, Slovakia, Japan, and India. Okay, none of these other places appears on the Wikipedia list of cannibalism incidents even twice, yet people from Florida are there three times. But still.

There are shark bites and alligator attacks recorded in Louisiana, Georgia, and the Carolinas as well as in Florida. Florida just has more of them than anyplace else. As for political corruption, incompetence, and shenanigans, *Fortune* magazine has provided a listing of the ten most corrupt states, and Florida barely squeaks onto the list. The nine states more corrupt than

Florida, in order (starting at the bottom), are Kentucky, South Dakota, Alaska, Alabama, Pennsylvania, Illinois, Tennessee, Louisiana and Mississippi. Clearly, Florida has no monopoly on this particular bit of weirdness either, although we did make the top ten.

Both my children have lived in California for decades, so it is a place I visit often. If any one state rivals Florida for total weirdness, California would be it. But California weirdness usually has some political or ideological edge to it, whereas the Florida variety is just plain crazy. In California, ordering a cup of coffee, going to the grocery store, shopping for clothes, or buying a car are exercises in ideological purification. Californians' politicization of virtually everything is definitely weird.

According to the Bigfoot Field Researchers Organization, abominable snowman sightings in Florida number maybe three hundred over the decades, a count that includes sightings of the equally elusive "skunk ape" (either the same creature or a closely related one, according to "eyewitness" accounts). But Northern California alone has 437 bigfoot sightings—just as weird as Florida. Per capita UFO sightings are also similar. So no clear winner in the weirdness sweepstakes here.

California is a land of ghosts, legends, and curses, of necromancers and tarot card readers, the home of Death Valley and the Salton Sea and any number of roadside oddities that rival the best that Florida has to offer. So someone could make an argument that per capita strangeness is higher in California than in Florida. But in the serious weirdness sweepstakes, it is at best a runner-up. California's first state flag shows a grizzly bear and the legend CALIFORNIA REPUBLIC. Florida's first state flag bears the legend LET US ALONE. Really, is this even a contest?

Craig Pittman's book about Florida opens with an epigraph, a quotation from writer Lawrence Lessing: "Florida is a study in abnormal psychology." The quotation appeared in the *Fortune* magazine article "State of Florida," and was published in 1948. Apparently, Florida has been out front in WQ (weirdness quotient) for at least seven decades. Then consider business consultant Tiffany Madison's indictment of California: "Political corruption, social greed, and Americanized quasi-socialism can ruin even the most wonderful places. California proved that." Florida's distinctions fall in the realm of abnormal psychology—in the deep recesses of depression, psychosis, aberration, and deviance. California's distinctions are political and socio-economic. California harbors the greedy; Florida harbors the mentally ill. Carl Hiaasen has said, "I think in the old days, the nexus of weirdness ran through Southern California, and to a degree New York City. I think it's changed so that every bizarre story in the country now has a Florida connection. I don't know why, except it must be some inversion of magnetic poles or something."

Setting aside possible inversions of the magnetic poles, what other explanations have been advanced? Some have argued that there is no more weirdness here than anywhere else, but Florida weirdness is easier to uncover and report because of the state's extremely strict sunshine laws, which give the media unrestrained access to police files. True, the Florida sunshine laws are strict, but there are similarly strict laws in many other states, and perhaps the strictest law of all, the federal Freedom of Information Act, applies equally to all states. Open-access laws similar to Florida's are on the books in Michigan and Oregon, for example, but when's the last time you came across a magazine article or internet story about how weird Michiganders or Oregonians are?

Another common theory is that the media delights in Florida-bashing, particularly the media in the snootier states, who want desperately to portray Florida as the haven of drug dealers, crazed retirees, rabid anti-Castro Cubans, and endless traffic snarls. But most of the weirdness covered in this book was initially reported in Florida papers and news outlets, not as much in *The New York Times* or *The Huffington Post*. So if there is a media bias against Florida, it is embraced as much by local media as anyone else.

That said, it is true that the 2000 election debacle made Florida a national laughingstock, and very little has happened since to change that perception. The wide media attention given to @_FloridaMan certainly helps sustain the image of Florida as a basket-case state. CraveOnline once remarked, "It wouldn't be a complete week on Planet Earth without some sick, twisted, 'hillbilly humping something that isn't human' story out of Florida." If some "sick, twisted hillbilly" from western Massachusetts was found in flagrante delicto with a goat, would anyone care or even bother to cover the story? Maybe Florida *is* everybody's favorite whipping boy, so the weirdness that surfaces here gets more prominent play than weirdness in

California or Indiana or Connecticut. One commentator, Allison Ford, writes, "Florida's reputation as a weirdo wonderland propels its news into the national spotlight more often. . . . We love to laugh at Florida, but we also love to go there and give them our money. That makes Floridians laugh, too—all the way to the bank, where there's probably an alligator in the toilet."

Still another line of argument is that there are twenty-one million people all jammed into the habitable parts of the peninsula and another hundred million or so that show up annually for periods ranging from days to months. And maybe that is just too many people bumping up against one another. Lab studies with rats do show that aggression increases with overcrowding. But Florida is not the most densely populated state. New Jersey, Rhode Island, Massachusetts, Connecticut, Maryland, Delaware, and New York all have higher population densities than Florida does. And even making generous allowances for the daily tourist load, Florida's density (365 people per square mile) would have to triple to rival New Jersey's 1,210 people per square mile or Rhode Island's 1,017.

Local densities do swell dramatically when the tourists descend. Even more to the point, people on vacation often do dumb things; they are, after all, on vacation. But many other states also witness annual tourist influxes without any corresponding increase in the WQ. Nevada may be an exception, but then the very concept of Las Vegas strikes me as weird.

Pittman has also posited the state's unique geography as an explanation. The argument is that Florida is "the drainpipe of America"—the end of the line or the bottom of the barrel for everyone in America who is fleeing something. Miami observer Karen Russell puts it this way: "The shape of [Florida] too, it's like a lot of strangeness just travels down the spine of the country and seems to land there. . . . I think there's some physics to it." If you look at a map, Florida does seem to be the nation's spigot, and it is obviously the southernmost part of the continental United States. Maybe weirdness, like water, runs downhill and an outsize supply puddles up in Florida. It is a delightful metaphor even if unlikely as a serious explanation.

Some authors have even laid the blame on Florida's tenacious foliage, said to be relevant because everyone in the state owns a machete to beat back the shrubbery and that often makes machetes the nearest weapon at hand. That might explain the Lake Worth man who attacked his roommate with a machete for changing the radio station, or the West Palm Beach guy who attacked his neighbor with a machete because the neighbor's dog pooped in the yard, or the drunk and naked Palm Beach man who destroyed his neighbors' mailboxes with a machete, or the four Florida students who used machetes to hack up a seventeen-year-old boy, bury him alive, then have sex at the scene to celebrate. Yeah, okay, there's a lot of machete weirdness, and maybe the "machete hypothesis" should not be dismissed out of hand.

To my lights, the most promising lines of explanation for the strikingly high Florida WQ involve, first, the very large number of people in the state at any one time who were born or currently live elsewhere; second, the widespread perception that "the rules" are different here, that in Florida, pretty much anything goes; and, third, the incessant heat and humidity. Herewith, my reasoning:

The percentage of Florida residents born elsewhere is second highest in the nation. (Nevada is first.) Granted, a large share of Florida's WQ is provided by crackers, the distinguishing feature of whom is that they have been in Florida for a long time. On the other hand, immigrants, tourists, vacationers, and retirees usually leave their social networks behind and, with them, the behavioral restraints that social networks provide. This is a variation on the mass-society argument that mobility produces normlessness and normlessness generates deviant behavior, a standard explanation for everything from the rise of fascism in Europe to the defeat of water-fluoridation referenda as a method to combat tooth decay. I think it also helps explain Florida's outsize WQ.

To indulge in a sociological speculation, it is remarkable that no matter what situation we find ourselves in, we (almost always) know what to expect and how to behave. Whether we are standing in line at the grocery store, getting on an elevator, queuing up to buy tickets to the movies, or attending the funeral of a loved one, we always know just what to expect— of ourselves and of others. There are social rules ("norms") that pertain to virtually every social situation, rules that almost everybody knows, respects, and obeys, at least most of the time.

For the most part, these social rules are enforced by informal mechanisms of social control—by the disapproval of one's social group for behavior that violates its norms. All social groups maintain an elaborate set of social controls, many informal but some formal, whose purpose is to sanction those who break the group's rules. Socialization about common values that occurs within the family or within religious institutions is one source of informal social control ("people like us just don't do that!"); the criminal justice system is a more formal mechanism.

In modern societies, the principal mechanisms of informal social control are the values and behavioral expectations imparted in families, in schools, and in religious institutions. The seven deadly sins and the Ten Commandments are familiar religious behavioral proscriptions—justified more as what God expects or wants of us than as what society needs, but the latter is surely relevant. Schools teach patriotism as surely as they teach arithmetic, reward conformity to social expectations, and punish deviance. And families are where children are taught what "people like us" say, feel, think, and do. All this renders social life predictable.

Deviance, nonconformity, criminality—in short, weirdness—are what result when the informal mechanisms of social control lose their grip on behavior. And this often happens when people are away from their primary social groups. This is why explanations of Florida's weirdness that focus on the large number of people who moved here from out of state are plausible. When people move to Florida, they leave behind not only icy winters but also religious institutions, social networks, kin, and other primary social groups and group ties, in other words, the mechanisms of informal social control that normally constrain behavior. When nearly two-thirds of a state's residents come from somewhere else, one expects group ties to be somewhat weak, and weak ties lead to weird behavior.

The same may be said of tourists who come to Florida on vacation. No one seems to know how many tourists are in Florida on an average day, but daily attendance at Walt Disney World alone is near sixty thousand people, and on any day that Disney is full, so are SeaWorld and Universal and all the other theme parks in the Orlando area. Ditto the theme parks, water parks, and tourist attractions throughout the state. No matter how you count, it adds up to a very large number of people in the state on any given day who are not being "watched" by neighbors, friends, kin, and other primary groups, but rather by strangers, if indeed they are being "watched" at all. Perhaps it says too much to claim that being on vacation and away from your primary social groups causes weird and deviant behavior, but it is surely easier to get weird when no one you know is watching. So in that sense, the rules really are different here. The usual rules of behavior weaken, and that at least allows people to do wacky things.

And that brings me to my second point, the widespread perception that in Florida, the rules of behavior are different. The state's official promotion of Florida's laissez-faire lifestyle began in a mid-1980s tourism campaign based on the slogan "The Rules Are Different Here." The idea was to promote the state as a carefree, hassle-free vacation paradise, but it is now used derisively by anyone seeking to break whatever rules there are. Florida spent $4.5 million on this campaign.

Even when the slogan was first announced, state officials acknowledged that it could generate wild misinterpretations. No, it is not okay to shoot your husband here, or drive while intoxicated, or smoke pot in public, or pick a fight in the bar, or pull the bikini tops off Florida beach bunnies. Pretty much everything that is against the law elsewhere is against the law here. But some people seem to interpret the slogan as meaning that in Florida, there are no rules at all. And maybe that puts a lot of fresh points into the state's WQ. Florida does encourage its guests (and even its residents) to kick back, relax, have a good time, and maybe that mentality does promote weird behavior.

And in some cases, the rules truly *are* different in Florida. Florida has a very loose regulatory environment and an "anything goes" attitude about most things (marijuana smoking and welfare fraud excepted), and in the words of one commentator, this has made the state "a sunny place for shady people." Florida's gun laws, for example, are notoriously lax (as gun laws tend to be throughout the South—so lax that Pittman says we should call ourselves the "Gunshine State"). Drugs are also readily available and alcohol is sold everywhere. And there is no state income tax. All this adds up to a strong attractor for misfits, losers, deviants, and rebels from all corners of the country.

Then finally we have Florida's insufferable heat and humidity, which can drive people crazy or make them do crazy things. There was a study done in Australia, for example, that found a positive correlation between "ambient temperature and hospital admissions for mental and behavioral disorders." Florida's mean annual ambient temperature is 70.7 degrees, first among the fifty states. And there is an ample research literature linking high heat and humidity to deviant behavior. Also favoring the hypothesis is that Louisiana ranks third in average temperature and is also high in WQ, as anyone who has been there during Mardi Gras will attest. (On the other hand, Hawaii ranks above Louisiana and just below Florida, and *HuffPost* has yet to run a story about weirdness in the fiftieth state.)

One well-established fact is that homicide rates are higher in the South than elsewhere, and all the southern states are warm-weather states. More than a few criminologists have linked the region's excess homicides to the hot, muggy weather, where tempers flare and minor altercations turn deadly. And it is not a long logical leap from homicides to other forms of deviance.

For half the year or more, Florida's daily high temperature will be in the 90s and the humidity will be suffocating. People often compensate by wearing as little clothing as the law allows. Add to the near-nakedness thousands of tourists who aren't going to be around very long, the idea that "the rules are different" in Florida, and a widespread "you only live once" attitude, and you have a formula for illicit sex, some of which turns pretty weird.

Research shows that when the heat and humidity go up, people are more likely to die, are more likely to be hospitalized, report more fitful sleep, become less productive at work, skip work more frequently, tend to argue more with others, become more violent, commit more crimes, are more aggressive, tend to have more and steamier sex, and are generally nuttier (i.e., mental illnesses are exacerbated). And that is only a partial listing. A quick review of the relevant scientific literature suggests that there is scarcely an element of human behavior that doesn't change when the heat index goes up.

So there you have it: lots of immigrants and tourists who lack the constraining influence of their informal social groups, a common belief that Florida's rules of behavior are different, and month after month of "straight-95" days—that's the temperature, humidity, dew point, and chance of an afternoon shower. *Et voilà:* Florida!

I conclude with a quotation from the incomparable Tim Dorsey's novel *Pineapple Grenade*: "A prosthetic leg with a Willie Nelson bumper sticker washed ashore on the beach, which meant it was Florida. And then it got weird."

INDEX